"Knowledge is a garden. If it isn't cultivated, you can't harvest it."

African Proverb

Comments About This Book

"My grandmother (Mama) authored an amazing book detailing her personal experience and those of others exploring how the resilience of Black people is unmatched. As I was reading, I felt transported through multiple eras of time while seeing the same inequalities. The eloquence and grace of Mama's words throughout her story is captivating. This book was yet another reminder that despite how far we must go we as a people have what it takes to get there. The book is a symbol of affirmation and reassurance through the turmoil and turbulence that our country is plagued with."

> Aaron M. Williams,
> Undergraduate University of Miami
> Professional Freelance Photographer

"I read this book and exclaimed, 'Wow, this is an historical read that neither scholars nor children should miss!' Dr. Portis accurately presents how social barriers, and legal systems impede Black families' progress as well as the progress of the agencies that train staff in group homes and residences. She reminds us of the determination of our Black ancestors to make this nation one of equality and justice for all people and encourages us to continue progressing."

> Joyce Carter, (ret.)
> LMSW Deputy Commissioner, New York City Administration for Children Services, Vice President for Programs/Research Development, and New York City Foster Care and Adoption Agency (Not-For-profit)

"Through the Eyes of this Black Woman" gives us unique and valuable insight into the life and experiences of a Black woman in a systemically racist society. From her rearing in the South, parenting and community guidance, dedication to education and life-long learning, and Christ centered modus operandi for helping others, to her uplifting work as a teacher, international consultant, institutional administrator, a mother, godmother, and theologian, Dr. Portis hands us a gift. It identifies nettlesome philosophical disconnections and reflects the intellect, gender, strength, faith, fire, and *Steadfast Resolve* needed to address and heal our dangerously imbalanced society. This incredible history, firsthand experiences, and insights will inspire generations, current and future, and encourage all people to stand upright and meet these psychological, emotional, and physical challenges head-on. Through the Eyes of this Black Woman can serve as a teaching tool about the hard-to-see and define effects of *Systemic Racism*, in one's childhood, education, and professional development."

> Kevin A. Anderson, Commissioner of Commerce for the State of Maryland, and Former Chairman, Board of Directors NEA Foundation

"Dr. Portis' work commanded my utmost attention from the first word to the last. It is an in-depth lesson about the WHOLE story. An opus was so incredibly woven from a historical and generational context that I, an avid reader, am humbled by what I've learned. Riveting, accurate, genuine, this book tells the truth of an enduring hope known uniquely to Black people in America that is disturbing and uplifting at the same time. The message leaves us with a charge to love and not to hate; not easy to do. By telling her story, she has helped me understand my own and inspired me to "hold high the torch" because the torch was held high for me. What a privilege it is to know that the blood of the brave runs warm in my veins. How precious a gift this is to be reminded of our history in this great work. This book is a must- read for such a time as this."

Lele Sneed and True Eden Sneed Co-Author the book Be True to You

"Through the Eyes of this Black Woman" is the perfect book for this period. In the wake of George Floyd's murder and the resulting global outrage, America must deal with the original sin and the lasting effects on the Black community. And this time, the conversation has made its way into Corporate America. Management teams across the nation are seeking ways to understand, retain, and promote Black professionals. Diversity, equity, and inclusion programs are all the rage. White leaders want to become allies of the people of color within their organizations. Through the Eyes of this Black Woman is a perfect place to start.

Dr. Portis seamlessly weaves American history with autobiography and educational text. Corporation leadership looking for insight into the complexity of creating safe spaces to encourage retention, recruitment, and promotion of Black professionals should make this book required reading. Black young adults should also read this book to understand better *where* and *when* they can enter. Black professionals should read this book to help identify tropes, stereotypes, and other pitfalls at work and manage them together. Allies, and those who want to be allies should also read this book to situate themselves in their counterparts' shoes and help make their ally as meaningful as possible. Additionally, this should be assigned reading in every Black history class in America.

From a personal perspective, Through the Eyes of this Black Woman is relatable, attainable, inspirational, and aspirational. Dr. Portis told my story and that of so many other Black women. Yes, the voice and specifics are her own, but the history, struggles, and triumphs embody the spirit of the Black community. I am better for having read it, and you will be, too."

Radiah Rondon, JD, Entrepreneur

"Dr. Portis seamlessly twines together history and her own personal experiences to create an entirely realistic, yet hopeful, discussion on systemic racism in the United States.

Accessible to any readers regardless of professional or cultural background, this book is an emotionally impactful must-read for any citizen hoping to contribute to the healing of systemic racism in America."

Rachael Bindas, Editor

"This book is both timely and timeless. Dr. Portis masterfully addresses each issue with purpose and truth. Uncomfortable for some, cathartic for others. It is a must-read for any law student, professor, lawyer, or judge interested in civil rights law, criminal law, or constitutional law. Dr. Portis identifies the root causes rather than merely listing symptoms. Anyone who cares about justice will thoroughly enjoy this read."

Judge Ronald A. Wilson, Tribal Judge

*"If the **surviving lions** **DON'T** tell their stories, the **hunter** **WILL** take all the credit."*

An African Proverb

The contents of this work, including, but not limited to, the accuracy of events, people and places depicted, opinions expressed, permission to use previously published materials included, and advice given, or actions advocated are solely the responsibility of the author, who assumes all liability for said work and indemnities for said work and indemnifies the publisher against any claims Stemming from publications of this work.

All Rights Reserved

Copyright © 2024 by Dr. Thomasina M. Portis

All rights reserved. No part of this publication may be reproduced, distributed, or transmitted in any form or by any means, including photocopying, recording, or other electronic or mechanical methods, without the prior written permission of the copyright owner and the publisher, except in the case of brief quotations embodied in critical reviews and certain other noncommercial uses permitted by copyright law. For permission requests, write to the publisher, addressed "Attention: Permissions Coordinator," at the address below.

CITIOFBOOKS, INC.
3736 Eubank NE Suite A1
Albuquerque, NM 87111-3579
www.citiofbooks.com
Hotline: 1 (877) 389-2759
Fax: 1 (505) 930-7244

Ordering Information:

Quantity sales. Special discounts are available on quantity purchases by corporations, associations, and others. For details, contact the publisher at the address above.

Printed in the United States of America.

ISBN-13:	E-book	979-8-89391-184-8
	Hardback	979-8-89391-183-1

Library of Congress Control Number: 2024913097

Title page by Vernard L. R. "Ronnie" Portis

Book Lay-out And Design by Verenander L. F. "Randy" Portis, III

Editorial Assistance provided by Rita Lowery, Dr. Lois Poag-Ray , and Judge Ronald A. Wilson

Research Assistance by Marcelina James and Veronica C. Montgomery and Ayden Micah Williams

Definitions provided by Wikipedia, Black's Law Dictionary, and Webster's Unabridged Dictionary
Photo image provided by individuals and by Public Domain of Google

Author's Cover Photo by Aaron Marckell Williams

Other Works by the Author

The 21st Century Required Reformation: All Children are Gifted

God the Triune: Growing in the Holy Spirit

The Habit of Action: Fulfilling he the Great Commission

Women of Faith: Their Spirit; Strengthening the Ministry

Music: A Universal Language and Ministry

GLOSSARY

1. Ability – the physical or mental power needed to complete a task.
2. Altruism – the belief in the practice of selfless concern for the well-being of others.
3. Amoral – a lack of knowledge that exists to make moral or immoral determinations.
4. Anarchy – a state of disorder due to the absence or nonrecognition of authority.
5. Angstrom – a unit of length equal to one hundred-millionth of a centimeter.
6. Arc – a curved path as in the portion of a circle.
7. Autocracy – a system of government by one person with absolute power.
8. Authoritarian – a system favoring or enforcing strict obedience to authority, especially the government's, at the expense of personal freedom.
9. Bartering – simply the exchange of goods and services between two people for payment. The value is usually mutually understood as equal. Currency (money) is not involved at all.
10. Benevolence – the quality of being well meaning; kindness.
11. Capitalism – an economic system characterized by (a) lack of government intervention, (b) means of production owned by private firms, and (c) goods and services distributed according to mechanisms (as opposed to government price controls).
12. Caste System – A caste system is a fixed social order in which a person is born within a particular system of social, economic, and political strata. People who are placed into one are stigmatized.
13. Chattel – an item of property other than real estate.
14. Citadel – a fortress, a little city, where it is the defensive core. In the case of the United States, the United States Capitol is the nation's citadel because it is designed to defend the core of this Democratic society/nation.
15. Citizen – a legally recognized inhabitant of a state or commonwealth, either native or naturalized.
16. Coercive power – power-driven by fear of consequences and of what the person with the coercive power can do to you if you disobey.
17. Constituency – a body of voters in a specified area who elect a representative to a legislative body.
18. Convict Leasing – a system of forced penal labor historically practiced in the Southern United States that included Black women and children as it overwhelmingly included Black men.
19. Culture – is the customs, arts, social institutions, and achievements of a particular nation or another social group.
20. Debt – the amount of money borrowed by one party from another.
21. Dehumanization – the process of depriving a person or group of positive human qualities that can be horrific.

22. Despotism – the exercise of absolute power, especially in a cruel and oppressive way.

23. Disease – misuse of power causing abuse to people.

24. Disdain - implies strong feelings of disapproval and aversion toward what seems mean.

25. Democracy – a system of government by the entire population of all eligible citizens of a state, typically, through elected representatives.

26. Economics – the science that deals with the production, distribution, and consumption of goods and services or the material welfare of humankind.

27. Emancipate – to be set free, especially from legal, social, or political restrictions.

28. Equal – considered to be the same as another in status or quality.

29. Equality – the state of being equal, especially in status, rights, and opportunities.

30. Equity – the quality of being fair and impartial.

31. Family – any of the various social units differing from but regarded as equivalent to the traditional blood family.

32. Fascism– a political philosophy, movement, or regime that exalts a nation, and often race, above the individual. It stands for a centralized autocratic government headed by a dictatorial leader, severe economic and social regimentation, and forcible suppression of opposition, extremely Authoritarian, intolerant with oppressive ideas and behavior.

33. Folklores – the traditional beliefs, customs, and stories of a community passed through the generations by word of mouth.

34. Foment-to promote the growth or development of rouse, i.e., to incite a rebellion.

35. Freedmen -Blacks who had never known slavery.

36. Gerrymandering – manipulating the boundaries of an electoral constituency to favor one part of a class.

37. Good – having the qualities of a particular role.

38. Griot – a member of a class [African] traveling poets, musicians, and storytellers who maintain a tradition of oral history.

39. Forbearance – patience, self-control, restraint, and tolerance.

40. Hireling – a person employed to undertake menial work.

41. Hope – a feeling of expectation and desire for a certain thing to happen.

42. Humanity – all people.

43. Human Relationship - how we are connected, or our way of being connected [through feelings].

44. Immoral – a choice to disavow or disobey moral standards.

45. Indelible – impossible to subdue or defeat; not able to be forgotten or removed.

46. Inequality – the difference in size, degree, circumstances, etc., lack of equality, a symbolic expression of the fact that two quantities are not equal.

47. Inequity – lack of fairness or justice.

48. Insidious - proceeding in a gradual and subtle way with harmful effects.

49. Insurrection – a violent uprising against an authority or government.

50. Intellect – the faculty of reasoning and understanding objectively. It concerns academic matters, but it is not relegated exclusively to academics.

51. Jim Crow – the perpetual practice of segregating Black people in the United States.

52. Justice – just behavior or treatment, the quality of being fair and reasonable, the administration of the law or authority in maintaining this.

53. Kind - a good deed: favor.

54. Knowledge – facts, information, and skills required by a person through experience or education, awareness, or familiarity gained by experience by a point or situation.

55. Leverage – an economic term that involves using currency, i.e., money, to build wealth.

56. LGBTQ+- a culture shared by lesbian, gay, bisexual, transgender, and queer individuals.

57. Love is the most powerful force in the universe that propels benevolence. It is courage and goodness despite disputes and turmoil. It forgives while seeking good and punishing evil.

58. Mediocre – of moderate quality; not exceptionally good.

59. Mediocracy – dominant class consisting of mediocre people, or a system in which mediocrity is rewarded.

60. Meritocracy – holding of power by people selected based on their ability.

61. Meted – to give out by measure, i.e., to dole out.

62. Miscegenation – interbreeding of people considered to be from different ethnic types.

63. Militancy – The use of confrontational or violent methods in support of a political or social cause.

64. Minority – (a social science definition) is a culturally and ethnically distinct group that coexists But is subordinate to a dominant group. It does not correlate with population but with social and political status. In practice, 'minorities' are ethnic, religious, or linguistic groups living among a 'majority group in considerable and justifiable fear of persecution.

65. Modus Operandi – a particular way of doing something, especially a characteristic one.

66. Moral – a set of standards that determine right and wrong; good from bad; decent from indecent.

67. Mores – social norms that are widely observed within a particular society or culture. These norms determine what is considered morally acceptable or unacceptable within any given culture.

68. Motivation – the reason(s) one has for behaving in a particular way.

69. Multicultural – relating to or constituting cultural or ethnic groups within a society.

70. Multi-ethnic – relating to or constituting several ethnic groups.

71. Multicultural v multi-ethnic - is relating or pertaining to several diverse cultures while multi-ethnic is about, pertaining to, consisting of several ethnic groups.

72. Nationalism – A belief that some people are superior to others.

73. Peonage Slavery – the system of unfree labor in which people are employed against their will by the threat of poverty, detention, violence (including death), lawful compulsion, or other extreme hardship to themselves or members of their families. It was outlawed in Congress in 1887. Though outlawed then, Peonage Slavery in extreme ways of hardship and subtle forms existed until 1965.

74. Pluralism – a condition or system in which two or more states, groups, principles, sources of authority, etc., coexist.

75. Politics – the activities associated with the governance of a nation or other area,

76. Power – the capacity to direct or influence the behavior of others, influencing behavior.

77. Pride – a feeling of deep pleasure or satisfaction derived from one's own achievements, or from qualities or possessions that are widely admired.

78. Privilege – a system of material, psychological, and cultural benefits all members of a dominant social group have access to, in exchange for their support in power. (Political leaders intentionally construct systems to reinforce hierarchies of status, wealth and worth, and to foster division among those who lack political power.)

79. Profanity – indecent and pornographic language or irreverent behavior.

80. Racism – how discrimination is directed against a person based upon membership in a particular group.

81. Redlining – the refusal of a loan or insurance to someone because they live in an area deemed to be a poor financial risk.

82. Republic – a form of government in which a state is ruled by representatives of the citizen body and founded on the idea that sovereignty rests within the people.

83. Respect – due regard for the feelings, wishes, rights, or traditions of others.

84. Resilience -the capacity of a person to maintain their core purpose and integrity in the face of dramatically changed circumstances.

85. Sacralization – the transposing of an ideological concept into a tenet of religious faith to serve the vested interest of a particular ethnic group.

86. Secularization – dilutes a rich religious concept under the heavy influence of secular, social, or political pressure.

87. Sedition-overt conduct, such as speech and organization, that incite rebellion against the established order. It can include the subversion of a constitution.

88. Self-empowerment – an attribute that makes [us] strong and more confident, especially in controlling our lives and claiming our rights.

89. Serendipity - the occurrence and development of events by chance in a happy or beneficial way.

90. Slavery – the position of power that one person holds over another which controls their life and liberty.

91. Social class – a group of people within a society who possess the same socio- economic status. They may also be individuals sharing similar economic circumstances that have been widely used in censuses and studies of social mobility.

92. Sovereignty – the quality or state of having supreme power authority in government as possessed or claimed by a state or community.

93. Steadfast Resolve – the acquisition of determination and strength deliberately formulated by an ethnic group to withstand the duress and disenfranchisement brought on by overt slavery and the evil of covert Systemic Racism.

94. Sub-humanization – lower than human and considered property. When one is characterized as sub-human, its owners are not required to have a moral compass.

95. Swastika – an ancient symbol used in many diverse cultures for at least 5, 000 years before Adolf Hitler made it the centerpiece of the Nazi flag. Its present-day use by certain extremist groups promotes hate and represents White supremacy.

96. Suffrage – the right to vote in political elections.

97. Systemic Racism – the [nationwide] social by-product of hatred born out of an evil ideology purposed to systematically perpetuate power and monetary gain at the expense of another human being.

98. Thralldom – the state of being in someone's power.

99. Tenacity – the quality of being determined; persistent forward momentum with a plan; to never stop trying to achieve a goal even in the face of walls without steps to climb.

100. Tolerance – the ability to accept or endure forbearance.

DEDICATION
This book is dedicated to my sons:

Vernard L. R. Portis (Ronnie)   Verenander L.F. Portis, III (Randy)

Randy and Ronnie, my beloved sons, trust yourselves. You've survived a lot and have proven what it means to get up and to move forward. You have accomplished much and will continue to excel as you face what is before you. Now, you carry the mantle for generations to come. Let them see through you that with God, all things are possible. My love and gratitude extend to my grandchildren as well. This poem by Langston Hughes titled MOTHER TO SON depicts a truth that I pass on to you. I am so honored to be your mother.

I love you forever.
Mommie

Well son, I'll tell you:

Life for me ain't been no crystal stair.

It's had tacks in it, And splinters, And boards torn up, And places with no carpet on the floor- Bare.

But all the time I'se been a-climbin' on, And reachin' landin's, And turnin' corners,

And sometimes goin' in the dark Where there So 't you turn back.

Don't you set down on the steps Cause you find it kinder hard.

For I'se still going, honey, I'se still climbin', And life for me ain't been no crystal stair.

I am so honored to be your mother, and I love you.

FOREWORD

Barbara D. Parks-Lee, Ph.D., Author
Connection, Capital Punishment.
The Seasons:and The Day the Sun Got up Late.

Systemic Racism is alive, well, and living in the United States of America. It arrived in 1619, 401 years ago, aboard a ship that landed in Jamestown, Virginia, a year before the Mayflower landed in 1620 at Plymouth Rock, Massachusetts. In Dr. Henry Louis Gates' Many Rivers to Cross, he reports, there were both White and Black indentured servants on board, but within a few years of servitude, all the Black passengers did not meet with the same gift of freedom. Rather, they evolved into slavery, where they were viewed as sub-human chattel who could be forced to work from *"can 'til can't."*

Ever since the words of the old spiritual, "I've been 'buked, and I've been scorned" have characterized the lots of resilient Black people who have come this far by faith, perseverance, ingenuity, and making a way out of what seemed to be no way.

Without slave labor, this country would be unrecognizable and behave much differently today. Tobacco, rice, cotton, and sugar cane crops worked by Black enslaved people made White Europeans wealthy beyond belief. Some ethnic groups in Africa also profited by the sale of captives to White slavers, who then used their profits from the sale of enslaved people to proliferate the triangular slave trade back and forth across the Atlantic Ocean. These slave owners refused life, liberty, and the pursuit of happiness to Black people while amassing a fortune for themselves.

The White House and the U.S. Capitol, internationally recognized symbols of liberty and justice for all, would not have been built without the labor of Black enslaved people. The statue of Freedom atop the Capitol was the work of an enslaved Black man. There would not have been the White House's five-story, subterranean bunker where United States Presidents can be whisked to be sheltered in safety in the event of an emergency, without the forced labor of chattel enslaved people, whose work was unrecognized, thankless toil.

Black women and men could be torn away from family members, children even, and sold off. Black women were raped by White men, Black men were used as studs to produce more two- legged livestock to continue enriching White coffers. When children, who were born out of rape, could not be distinguished from their White siblings, they, too were enslaved.

"Them that's got, gets…but God bless the child that's got its own," the refrain from a song made famous by the late Billie Holiday reflects the status of Blacks in the United States today. Dr. Portis addresses inequalities in health, education, economic advancement, climate change, employment, police brutality, politics, religion, and housing that have all helped systemic racism's arms regenerate. These inferior systems are intentionally designed to keep Black people under the bottom of the barrel. *Systemic Racism's* greed, arrogance, feelings of superiority, and entitlement still thwart the pursuit of liberty, life, and justice for Black people.

Despite inadequate and sub-par or nonexistent facilities, Black people, with progress like that "of the little old inchworm," continue to struggle against the vagaries of Systemic Racism and a plethora of other isms, like classism, ageism, and sexism. Slavery has been realigned through incarceration, miseducation, and generational poverty. For instance, the White family's inherited wealth enriches many generations whose fore parents received 140 acres of Midwestern homesteads stolen from indigenous tribes after the Civil War.

Those land grant awards amassed —and continue to amass—generational financial advantages denied to generations of freed Black enslaved people's families whose forty acres and a mule were never to be realized. The U.S.A. is a country of haves and have- nots, where European immigrants can receive benefits denied by *Systemic Racism's* arms to Black people. 401 years of being treated as less than, other than, of not deserving of privileges White Supremacists have felt to be theirs alone, as inalienable rights have built up Black people's survival skills, strengths, and faith in striving on the road toward "better."

Despite ill-equipped schools, despite Post-Traumatic Stress Disorder (PTSD), despite inhumane and violent lawlessness and police brutality, despite being the last hired and the first fired, despite redlined and underserved neighborhoods, Black people still are the backbone who keeps the services of this country intact. Despite an overabundance of liquor stores and fast-food establishments in Black and poor ghettoes, despite the scourge of drugs and guns that enrich others while decimating Black communities, despite attempts to take away the vote, Black people still physically keep the services of this country intact.

What would happen here, in the United States, if, as in Douglas Turner Ward's play, Day of Absence, all Black folks suddenly disappeared? They have declared themselves privileged and superior to fend for themselves for a day. As in the telephone commercial, would meaningful changes occur when the masses shout, "Can you hear me now?"

There are conditions all Black people have survived, and continue to survive, namely, faith in the face of adversities, perseverance against mistreatment, and the strength gained from making a way out of no way. We thrive under conditions promulgated under the arms of *Systemic Racism* to break our minds, our bodies, and our spirits. Survival against all odds has strengthened. Our fortitude is gaining attention and causing trepidation. Since arriving in the U.S.A. Black people have used challenges as lessons and blessings for generations we may never know or see.

Yes, *Systemic Racism* is alive, living—but not as well as it once was—as cruel events shown around the world have inspired us American Black men and women to find our voices. Other ethnicities join us as we protest for justice, advance freedom, and insist that all people's worth, dignity, and value be affirmed.

Dr. Portis' book is a rich source of data suitable for explorations in the interdisciplinary humanities, education, history, law, political science, art, music, social studies, and economics— an often neglected but much-needed area, geography, ethnography, values education, theology, and communication between people of different ethnicities. She provides historical research and firsthand experiences as she explores the ramifications of One Woman's Story. It is a thought-provoking narrative that, in these times of chaos and change, is designed not only to explain why protests continue in the United States but also invites all Black people to learn; To understand how The United States of America can live up to its promises in The Declaration of

Independence and the United States Constitution and to recognize the contributions and worth of all people everywhere.

She continually encourages Black people "to walk together, chirren, and don't you get weary," and she invites White people to be willing to examine and to excise the arms of *Systemic Racism*. Progress, reconciliation, and peace are not as Hamlet would question "To be or not to be," but rather, "It's not yet what it ought to be, but what it must be." This book can be read easily once and again several times, for each section provides rich food for thought. Every rereading offers current information, new ways to understand, and new ways to address the eradication of *Systemic Racism*.

Table of Contents

COMMENTS

Other Works by the Author Glossary	iii
Dedication	ix
Foreword	x

SECTION ONE: RELAY TO LIBERTY AND JUSTICE – A Fractured Nation

Poem: In Times of Crises

Prologue — Page 4

Friends for a Lifetime - Change is Coming An Autocratic Government Inhumanity - Jim Crow - Who We Are Now? - What I Learned We are Essential American Logistics - Chariots Depart

Chapter One - Setting the Context — Page 16

The Issue? Exclusive White Rule - Our Indelible Spirit Reigns America Is Our Home - Fluid V. Constant - Cycles of Injustice Who are We? - Black Social and Economic Disenfranchisement - The Emancipation Proclamation- Slave Master Mentality - The Complexity of Freedom - The Beginning of Public-School Desegregation - Inhumane Control Never Again - Black Lives Matter

Chapter Two - A True Pledge of Allegiance — Page 33

Separate but Equal - Principal in South Carolina During Segregation - Table Talk - History A Chronicle of Racism in America - The Story Continued Our Call-to-Action - Legalized Inequities - Los Angeles Police Beats Rodney King - Our Relay to Liberty and Justice - Demonstration of Strength

Chapter Three - Making Our Lives Better — Page 43

Creative and Intellectual - Geniuses Chronicling the Lie - People with Purpose - We Make Beauty Out of Ashes Benjamin Banneker, a Freed Man - Frederick Douglass: the Courage of a Statesman - Why Tell Douglass's Story?

Chapter Four – Christianity V. White Christian Nationalism — Page 52

Christianity - Altruism, Christianity, and Democracy - Evangelical Racism – White Nationalism – Christian Evangelical Nationalism – Democracy V. Christianity – White Christian Nationalism V. Democracy – Social Development through American Religion – The Blac Church – What is Lacking? –

Chapter Five - Two Roads Diverge — Page 62

Two Roads Diverge Inside the Systemic Racism System – An Eye-opening Experience – Poem: Hold High The Torch

Chapter Six - Race and Racism — Page 66

Race – Racism – Manifestations of Racism - Penalties Never End - Racism – Impact of Racism – Addressing Racism – Pay Attention
-300 Year Guarantee to Suppress Black People: Their Disgrace – They Keep Coming – How Does this Happen? – A Sail to Freedom
–Never Forget

Chapter Seven - The Fearlessness of Hope — Page 73

A Moral Compass: Competence, Compassion, and Kindness – An American Intercultural Reality – American History Denied: Racism Grows Tentacles – Cheering Greatness – An Intrigue -

Chapter Eight - The Mania   Page 77

The Black Intellect Saga – Meritocracy – Systemic Racism Through Meritocracy – A Gift to Nixon – Black Intelligence is Innate – The Art of Oration

Chapter Nine - Blueprints   Page 80

Mrs. Wilhelmina D. Scott – School – Desegregation Forged Many Changes – A Different Culture: Relationship and Love – Listening Is a Valuable Asset – Firsthand Challenging Conversations – My Belief about Human Beings

Chapter Ten - Economics   Page 87

A Place Called Lack" – The Bartering System – The Power of Economics – Two Systems of Exchange of Good Intentions Require Better Choicer Goods and Services – Classism – The Nemesis Called Debt – Financial Bondage – Perspectives Navigate Sharecropping - Our Lives – Wealth Relay Runners – Begin with Small Investments

Chapter Eleven - The Birth of The Jim Crow Era   Page 92

Fasten Your Seat Belts – Denigrating Cycles Continue - An Urgent Reality – Decoding – Recapping Injustices – Picking Cotton – Policing to Protect Free Labor – Systemic Racism is Fertilized – Systematized Collaboration – The Jim Crow Laws: 1887-1967 – Sharecropping – Variations in Convict Leasing – Modern day Sharecropping – - Wisdom from the Mother - Decoding Jim Crow – Tulsa, Oklahoma – After the Massacre

Chapter Twelve - The Great Migration   Page 102

Creative and Locked Out of Mainstream – The Art of Memorization – Madam Stephanie St. Claire: Robin Hood, - Be The Change We Expect1920 – Renaissance Era: The Cotton Club – Finding a Way to Get Ahead – Mainstream Workforce Realities – Taking a "Chance" on Acquiring Funds – We, Too, Are America – From Perception to Truth

Chapter Thirteen - Vote   Page 109

The United States" Democratic P – Democracy is Not Process –What are the Types of Elections? – Historically, Who Holds Elected Positions – Our Republic? We Become Vigilant – Release of Hope – Innate Ability

Chapter Fourteen - Leadership   Page 122

Another Commentary from Me-Taking on The Next Relay – "We are the Leaders are Look for!" Drugs" An Arch-enemy – Opening Pandora's Box – Good Intentions Require Better Choices – Social Injustices – Dignity in Action

Chapter Fifteen - Generative Creativity   Page 129

What Affects One Affects All -Chronicling Black American Contributions – The Trend Continues – Democracy is Not Perpetual – Economics' Reality - Be The Change We Expect – Black Entrepreneurship in the 21st Century – We Rise – Wisdom From the Motherland

Chapter Sixteen - Poverty: A Human Crisis   Page 138

The Systemic Pain of Poverty – Greed and Supremacy – Wages and Compensation Packages – Poverty is Systemic Racism – Racism Continues – An Intriguing experience – Lifting People Out of Poverty – A Segue – Sharecropping People of Distinction - Some Powerful Black Women – Our Ancestral Story – A Peril

SECTION TWO: CONTINUING TO RISE – Family The Bond of Respect and Love

Poem: Family Heroes

Chapter Seventeen - Endurance   Page 149

My Story – Kinfolk Everywhere – Building an Estate With Less Money and More Resources – A Saga- Death From a Massive Heart Attack – A 30-Year-old Widow's Reality in 1925- TB's and Ms. Mae's Grandchildren – TB and Ms. Mae's Grand and Great Grandchildren – TB and Ms. Mae's Great Grand and Great and Great Grandchildren -Education was Next to Christianity for Us – Vignettes about Endurance – Segue Way to Section Three: Hard Work, Intelligence, and Benevolence – The Power of Benevolence- The Race –

SECTION THREE: BENEVOLENCE – Mending the Fractured Nation

Poem: Ancestors

Chapter Eighteen - General "Can't" Is Dead   Page 189

General "Can" Killed Genera "Can't"– A Hallmark of Benevolence – (Integrity – Congressman James E. Clyburn; Dedication – LeBron James; Determination – Judge Ronald A. Wilson – Perseverance – Katherine Johnson, Dorothy Vaughn, and Mary Jackson) – Feature of Grit

Chapter Nineteen - Our Best Selves   Page 195

"Our Rights: Our Responsibility" – The Age of Technology is Now! Teach Curriculum and Instruction - The Horseless Thing – Fast Forward – My Wish for Technological Transformation

Chapter Twenty - Home   Page 207

Honor and Loyalty to Home – The Indelible Spirit – America, Our Home – The Faithful Friend – America Our Home: The Sworn Oath - Buffalo Soldiers – The Montford Point Marines – A Salute to the Women and Men in Uniform – A Noble Act – Post Traumatic Stress Disorder (PTSD) –

EPILOGUE   Page 217

Appendices   Page 222

Appendix One: The Vanocur Interview with Dr. King –
Appendix Two: The Oration by Frederick Douglass call "What To the Slave Is the Fourth of July? –
Appendix Three :Early 1920s plots of land owned by Thomas Boston (TB) Wright in the city of Sumter, South Carolina

ACKNOWLEDGEMENTS   Page 255

ABOUT THE AUTHOR   Page 256

REFERENCES AND SELECTED READINGS   Page 257

"…and Still, We Rise!"

The Negro Mother
by Langston Hughes

Children, I come back today
To tell you a story of the long dark way
In order that the race might live and grow.
Look at my face - dark as the night -
Yet shining like the sun with love's true light
I am the child they stole from the sand
three hundred years ago in Africa's land.
I am the dark girl who crossed the wide sea
Carrying in my body the seed of the free.
I am the woman who worked in the field
Bringing the cotton and the corn to yield.
I am the one who labored as a slave,
Beaten and mistreated for the work I gave -
Children sold away from me, husband sold, too.
No safety, no love, no respect was I due.
Three hundred years in the deepest South:
But God put a song and a prayer in my mouth.
God put a dream like steel in my soul.
Now, through my children, I'm reaching the goal.

Now, through my children, young and free,
I realize the blessings deed to me.
I couldn't read then. I couldn't write.
I had nothing, back there in the night.
Sometimes, the valley was filled with tears,
But I kept trudging on through the lonely years.
Sometimes, the road was hot with the sun,
But I kept trudging on through the lonely years.
Sometimes, the road was hot with the sun,
But I had to keep on till my work was done:
I had to keep on! No stopping for me -
I was the seed of the coming Free.
I nourished the dream that nothing could smother Deep
in my breast - the Negro mother.
I had only hope then, but now through you,
Dark ones of today, my dreams must come true:
All you dark children in the world out there, Remember
my sweat, my pain, my despair. Remember my years,
heavy with sorrow -
And make of those years a torch for tomorrow.
Make of my pass a road to the light
Out of the darkness, the ignorance, the night.
Lift high my banner out of the dust.
Stand like free men supporting my trust.
Believe in the right, let none push you back. Remember
the whip and the slaver's track. Remember how the
strong in struggle and strife
Still bar you the way, and deny you life -
But march ever forward, breaking down bars.
Look ever upward at the sun and the stars.
Oh, my dark children, may my dreams and my prayers
Impel you forever up the great stairs -
For I will be with you till no white brother
Dares keep down the children of the Negro Mother.

SECTION ONE

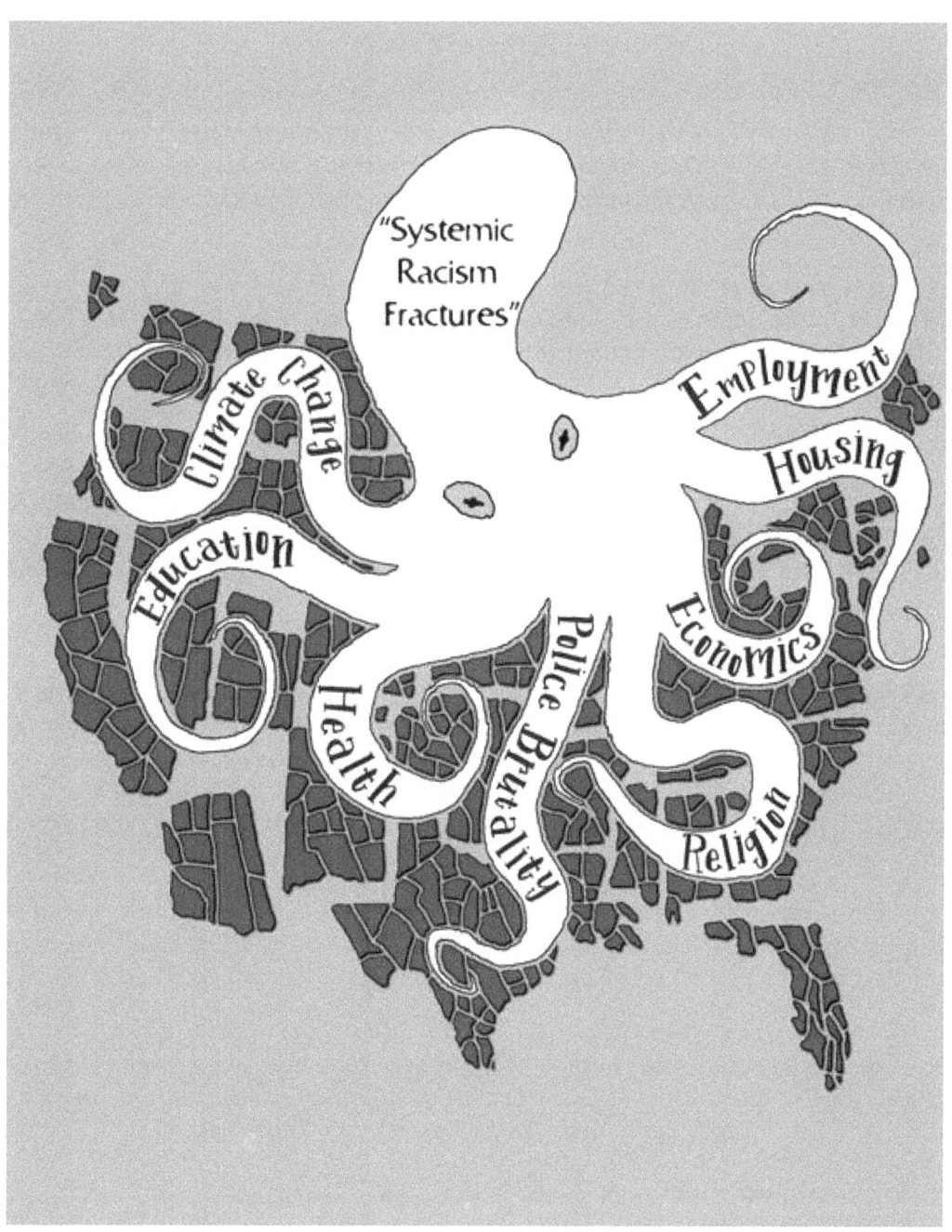

A Fractured Nation

Through The Eyes of This Black Woman

In Times of Crisis

I lie, half awake, half asleep, half watching, half listening to the television's Saturday morning accounting of weather, traffic, and other minutiae of the day, when I am startled out of my reverie by streaking, pulsating orbs, and vapor trails like I have never seen before.

I hear the newscasterssay that contact with Columbia has just been lost, and I instantly utter a call to the One Who Holds us All. My "Oh, my God" seems to be my life's stabilizing force whenever events too horrendous to contemplate happen.

My mind flashes back to catastrophes, to gut- wrenching times in the past when all I could do was to utter other "Oh, my God's, "and I remember the Challenger's Y- shaped vapor trail, Kennedy, King, and Malcolm X assassinations, National Guard troops standing in front of my neighborhood High's Store with rifles bayoneted, tanks in the streets of Washington, DC, and making my way home through smoke and flames and tear gas.

Then I remember other life-changing moments: the daily body counts from the war in VietNam, planes crashing into the World Trade Center, a man hurtling through space, his leg making a figure four, his hand still clasping his briefcase, the Pentagon in flames, a vaporized plane in a Pennsylvania field. I recall children killing children and the cottage industry of funeral tee-shirts saying RIP with a child's vital statistics listed along with a name.

And I am forced to wonder why we cannot hold in reverence all life on the planet, forced to question. Why cannot we teach peace instead of studying war? We are forced to think how hypocritical we are to mourn the lives of seven while, at the same time, planning the annihilation of thousands.

I am perplexed and saddened as I call forth again a prayer, "Oh, my God, Maker, and Ruler of us all, show us the way toward humanity and peace; lead us away from violence and the carnage of war and crime and hatreds allowed to fester for centuries.

Make me a person who practices peace, shows love, respects all life, and leavesthe understanding of crises to You, who understands what we cannot."

Amen

Dr. Barbara D. Parks-Lee

*"If we can open up a little bit more of each other as we share our stories, our real stories, that's what breaks down barriers. But in order to do that, you have to believe that your story has value. Be vulnerable.
Dare to be vulnerable."*

Michelle Obama

PROLOGUE

This conversation is for my sons and their wives, grandchildren, great-grandchildren, godchildren, Halifax family, siblings, nieces, nephews, aunts, cousins, and dearest friends. Universal family, I am thrilled to include all of you as well.

I am excited to share stories about our intelligent, resilient, and beautiful ancestors who left a powerful legacy. They lived in a world ruled by White supremacists, where beatings, maiming, and murder were common punishments that enslaved people endured in the South.

My aim is to share these stories with you and explain why love, family, and healthy relationships are so important. I love my family as you do yours. It is crucial that we share our stories because one day, we will be the ancestors.

I am a proud Black woman, and this book tells you why. One day, books may no longer be popular or even available. Even so, please document your stories for your children and their descendants. Our duty and responsibility is to record our stories; otherwise, someone else will tell them incorrectly or not at all.

Friends for a Lifetime

As I speak of the importance of relationships, thanks to Joyce Doty, I can share this photo. We started our journey together as ninth graders at Mather Academy, Camden, SC. These ladies are my three remaining lifelong high school sister/friends. Their support is still comforting, and I am eternally grateful for them. Their lifelong friendships are like anchors. They are forever dear to my heart.

Here I am with Joyce McCain Doty, Joyce Carter, and Ercelle Hill Pinckney. Joyce Doty wrote: "Ain't we cute?"

Change is Coming

I want to share a story that foretells our community's need to employ and build upon Democracy as our system of government. Today, there remain several major social and humanitarian issues that adversely impact Black ethnicity. When I was born, Democracy and equality were not provided to Black people in America.

I am among those who dismantled the metaphorical wall of segregation. Between 1966 and 1968, our community at large integrated into mainstream American society. This period coincided with President Lyndon B. Johnson's Great Society initiative, which aimed to expand civil rights, public broadcasting, access to healthcare, education, and the arts, as well as promote urban and rural development and public services. The Great Society sought to improve living conditions for low- income Americans by declaring a war on poverty.

For the first time in American history, Black people were recognized as citizens with voting rights, fully participating in American democracy. We entered this new world without any orientation, uncertain of what integrating into mainstream America would entail. The judicial and legislative systems had to grapple with a U.S. Constitution that, until 1965, had not confronted the tensions between its intent and its content. The excitement we felt when all Black people gained the right to vote is indescribable. Both Black men and women could now participate in elections, and our children became the first generation born into mainstream America.

The next objective was to have our children educated alongside their White peers, sparing them the "hand-me-down" education many of us Southern-born Black children endured. This generation would not have to watch White children ride buses while they walked to school, nor would they have to sit at the back of the bus on long trips. They would become more integrated into mainstream society. Their formal education, combined with life experiences from the "University of Hard Knocks," would aid their understanding of America alongside their parents.

Before our community entered mainstream America, Black griot lectures and dinner table history were integral parts of our lives. Today, however, many in our community may not make these vital connections. Although we were forcibly removed from our homeland and enslaved, stories have been handed down through generations.

I am compelled to share the reality of a Southern-born woman who understands the consequences of not connecting our heritage with our present-day realities. We must remain aware of the subtle yet blatant truths that emerge when we recognize them. It is crucial to understand that being connected to our history provides a perspective often missing from the American narrative. If we fail to do so, our viability in this democratic nation is at risk. Making logical decisions as Black people in America requires us to draw correlations between the past and the present. As my grandma would say, "Now, listen to what I tell you."

An Autocratic Government

The men who wrote the Declaration of Independence and The United States Constitution wanted to create a republic and a Democracy that would be the greatest the world had ever seen. We know that among these men were segregationists and enslavers who neither gave any thought to the rights of the American Indians, women, or Black people nor to any other Indigenous culture. The segregation that existed in the South during this time and the names of the signers of the Constitution are evidence that the Framers of the Constitution formulated these two documents. Their focus was to establish standards that could govern the rights of White men.

Never forget that some of these men were enslavers. If many of them were alive today, they would oppose our progress, just like they opposed it back then. Some of us can still remember the dreadful pain we endured as well as how ecstatic we were when we tore down the proverbial wall of Jim Crow in the 1960s so that our descendants would have the opportunity to enjoy all the benefits, rights, protections, and freedoms of being an American citizen.

An autocratic government system is led by one person with absolute power and longevity in office. There is no voting to elect people to office. There is no professional requirement for the people chosen to help lead the country except loyalty to the person in power. Protests are not allowed.

Autocratic governance existed in America for Black people until 1965. Since 1619, Black people have overcome three forms of slavery. If America becomes an Autocracy, the levels of inequality and injustice in the United States will multiply exponentially. Many of the atrocities committed during the Jim Crow Era could easily return. For instance, today's Penal System is a form of oppression that is a remnant of Jim Crow. It is a system created by Autocracy.

The convict lease and criminal surety systems that were outlawed during the Civil Rights Movement continue to be practiced today. Inmates all over the country perform various tasks for free to the government and corporations. The inmates work extraordinarily long hours per day under inhumane conditions. It is one of the many reasons why the United States has the highest incarceration rate for non-violent offenders in the world — more than China, India, and the continent of Africa. Inmates are abused, tortured, and killed regularly. Those who complain are labeled as snitches and suffer severe consequences.

The Prison Industrial Complex and inmates have replaced plantations and slavery in many communities. It has become a revolving door for inmates who have lost all hope, sanity, and support. Prison generates revenue and profit for communities and corporations, and the inmates have no rights. This is a way that Autocracy works.

Countries governed by autocracy often exhibit stark social divides between the privileged and the disadvantaged — commonly referred to as the Haves and the Have-Nots. This division primarily reflects systemic classism rather than racial distinctions. However, it remains evident that in nations where Black populations coexist with White authoritarian leadership, a disproportionate number of Black individuals experience profound poverty. Black communities typically lack access to significant socioeconomic opportunities and hold limited positions of power within these societies. Furthermore, dissenting voices are often suppressed through imprisonment or extrajudicial killings when they challenge the establishment.

There are various forms of democracy practiced globally. In the United States, our republic is founded on a system of checks and balances. The three distinct branches of government — the Judicial, Legislative, and Executive — exist to mutually hold one another accountable and prevent the concentration of power akin to tyranny.

The Executive Branch, where "the Buck stops" with the President, shoulders much of the public discontent due to its pivotal role in governance. The U.S. Congress comprises two chambers: the U.S. Senate and the U.S. House of Representatives, collectively responsible for legislating federal laws and regulations. The third component of this tripartite system is the U.S. Supreme Court. Tasked with interpreting the U.S. Constitution, the justices play a critical role in upholding the principles and legal framework of the nation.

In the 50 states of the United States, Governors preside over the executive branch of government, while the state legislative branches mirror the structure of the *United States Congress*. The judicial branch of the state government is led by the State Supreme Court or Court of Appeals. Our elected officials pledge to uphold the desires of "We the people." However, they are not required to prioritize the interests of the Country. They care only about their political futures, political party, party's constituents, donors, special interests, or lobbyists. Historically, affluent constituents have effectively preserved their wealth by electing compliant politicians who are susceptible to influence.

It is very important to know the functions of these three branches because it is possible that one branch can be blamed for a problem that they did not create or control. These three Branches are equal in authority. 2024 is the year for the U.S. Presidential election. For the first time since the Civil War between the States, this nation is facing the real possibility of becoming and autocracy again.

One can argue that the U.S. democratic system of governance has persistently misrepresented the inclusive principles of the U.S. Constitution since its ratification in 1788, indicating inherent flaws within the system. In 2024, our government faces substantial challenges as it encounters mounting criticism and resistance.

The following issues illustrate the consequences when marginalized groups resist systemic neglect and underrepresentation, while those in authority strive to preserve their positions of power and privilege. These national and international humanitarian concerns provoke anxiety among American citizens within our current governmental framework.

These issues include:

- Taxes
- War
- Genocide
- Pandemics
- Human Trafficking
- Women's Rights
- LGBTQ Rights
- The Prison Industrial Complex
- Economic disparities
- Judicial Reform
- Healthcare
- Housing
- Support for our Veterans
- Immigration
- The rising cost of higher education and student loans

Our democracy is under siege because Americans are not happy with the path our country is on. They are angry, frustrated, distrustful, traumatized, and tired. White supremacists who feed off the pain of others always try to find a way to capitalize on the suffering. They tapped into a population of Americans who were vulnerable enough to be misled. They were fed lies about the security of the voting machines. They were lied to about allegations of voter fraud. They were lied to about many things on conservative television shows, podcasts, and pulpits. They attempted to disguise a coup as an exercise of their First Amendment rights. Our country was not fooled, and now, hundreds of those who stormed the capital are in prison.

I have experienced life under authoritarian rule. In Chapter Two, I discuss some experiences from my southern way of life. I also propose that alternative approaches may be considered before contributing to the country's decline. Those of us who remember life in America before 1965 acknowledge that the nation is imperfect and requires further progress. We unequivocally condemn all inhumanity in any form.

Through The Eyes of This Black Woman

It is important to share with you my experiences and my viewpoints. I believe that cultures that do not preserve and teach their people's values, traditions, and history will one day lose their identity, pride, and dignity. We must teach the value of knowledge and respect for history. If we do not, we will have a divided community. The majority of Black Americans currently alive did not experience, Jim Crow. Many did not experience segregation. They do not know what it is like to live in an autocracy. As I write, tensions are very high here as we move closer to the 2024 elections. Please understand that we cannot make the mistake of returning to an autocracy in 2025. Some of us who lived under authoritarian rule remember what it was like. The Black community must take an aggressive position.

The omission of Black people from American History has crippled all Americans. This has left White people who may not subscribe to the White Supremacy Ideology of segregation and power do not really know our contributions to this nation. The overt and covert behaviors to render us inferior are the intentional behaviors of White supremacists. Therefore, the rights of Black people have never fully been recognized. Political differences of opinion should not, however, prevent our community from identifying solutions that make our democracy stronger. Our path forward is to elect more Black politicians who will vote for what's best for the country, not just for us or what's best for the wealthy and the White.

In 2023, the U.S. Congress refused to vote on The John Lewis Voting Rights Act because it would protect the voting rights of this nation's most oppressed and disenfranchised communities. It is important to know that John Lewis almost lost his life during the Civil Rights Movement. He led a march across the Pettus Bridge in Selma, Alabama, and was brutally beaten by the police as they marched.

I suggest that today's issues will not matter if the fight for our democratic system of governance is lost. It is understandable that any generation of Americans who has not lived in or heard stories about our ancestors' genius, courage, and sacrifices may refuse to listen. The best way to prevail is to fight for what our ancestors died for - freedom and liberty. They were determined to fight for the freedom of all disenfranchised people. Liberty is not just for Black people. Black people fought and died so that America would someday be the greatest country in the world. Remember, we are descendants of genius. We built America. It would not exist without us. It is our child as much as anyone. No people's blood has stained the soil of this country more than ours.

The first Black African slaves arrived in the American colonies in 1525. Over the next 340 years, more than 12 million Black Africans were transported to America as part of the Transatlantic Slave Trade. Tragically, over 2 million slaves perished during the journey known as the Middle Passage. Our sweat, blood, tears, innovation, creativity, and resilience-built America. We cannot let others who only care about themselves tear it down. Our blood, sweat, and tears stain the ground of this country.

Have you ever worked tenaciously to achieve a personal goal? If so, you can appreciate our parents' determination to provide a better life for us. When you look at our history, it's hard to comprehend the depth of their sacrifice, fear, pain, faith, and hope. Their efforts to provide us with better opportunities in America serve as a model I hope you embrace. Our history teaches us to let our indelible spirit guide us in all endeavors. From The Plantation to Jim Crow

White supremacists have continued to perpetuate segregation between our two ethnicities. Following the era of slavery, our ancestors transitioned from the cotton fields into the segregated society of Jim Crow. Systemic racism was perpetuated largely through mechanisms such as segregation and sharecropping. White supremacists ensured that at least 85% of the Black community remained undereducated.

Then, in the 1980s, illegal substances flooded the Black community. The illegal recreational drug market became an attractive yet deceptive way for some to make big money quickly and easily. However, the devastation and destruction drugs did to families and communities would take decades to repair. Systematically, entire cities were stripped of their dignity, freedom, cultural cohesion, and sanity. Today, the inequalities in these areas below continue the cycle of Systemic Racism in America.

They are…

- Education.
- Health education.
- Police brutality.
- Versions of the Christian religion.
- Economics.
- Climate change.
- Housing.
- Employment.

Their aim was clear. The legislative, executive, and judicial branches of government would write, interpret, and enforce laws that would perpetuate White supremacy. Systemic Racism was designed to create roadblocks that keep Black people marginalized and disenfranchised. White supremacy lost a battle when this country tore down the proverbial walls of Jim Crow. However, this did not stop them. They would wage a war on the Black community and call it a War on Drugs.

Due to Systemic Racism, my ancestors were compelled to struggle for the same equality that White people enjoyed. They believed that democracy would ultimately secure "fairness for all people." It should be no surprise that the incremental gains that we made toward achieving equality are often absent from history books.

Hundreds of Black people were lynched during Jim Crow. Many more were beaten by gangs of White people. We were spat on and attacked by large dogs. We were shot by the police for no reason. Our homes were burnt to the ground. Crosses were burned on our lawns. Black people could not testify in court against a White person. It was not illegal for a White man to rape a black woman. Black men could be arrested for being unemployed. The pains we endure today pale in comparison to what our ancestors faced. They did not abandon hope. They had faith. That is what we must do. We must hold on to our hope and our faith. We must not lose sight of the imminent reality that our rights, freedoms, and liberty can be taken from us if our country returns to an autocratic form of governance. We must remain focused on the real issue, our freedom. Don't let social issues keep you from understanding the importance of keeping our democracy alive.

The progress that we made over the past three generations in mainstream America will not matter if we do not vote to keep our Democracy intact. Our ancestors started this race to equality, and we must continue it until all American citizens are treated equitably. Our form of government is the foundation upon which all of our institutions are built. If the foundation collapses all that we built upon it is destroyed. All the progress is lost. All of the pain, sacrifice, and struggle was in vain. The Constitution and all the amendments are no longer guiding principles or laws that can protect us or our interests. If we do not vote to preserve our democracy now, there is a strong possibility that we may never get a second chance in our lifetimes.

The late Reverend James Cleveland was also a great gospel singer. The opening line in one of his songs says, "I don't feel no ways tired. I've come too far from where I started from…." While it may be grammatically challenging, its intent is to remind us that we are not quitters.

Jim Crow

Jim Crow laws persisted in America for over a century following the signing of the Emancipation Proclamation. These laws, instituted in the late 1800s, remained effective until the Civil Rights Acts of the 1960s and 1970s. Jim Crow served as a crucial social and political mechanism of segregation. For instance, while African American men could enlist in the military, they were segregated, even when fighting alongside White soldiers in the foxholes during World War II.

For over a century after the abolition of slavery, America continued to systematically practice and endorse legal segregation, violence, and discrimination. The governments in power refused to grant Black people the same rights, protections, and privileges as Whites. White supremacists designed systems to disenfranchise people based solely on their race. Institutions like the U.S. Census, IRS, and credit bureaus were established to uphold these mechanisms of oppression. All three branches of government enacted policies and laws that established White supremacy as both legal precedent and constitutional.

In 1857, the United States Supreme Court ruled on the Dred Scott case. The landmark Supreme Court case further entrenched racial discrimination in America. The Court ruled that Black people, whether enslaved or free, could not be considered American citizens and, therefore, had no standing to sue in federal court. The Black man had no rights that the White man was required to observe. Chief Justice Roger B. Taney wrote in the majority decision that the Founders' words in the Declaration of Independence, "all men were created equal," were never intended to apply to Black people. Judge Taney also declared the Missouri Compromise unconstitutional, effectively allowing slavery to spread into new territories. The ruling intensified national tensions over slavery and became a legal precedent. It reinforced our belief that racism was systemic. This decision, in part, contributed to the outbreak of the Civil War.

Although the Emancipation Proclamation that President Abraham Lincoln signed on January 1, 1863, led to the abolishment of chattel slavery, less than eight years later, White people devised and implemented a set of Jim Crow Laws that would perpetuate the slave culture for another 100 years reinforcing the systemic racism permitted by the U.S. Supreme Court in the Dredd Scott decision.

Jim Crow laws were an extension of the slave codes and black codes forged by autocratic leaders and supported by the United States Supreme Court. Physical enslavement was replaced with economic and social enslavement. Debtors' prisons, redlining, convict lease systems, criminal surety systems, and high interest rates led our people into the arms of economic enslavement. These Jim Crow Laws allowed White Supremacists, the right to steal our land, money, freedom, and lives without redress or compensation to the victims. Jim Crow ushered in the second era of slavery.

During the Jim Crow Era, most Black people in the South were sharecroppers who lived in cabins, shacks, sheds, and small, crowded homes without indoor plumbing or running water. Water came from pumps, wells, and streams. Without washing machines or dryers, clothes were washed and rinsed in large tin tubs, then hung on clotheslines, fences, and doors to dry. Bed frames were typically made from iron or wood scraps, with mattresses that were crafted from coarse cotton cloth filled with straw. Pillows were often fashioned from potato sacks stuffed with bird feathers. Many families lacked kitchen tables and chairs, eating instead from tin pans with wooden utensils. Those with lamps used kerosene and cotton wicks, while others relied on homemade candles or the light from the fireplace. Many homes lacked windows, and the floors were made of dirt or clay, covered with sawdust or straw. Roofs were often constructed from tin, and none of the homes had insulation.

The wind and rain beating on the tin roofs of their homes caused concerns about water leaks and damage that might require money for repairs. For the sharecroppers, on many days, food was scarce. Our people believed that Jesus Christ and education were our deliverers. They worked tirelessly to make Christianity and Education the path forward.

As a little girl, I remember visiting the Northeast. I traveled to Manhattan and Brooklyn. I also visited Newark, Philadelphia, and Pittsburgh. I still remember feeling suffocated and overwhelmed by the big cities. Jim Crow in the North was different. I remember the stale air, the close buildings, and the heavy grease smells seeping out from the cracks underneath or around apartment doors. I remember the dim lights on stairwells with feces and urine underneath and the sirens from police cars zooming through the densely populated streets. For a minute, it made me see my life in the country very differently. Visiting the large Black communities of the Northeast was a culture shock to my system.

I also traveled to the Midwestern States of Michigan and Illinois. They were also different from the South. I remember noticing the difference in land and building configurations. Unfortunately, the living conditions for Black people were also devastating. I can still remember feeling an indescribable trepidation that would make me cry.

Jim Crow was devastating us regardless of where we lived. The conditions forced upon our communities during the Jim Crow Era were not just inhumane; they were ruthless, evil, and cruel. It was the malice of White supremacy that created these conditions. This experience inspired me to alleviate people's suffering. I vowed that when I grew up, I would help people in any way I could.

Unemployment and poor education were a problem during Jim Crow, and they continue to be a problem today. Largely in part because it wasn't until 1954, with the U.S. Supreme Court decision in Brown v. Board of Education, that Black people were granted the right to a public education. In fact, in many states, it was illegal for a Black person to read.

Hard work and staying out of trouble was non-negotiable. Whether a child lived in a home that spoke broken English or lived in a home that spoke the queen's English, all children were expected to work and be respectful. We would work from sunup till sundown with the determination to succeed and help each other. We did not receive any financial aid from the local, state, or federal government, so we did not grow up expecting or knowing how to apply for loans, grants, or public assistance. Only White people were provided public assistance and aid from the government. There were no help or handouts for Black people.

In the spring of each year, before attending school, our work included milking cows, sweeping yards, cleaning night cans, feeding pigs, taking cows out to graze, and manually plowing the fields. In the Fall, we tilled the soil. We also picked cotton, cut corn, pulled potatoes, and cropped vegetables to take in the markets on Saturdays.

We rarely watched television. Cable, cell phones, and video games had not yet been invented, and computers were also not invented at this time. A few of us owned radios and listened to music during the week. On Sunday nights, we hovered around the radios at 7 p.m. We listened to gospel and old-time music.

After dinner on Sunday, many of us visited the sick or other family members. If we were old enough, we could "Court" on Wednesday and Sunday evenings. During the week, after chores, we played outdoor games until "first night"- dusk and bingo, Bid Whist, or Pic-up 52. During the week, we would recite our math, say short sentences, and describe the function of each word. We would often crowd around our elders and listen to them tell us stories about their upbringing.

Most of us had one pair of school shoes and one pair of "Sunday" shoes. Some children wore shirts and dresses made from the Purina sacks that once held fertilizer for farming. Generally, boys made skates out of soda cans and basketball rims out of tires and tire rims. They used yarn to make the strings for the rims. They found old farm tools to make other games. They would often use pipes for baseball bats and crocus sacks filled with sand for their bases. Most girls learned how to make dolls from corn cobs and grass. Colors of Rit dye were used to color the doll's cheeks and lips. Their clothes were made from the scraped cloths left from quilting. We learned to braid hair using weeds. Our creative juices were always flowing. Our community at large may not have been from the same bloodline, but our relationship was so interwoven that all of us were family.

Who We are Now

Tensions are very high here, as we move closer to election season. Please understand this governing system so that we do not make the mistake of going back into an Autocratic rule of governance in 2025. In the Black community, there remains a group of people who lived in this country under an Authoritarian governance while White America enjoyed the Democracy gleaned from the intent of the U.S. Constitution. Our community must take on an aggressive role. National and international issues must never override our need to hold fast to America's White Democracy. Black citizenship remains tentative because we have never had enough people in the halls of Congress to make voting a Law for us. In 2023 the U.C. Congress refused to vote on The John Lewis Voting Rights Act.

Later, we will differentiate between Acts and Laws later. It is important to know that John Lewis almost lost his life during the Civil Rights Movements. He led a march across the Pettus Bridge in Selma, Alabama and was brutally beaten by the police as they marched.

I suggest that *issues* will not matter if the fight for our democratic *system* of governance loses the ballot box in 2024. It is understandable, that any generation of Black American citizens, who have not lived in or heard stories about the genius, courage, and sacrifices of our elders may refuse to vote for Democracy. The best way to ensure that it prevails is to continue the fight our ancestors began for freedom and liberty. Their determination to fight for freedom and liberty was not just for Black people, our people fought so that humanity would someday have its direly needed value among all people. Remember, we are born from the loins of Warriors who are seasoned in what divisions and inhumanity yield. They came to America physically enslaved but endowed with millions of years of knowledge around building civilizations.

Have you ever worked tenaciously to achieve a goal that you set for yourself? If so, it gives you a vantage point from which to grasp the determination our fore parents must have had toward leaving a legacy that we could grasp. Try to process their leg of our history even though you may not understand how they processed their commitment to succeed. The fact that they worked for us to have better advantages in their New World is the model that I hope you grasp. They passed their contributions forward as steppingstones for us in this generation. Our history has been to ensure that in all things we always allow our indelible spirit to guide us.

In 2024, Black Americans are a multitude of ethnicities and identities. Many have native American, Asian, European, and Hispanic family members or ancestors. Many Black girls and women were also raped by the enslavers or other White men. Very few Americans who are not first-generation immigrants are not "mixed." The African American spirit embodies the true American spirit. We are a people of many backgrounds, religions, ethnicities, sizes, shapes, hair textures, and features. Many of us have family members, past and present, who pass for White or are considered ethnically ambiguous.

This diversity of background, culture, DNA, and experience makes us one of the world's most creative, innovative, resilient, athletic, talented, and adaptable ethnicities. We are highly energetic, with strong lungs for talking, speaking, singing, and laughing. We are equally rhythmic and excel in the entertainment industry. We are poetic. We instinctively care and are both compassionate and empathetic.

For years, I enjoyed public speaking at national and international conferences. Many of the attendees would be predominately White. If there was feedback from the sessions, invariably, the question would be, "Are you a preacher?" This happened many years before I actually began preaching. I decided to ask, "Why am I asked about preaching?" Almost always, the answer would be something about my cadence, volume, and animation. I started paying attention to speakers from other ethnic groups. I was tickled to learn that the question, "Are you a preacher?" Was a code term for "Why must you be so loud?" They were really implying that I was different. I spoke too fast, and my physical movements looked like gyrations to many of these inquirers. The fact that creativity has its own uniqueness was not permitted. I was too loud and too animated by their standards. My accomplishments that brought me as a headliner to their conferences, conventions, and school systems were not enough, I guess. There had to be something to critique. Now, I smile.

Years earlier, someone said something harsh about my grandmother (Mama). I was furious and perplexed when I saw Mama treating the person so kindly. She explained that forgiveness relieves the person who has been offended of a dark burden. So, forgiveness is in my best interest. I reserved trusting him because, according to Mama, trust and forgiveness are two very different things. You can forgive a person, but that doesn't mean you must trust them.

I suspect that if I had not been given that lesson years earlier, I might have been insulted and refused to share the wealth of knowledge that led me to this phase of my professional life. But our fore parents understood that to be successful, they had to think clearly and focus on the future. It is difficult to think clearly when you are angry. It is even harder to focus on the future when always ruminating on the past. A clouded mind does not produce the best results. I have come to understand that our ancestors would never have left us with this rich legacy if they did not forgive. The dark weight would have diminished their ingenuity and creativity.

What I Learned

I learned to be creative and to not expect others to give me what I can obtain for myself. I learned to share what I have, not because others are entitled, but because giving is a value of benevolence. I learned that expecting appreciation leads to disappointment, and not receiving it must never stop me from appreciating others. I learned that dignity is earned, tenacity comes from pressing onward when things seem to crumble, and success triumphs over fear. I learned that facing challenges is not a reason to harbor ill will, and that I can voluntarily love my offenders and require them to earn my trust. I learned that I must define myself and to never allow some else to do it for me. I learned that seeking accolades by impressing others is a waste of time, and that focusing on the weaknesses of others without working on my own is a recipe for disaster.

I do not quit. I do not compromise the ethical standard I agree to live by. While other people do not have my life story, theirs is likely to be comparable. I know what happens when we grumble less, work more, use our creative juices often, and refuse to allow excuses to justify our failures.

Much of what I learned growing up in the Jim Crow Era down south were lessons that have stuck with me for life. The deliberate focus on and dedication to excellence has taught me a lot and brought me into experiences I never knew existed. After all, I am the statuesque Black girl from rural South Carolina who has traveled to six of the seven continents. I believe in Jesus Christ and chose to incorporate him in every facet of my life. I also chose to believe that good people exist even when they are not of my ethnicity, race, intersectionality, political identity, religion, age, ability, gender, tax bracket, or culture.

We are Essential Americans

Questioning what it means when we refer to ourselves as a "Black community" has obligated setting the context for this conversation. Our present generations need to know our history. They need to know that there has never been a time since we came to these shores that we have not been indispensable to this nation's growth and development. There has never been a time when the economic machine that propels this nation has not known us to be an imperative. Our fore parents knew this. Our professional athletes must know this. They must know how vital they are to the economic development of this country. Our scientist must know this. They must know how necessary they are to the health of this nation. Our educators must know how crucial they are to the development of all minds in this nation. Continuing to rise requires diligence and commitment to our American citizenship.

Logistics

I like Milton Friedman's quote, which says, "A society that puts equality before freedom will get neither. A society that puts freedom before equality will get a high degree of both." Deliberate social misinformation and unjust policies have allowed inequities to remain the historical axis from which American judicial and legislative systems rotate. This conversation chronicles the plight of Black Americans from slavery: 1619-present.

Definitions in the glossary denote the most specific intent of words used in this conversation. Throughout this conversation, the words White and Black, when referencing people, are deliberately capitalized and the term *Systemic Racism* is in italics and capitalized for emphasis.

Chariots Depart

Please join me on a journey as I share tales of the tenacity, strength, and determination of our ancestors' indelible spirit. The greatest responsibility each citizen has to America is to vote for equality. We must remain diligent and focused on building a country that is fair and equitable for everyone. Democracy is not dead. Like our ancestors, we must use the tools we have to create the world we want. For the Black community, the most powerful tool in our toolbox is our right to vote.

We can be manipulated by White supremacy and lulled into another era of darkness, or we can fight for freedom. It cannot be overstated that the vote of every Black citizen of America must always appear in the ballot box as we fight for a better way of life for everyone. We are a people of varied learning styles. We are rhythmic. I will share patterns, prose, and poetry. Please give yourself permission to listen and learn. We are also visual artists, and I will share photos and images. The various ways I share are intended to connect with different types of learners. Some will take this journey with me intuitively, others cognitively, visually, or spiritually.

Listen for and to the spirit of our ancestors as they tell us about Our story, not His story. Become a participant and travel alongside me. Finally, consider how you can ensure our country

Prologue

does not take steps backward. We are all runners in the Relay to Liberty and Justice. The baton is yours.

"If we do not act, we shall be dragged down the long, dark and shameless corridors of time reserved for those who possess power without compassion, might without morality, and strength without sight."

Dr. Martin Luther King, Jr.

Family, you are members of the three generations of men whose lives represent the progress of our ancestors. You Continue to break the myths and proverbial shackles of the post enslaved as you demonstrate the strength, dignity, and determination to succeed. You are a source of Light in the Relay to Liberty and Justice as you, too, are Continuing to Rise.

CHAPTER ONE

Setting The Context

"Things that we have heard and known, that our fathers have told us. We will not hide them from their children but tell the coming generation the glorious deeds of the Lord, and his might, and the wonders that he has done."

Psalm 78:3-4 King James Version

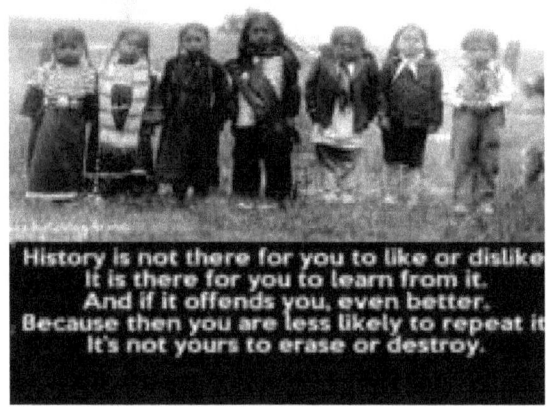

When the U.S. Constitution was written, its Framers, some of whom were White supremacists, did not consider that Black people would ever enter its Democratic framework. Democracy is an ideal that can work if we aspire for liberty and justice for all of its citizens. Over time the content of the Constitution has been challenged. The wording still brings duress to members of this nation who believe that its intent supersedes its content. I wonder if we understand the tension between the wording of the Constitution and the stilted ideology that continues to drive the actions of the congressional members.

The U.S. Congress is still structured by the Constitution, and it is still the Rule of Law for all Americans. Congress' leaders are voted into office to enforce its governance for all citizens. According to the Constitution's written content, the benefits are equal. White supremacy ideology declares that the intent the Framers wrote was for "Whites Only." The inertia of the U.S. Congress in 2024 is proof. When the duties of Congress are overrun by political fanaticism, chaos is inevitable.

While the dilemma of human inequality may apply in ethnic groups, through my eyes, the focus of our conversation is specific to the history of Black people. It is omitted in the history of America as White people wrote it. We believe that equality is based upon the content of the Constitution instead of the intent of its Framers or present-day White supremacists.

America's History left out the contributions of all ethnic groups who contributed to the development of American Culture, not American White Culture. This creates a deficit for this entire American society. In 2024 it causes much consternation for White supremacists. They would rather destroy the Constitution than to accept Black people as human beings who are

Chapter One - Setting the Context

equal to them. Many of the supremacists may be the Evangelicals who subscribe to what is known as White Christian Nationalism.

After coming through enslavement and Jim Crow, the next step was for our ancestors to become free and take their rightful places in America. They began to run a Relay for Liberty and Justice for all American citizens. Each step in their relay was met with violence and hatred. The White supremacists did not give Up, nor did we. We moved out of struggle into victory. Each time, our motto prevailed, "Watch as well as pray."

Our conversation is rooted in the genius and ingenuity of our ancestors. Each leg of the relay required them to be innovative, creative, resolute, and resilient. Our ancestors learned how to channel their anger and be productive. They refused to let anger keep them from moving forward. They knew that if they quit, the White supremacists would win. We must stay in the race. We must become and remain informed about ways to stop evil.

White people are privileged by default. All of them, however, do not subscribe to the White supremacy ideology. They seem to make up at least four major categories in America. The first category has lived in an exclusive White America most of their lives and is unaware of the insidious effects of racism on the daily lives of Black people. The Second category recognizes these effects and remains detached from the mistreatments Black people suffer. The third category actively participates in the destruction of Black people. The fourth category's aim is to support the notion that Black and Brown American citizens have equal rights in the democratic process. During chattel slavery, White abolitionists helped Black people escape to the North, where slavery was not as prevalent. In later years, many more of them were allies during the Civil Rights Movement.

Our story must be told and retold since so much of it has been left out of American history. Each of us must be able to recall our history and recognize the evil that prevails through the White supremacy ideology in this country. It is why we must continue fighting for Democracy. All people should be treated with dignity regardless of their race or skin complexion. Below are examples of atrocities perpetuated against Black people that must not be tolerated.

- On January 1, 2020, in Washington, D.C., millions of us watched as thousands of radical supremacists, who believed that the national election of the sixth President of the U.S. was rigged, stormed the U.S. Congress with the intent to stop the ratifying of his presidency and to kill certain members of Congress.

- On March 13, 2020, Breonna Taylor was shot into unrecognizable shreds in her home as she slept. This happened in Louisville, Kentucky. Three police officers stormed into Breonna's home unannounced under the auspices of a "no knock" search warrant. The assailants were not charged initially.

- On May 25, 2020, in Minneapolis, Minnesota, three police officers executed George Floyd for supposedly paying for some items with a fake $20.00 bill. One White police officer kept his knee on Mr. Floyd's neck for three and a half minutes. Bystanders were begging for Officer Chauvin to remove his knee from Mr. Floyd, who was crying out, saying, "I can't breathe." The two other officers on the scene kept the bystanders at bay.

The flurry of violence that Black people endure continues in America. It reminds me of the interview that the newsman Sandor Vanocur had with Dr. Martin Luther King, Jr. During the interview, Dr. King said, "Well, there was no doubt about the hypocrisy of large segments of the nation on the whole question of racial equality." (See Appendix one.) Then, the ancestral inner voice's questions were, "Who really knows our personal experiences throughout our history? How many parents tell their children the story of our past?" I pondered and thought, if you are under

55 years old, how many of you know it?" Could Marcus Garvey have been right when he said, "People without the knowledge of their past history, origin, and culture is like a tree without roots?"

The tentacles of racism continue to strike with a vengeance. Although we face the evil of White Supremacy, we are steadfast in our conviction and unwavering in our faith. We know that on the horizon is an American Democracy built by all of us for all of us.

The immediacy of my conversation is a result of hearing the discontent of Black people. Many have said that they may not vote in local, state, and national elections. The reason our ancestors never stopped moving on their Relay to Liberty and Justice was because White supremacists never stopped trying to dehumanize them. They understood that a fragile Democracy was better than an Autocracy. They continued the relay out of slavery and the Jim Crow Era. Their indelible spirits are urging us to continue the relay. Our ancestors called it Liberty and Justice; we know it as Democracy. We can never stop our relay because the White supremacists never stop trying to return us to a subservience that dehumanizes us. As the possibility of Autocracy looms large in our country in 2024, nothing must keep our people from voting for Democracy. A determination for any Black person not to vote affirms the White supremacy ideal. Voting can never be an option; it must always be a responsibility.

Through the Eyes of This Black Woman takes a three-pronged historical premise. The first premise purports that White Supremacy is manifested and perpetuated through Systemic Racism. The second premise acknowledges that all White people do not believe in White Supremacy. Most White people do, however, receive the social and economic privileges this society affords. Some segments of this group join the Black struggle while others may remain oblivious of our community's perpetual Relay to Liberty and Justice in this country. The third premise declares that Black people are born with an indelible spirit. Our history proves that we are Continuing to Rise despite the barrage of injustices and inequalities imposed upon us through Systemic Racism. These three perspectives are intentionally reiterated throughout this conversation.

Exclusive White Rule

The U.S. Constitution remains in conflict between the intention of its actual wording and who it was meant to guide. It states that all people are equally endowed with the right to liberty and justice by birth. When it was ratified, the social structure of America meant for the Constitution to apply to All White European men. To ensure this social structure in 1790 the Naturalization Act was passed. This was the first law to define the eligibility for citizenship and to establish standards and procedures that immigrants must follow to become citizens. Congress limited this important right to "free White people." Over time, things in that society have changed to include multiple ethnic and cultural groups. Enslaved Black people are now full citizens of America with the legal rights of the "free White people." We have the right to enjoy the benefits that were intended in the actual writing of the U.S. Constitution. We have moved from enslavement to leaders of this nation.

There is a movement toward the return of White Supremacy in this nation. The people who led this rebellion are determined to resurrect the "Thing-I-fy" Dr. King described. See the second Appendix. This insurgence is led by a group of White people whose goal is to deconstruct the U.S. Constitution and to become an Authoritarian government. There are many of us living who have experienced this behavior before.

America is our home, and as we defend it, we refuse to be labeled or to accept the unbecoming labels that do not define our humanity. We are strong and resilient Black people who overcame the barriers of language and culture. The physical segregated life of our past did not include us in the American workforce or education system. It paid us meager wages for essential jobs. We continue to experience the inequities of poorer education from pre-K through college, lower wages, and poorer housing. These are among the inequities that persist today. Yet, we refuse to return to yesteryear or to subscribe to the notion of a God, defined by White nationalists, who justifies socio-political dominance.

As we travel through compelling examples that our ancestors endured while Continuing to Rise, this conversation's purpose is to excite our community to remain focused on our ability to succeed despite physical and emotional injuries. We must remain focused as we celebrate our successes. Our ancestors taught us that our best weapon is success and to remain guided, through what we will call the indelible spirit's guidance. We must not fear or become stuck in anger from White supremacists' legislative, judicial, or physical weapons of destruction.

Our Indelible Spirit Reigns

There is an indelible spirit that Black people relied upon as our guide. It existed long before we came to America. This spirit continues to guide us, ignite our endurance amid struggle, and remind us of our quest for the humanity and dignity of all people. Today, our belief system remains antithetical to some of the generations of enslavers who took our ancestors away from the land where civilization had existed under Black people for millennia.

In his book, The Hidden Roots of White Supremacy, Robert P. Jones links Systemic Racism and White supremacy ideologies with Christian nationalism. He describes, from a historical context, a reason White people who believe in White supremacy may have a sense of superiority. Many of their ancestors came to American because they had been oppressed in Europe based upon the European socio-political stance on Christianity. How could this be? They came to this soil, took it from the native Indians, then joined thee writers of the U.S. Constitution, and the Declaration of Independence who were their atheist or agnostic counterparts.

Dr. Jones tells us that around the 1500s, White Christian leaders declared a sector of humanity as inferior to them as the will of God. It seems that some Europeans, who immigrated to these shores, may have abided by this declaration. Their idea of superiority may have been to do to others what they endured in Europe. So they continue taking from any ethnic group they declare subservient to them. This appears to be the ideology of the first settlers and it continues through their generations! Black people know these theatrics.

If the indelible spirit did not continue to reign in us today, Black people may have become extinct like the Mayans. They were a civilization who was conquered by the Spanish colonizers between 1517 and 1545. We are members of the African civilization that taught us how to sustain ourselves amid the adversities we continue to face. This has been true through generations. The issues of "fair" and "unfair" do not drive us to success. We have remained on these shores, and we are Continuing to Rise in America. Thus, in this generation, we continue the Relay to Liberty and Justice.

America is Our Home

The structure of the present American public education can subliminally build racist constructs as early as pre- kindergarten. The issue in the Black community is not the lack of intellect. It is usually the poorly kept facility and the biases in curriculum and instruction in the public schools where Black children populate. This American public education system lends itself to the systemic schemes, plots, and conspiracies perpetuated by this American White Supremacy Ideology. Despite this reality, since 1619, we have continued to be great contributors to this country while Continuing to Rise. Believe it! America is our home!

Through The Eyes of This Black Woman

Is it possible that the present public education system is designed so that most community members cannot compete in the American Marketplace? Is our invisibility so crucial that all students cannot have the advantage of the "Ivy-League" curriculum from pre-kindergarten through college? Do the "powers that be" really believe Black people have not figured out what perpetuates the White supremacists' need for us to remain invisible in the public school's curriculum? The lawsuits that combined the landmark Brown V. Board of Education Supreme Court case outlawed segregation in schools in 1954. Yet here we are in 2024. What was once the separation of physical bodies is now the blatant distinction between public and "Ivy-League" curricula. What one learns generally determines one's lifestyle.

Our ancestors taught us that equality for all humanity must remain our guiding principle. As we travel through compelling examples of turmoil our ancestors endured, we will see why the enigma of generations of our community Continuing to Rise remains. The intent of this conversation is for us to remain focused on our genius and our abilities despite these realities.

There are people who continue to employ inequality and injustice. They are perpetuating racism by changing voting maps throughout this country to restrict the Black voice—our legitimate voice as American citizens to be recognized. We must not lose hope because of the tenets of racism as we continue to rise. Black people must pay closer attention to things that inform and prepare children for today's marketplace job requirements.

Our ancestors understood the need for a change in our mainstream governmental structure and found ways, amid turmoil, to get this achievement. We must increase our membership in local, state, and federal legislative and judicial structures. Regardless of intent, the writers of the Declaration of Independence and the Constitution pinned and signed these documents by saying, "We hold these truths to be evident that all men (meaning people) are equal..." Places to make changes can be our education, legislative, and judicial systems.

We cannot fear or become overwhelmed by the White supremacists' legislative and judicial structures. We must take our rightful places among them. People from our community must become members of the local, state, federal, and judicial systems. Since the inception of this democratic process, leaders in positions of power have rendered verdicts of separate and not equal. We know their attempts and our accomplishments.

Constant V. Fluid

Black History is constant. Things that dictate economic and social changes in our lifestyles are fluid. This society has moved from the Age of Agriculture and Industrial systems into the Age of Technology. In the Age of Agriculture, our ancestors brought to this country many skills that have withstood the age of time. Fifteen of the American landmarks they built are standing today. They grew cotton and harvested what became the first commodity on the Wall Street Stock Exchange in the same year, 1792. They built the railroads and docks and participated in trade unions during the Industrial Age since 1869. Today, 17 Black inventors changed the Tech world/Digital Trends in the Age of Technology. The evidence of our participation in the constant growth of our America remains fluid. We know that we must remain vigilant.

In our community, there are two and a half generations (50 years) of Black people who may not know about our ancestors' richness. They may not know their link in the continuum of our journey to freedom. From the grave, our ancestors cry out, telling us that truth cannot die. Whether we are Black, Brown, or White, those of us born into this world are human beings; those of us born in America or immunized are citizens.

Black people were physically enslaved from 1619 until The Emancipation Proclamation was signed in 1886. From 1877 until 1964, "The Jim Crow Laws" terrorized, marginalized, and made us socialize mainly by ourselves. The Civil Rights Movement of 1965 moved us into another form of marginalization. This time, we had to compete in a mainstream that had been established by White people for White People since the 1700s. In this position, many of us survived while others of us thrived. We began to build lives that isolated us from each other. We became members of classism. Some of us ask, "Who is the Black Community?"

These current national and ethnic tensions are requiring our community to come together and take note of the overt hatred that is being evidenced in America. It directly impacts our community. As I have this conversation with you, violence and hatred in America are real and appear to be perpetuated by a provincial Christian indoctrination that historically promotes anti-Semitism, ethnic separation, and the insistent political and historical cycle of White Supremacy Ideology. In his book Race, Religion, and Racism, Vol. 1, Dr. Fred Price said, "Slavery would not have existed if the White church did not allow it." There is a distinction to be made between patriotism and nationalism. Philip Gorski, chair of the Department of Sociology at Yale, says, "Patriotism is an adherence to ideals of the United States, and Nationalism is loyalty to your tribe and not the nation." There is a full-court push to have this nation ruled by the guidelines of the insurgence of Nationalism. Nationalists are traitors rather than patriotic Americans. They are trying to find ways to destroy our Constitutional Rights.

It is fair to say that today's White supremacists are also Nationalists and traitors. They are indeed organized and are a community. The current unrest in America is a historical cycle that continues to maintain a dual governmental process. According to Dr. Gorski's definition of Nationalism, it appears that White Christian Nationalism is tribal. There is a need for a clearly defined Black community in this era that willingly works and socializes with people of all ethnicities. For those of us who believe in Democracy, we need each other.

After the Emancipation Proclamation Era, Jim Crow has plagued our lives. It began as the heinous Jim Crow Act of 1877. It used terrorizing and killing by hooded men who were pillaging the Black community, hanging our men, raping our women, and denying us public education. The second phase of Jim Crow was sharecropping and separate and unequal education. Today's phase of Jim Crow works through the lack of economic and financial solvency education for all members of the Black community. In all three stages, many members of our community remain relegated to sub-standard housing; young men remain incarcerated without a timeline for court or subjected to police violence; and death through the proliferation of guns on the streets. These are only a portion of our institutionalized realities. Yet, we continue to Rise!

The marginalization of Black people prevails through legal and legislative bodies of governance and remains part of the cyclical belief system that feeds the White Supremacy Ideology. It strives to prove us to be intellectually inferior to them. Here we are in 2024, and journalists continue to probe with questions that have the same tenor as the Sandor Vanocur/ Dr. King interview 67 years ago.

Cycles of Injustice

The insult of the supremacists' inhumane behavior manifested throughout the slavery period was made clear as a judicial inclusion when in 1857, Roger B. Taney, the Chief Justice of the U.S. Supreme Court, said, "The framers of the Constitution had no rights which the White man was bound to respect; and that the negro might justly and lawfully be reduced to slavery for his benefit. He was bought and sold and treated as an ordinary article of merchandise and traffic, whenever it could make a profit." Referring to the language in the Declaration of Independence that includes the phrase, "all men are created equal," Taney reasoned that, "it is clear for dispute, that the enslaved African race was not intended to be included and formed no part of the Taney could have believed his statements to be true because, as this cycle continues, he may have taken his position from the founders of the Constitution. According to Dr. Claud Anderson, the 1790

Naturalization Act said, "White people are to be citizens of America." Dr. Anderson says that the writers of the Constitution held a meeting the day after the Constitution was signed and wrote the Naturalization Act. Dr. Anderson also contends that "this was the first Act approved in the Congress after the Constitution was ratified. This insidious arrogance remains in the White Supremacist Ideology today. It is part of the cyclical remnant that Taney cited from his ancestors.

Who are We?

When our African family was enslaved, many members were royalty, some were well-educated, and most were politically savvy. Many of our people were inventors, engineers, astronomers, politicians, etc. Some of them were Christians or Muslims. This information was never recorded or spoken of by slave owners because we had to be portrayed as brutal, heathens, and other enigmas.

We are a brave people of integrity who have withstood the rigors of civilization, including its greatness and inhumanity, for millions of years. Our Ancestors, who were enslaved by White Americans, were not illiterate or unintelligent. The differences in language and culture where communication barriers. These African people were met with the same challenges each of us faces today when we visit countries or cultures, and we do not know how to read, write, speak their language, or understand their culture. American culture was as peculiar to them as African languages and cultures were the slave owners.

Black Social and Economic Disenfranchisement

Only 67 years ago, time once shared in the Black community became energy used in the public square. Many of us advanced into economic solvency, higher education, and classism independent of the interrelationship of our community. In doing so, some of us lost the connection to the constructive collaboration that focused our ancestors on a socio-political consciousness, which envisioned that Black people would make a better life for the collective of us.

On our journey, a portion of our people were traumatized and chose to forget our social plight. Others got angry and demanded that we make White supremacists give back what they took from us over generations. Some decided to drop out of the mainstream. While these varied realities were understandable, most of us continued our Relay to Freedom. The latter segment of us understood that the power of our intellect and genius had never been annihilated. Our power and constructive interaction remained connected in the oral Black history we shared around dinner tables, in our worship centers, and heard from elders.

The hard work of our fore parents reminds us of their hope for a life better than theirs. Even when their reality was poverty with indescribably deep struggles, many of their stories began with them saying, "One day…."

It was as if they were looking at their victory. The resolution on their declaration would be, "Now, watch what I tell you. You will see." These were stories that lived in their forecasts. The progression into Democracy in this conversation begins in the 1800s with Harriet Tubman, who escaped slavery and went to Philadelphia in 1849.

Harriet resolved that we, as human beings, had to be protected. She became an American abolitionist and social activist. In the late 1850s, she started what became known as the Underground Railroad. With a musket for protection, courage, and ingenuity to follow the North Star as her astrological guide, it is alleged that Harriet walked back to the South with her bare feet. Undaunted by threats, this warrior walked over 300 Black men, women, and children to freedom and became known as the woman called "Moses." This incredible act of courage and its ultimate success became one of the agitations that led to the Civil War. After that war, the Emancipation Proclamation was signed on January 1, 1863.

Harriet Tubman reaches out to us to be agitators of change

The Emancipation Proclamation

Since 1619, the separation of White and Black ethnicities existed. In 1863, President Abraham Lincoln signed The Emancipation Proclamation that released our formerly enslaved ancestors into a more devastating, impoverished situation. Our formerly enslaved fore parents had no place to go, no way to get food or shelter, no place to work, and no land. These people had never been responsible for American money and never had to look for employment. Many had never been away from the plantation where they had lived and worked.

180,000 Black men immediately signed up for the Union They comprised 10% of all Federal Forces. They were paid $10 per month (minus a clothing allowance in some cases)) yet White soldier got $13 per month (plus a clothing allowance in some cases). This was the first time most of them had been responsible for money on American soil. Others pooled their resources and purchased land from former slave owners. This too was short-lived. Jim Crow began in 1884.

For two hundred and forty years, our enslaved people survived the remnants they received from their former slave owners from 1619 – December 31, 1862. The next day, on January 1, 1863, our ancestors became wanderers. They were free without any provisions. They had to find work: they had no idea where to go because their lives had been sequestered when they were in slavery by their slave owners. Conversely, these southern slave owners were becoming poorer because their land was left untended. They had no money to pay for hires because their funds were used to fight the North regarding the issue of slavery. The slave owners lost.

This insult occurred when the South seceded from the Union. Southern slave owners lost the War and were left destitute with no idea how to deal with their farms. The system of government, however, remained what I call White America's Democracy. This dilemma led our community into the first Jim Crow Era. The name Jim Crow came from Thomas Dartmouth, a White actor who performed in blackface makeup as "Jim Crow." The Jim Crow Era lasted from 1868-1965.

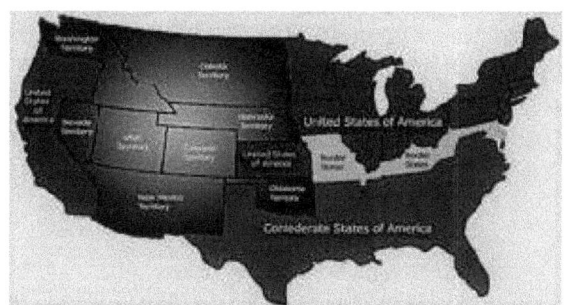

The U.S. Map of 1864

Slave Master Mentality

The White supremacists are a segment of the White ethnicity who believes that America is their Nation. They believe that they own the contributions that Black and Brown people have made, since its inception. Their psycho/spiritual mindset is that of the quasi-slave masers. The atrocities they heap upon Black people since 1619 is steeped in their belief that God gave them this privilege. Many of them are so blinded by power and privilege, that many of the Systemic Racism roadblocks our people incur are because of the standards of White supremacists. This mentality is not the sentiment of many White people. But, among this group, unfortunately, are those who cannot believe this to be our reality.

Not long after the Emancipation Proclamation was signed, for the first time on the American shores, formerly enslaved black men from southern states who chose to secede from the Union became citizens and members of the democratic process. Reconstruction history.com reports that "all persons held as slaves within the rebellious states are, and henceforward shall be free." This Proclamation exempted parts of the Confederacy that were under Northern control, and 300,000 enslaved people were freed. Additionally, 179,000 of our men enlisted in the Union Army.

The limitations of this Proclamation applied only to states that had seceded from the Union, leaving slavery untouched in the loyal border states--Delaware, Maryland, Kentucky, and Missouri, then, after 1863, West Virginia. It was not until June 19, 1865, that the word about their freedom reached Texas. On June 17, 2021, President Joe Biden signed a bill into law making the day known as "Juneteenth" a national holiday.

There were a few Black people in this nation who were never enslaved. They were entrepreneurs and financially solvent. However, they were not insulated from the racism that that all Black people the ruling factor for all Black people of that era. They were not allowed any civil privileges, even with their elaborate lifestyles

Trema, Louisiana in the 18th century was a place of pride, ownership, refuge, and wealth for free Black people.

Like the lives of the Black people who were never enslaved, the progress our former enslaved men made was astounding. Their courage, intellectual genius, and intergenerational connection to our history speak to the indelible linkage to leadership passed on by our ancestors who built the first civilizations on Earth. Some of our men went from being enslaved to being state and national representatives in the U.S. Senate, the House of Representatives, and State legislatures. However, that representation was short-lived for us. The backlash of White Christian Nationalists was swift and without mercy. Thus, most of our ancestors were forced to return to a lifestyle similar to living in a third-world country.

The Complexity of Freedom

After more than two hundred years of living on the property of slave owners, receiving the residuals of their land for food, as well as clothing and shelter, our former enslaved ancestors were forced off the land they had worked for generations without any food, housing, or possibility of work once slavery was abolished. Conversely, the former slave masters had no idea how to work their crops, and they needed free labor.

Blanche Bruce, 1867

Hiram Rhodes Revels, 1867

These two geniuses who had been enslaved four years earlier became national politicians from Mississippi. How could they have become prepared such positions just out of slavery? What prompted them to run for these offices? We may never get full answers to these questions, but we can see that it does not require much time to become responsible citizens.

White supremacists solved this problem by creating Black Codes and laws that criminalized unemployment, homelessness, and vagrancy. The courts, police, and politicians created a justice system to give former enslavers the needed free labor. This convict lease system and criminal surety system exist today.

Former slave catchers were hired as police officers, formerly enslaved were appointed as judges, and politicians were chosen by plantation owners to make laws that served their interests. Even in this situation, our ancestors never stopped working to make life better for upcoming generations. During this heinous era, Black people were lynched, tortured, castrated, raped, beaten, and murdered. Innocent Black people were arrested and incarcerated for decades over fabricated charges in attempts to force us physically and psychologically into submission. A freedman who was unable to find work could be sold into bondage to pay his debts. This tactic is still used in child support cases around the country. Thousands of people are currently in prison for failure to pay child support to the courts for children that aren't even theirs. Laws were implemented that exist today. They prevent those who are convicted of crimes from exercising their right to vote. These are just some examples of how enslavers and White supremacists use the courts and politicians to marginalize and disenfranchise thousands of innocent Black people.

Young White people enjoying the scene where a Black man hanged.

Relay to Liberty and Justice

A freed man who was unable to find work was sold to pay his bills.

Some of our ancestors were overwhelmed by the persistence of these inhumane practices. They became weary and died from the punishments. However, many lived to tell the stories and warn us of what could happen if we did not continue to fight for freedom and equality. They survived the social, physical, and mental atrocities of Systemic Racism.

The choice of all eligible Black people not voting today is a cry of despair from the graves of our ancestors. Even the Ku Klux Klan couldn't stop our ancestors from voting. These hooded Christian White people burned our properties and churches. They murdered our children and were never held accountable for any of the Klan's leaders or members were local White police officers, clergy, politicians, judges, bankers, schoolteachers, and capitalists.

In Perth Amboy, New Jersey, the first Black men voted after the 15th Amendment was enacted.

The Beginning of Public-School Desegregation

Seventy-three years into the Jim Crow Era, Reverend Joseph A. DeLaine, a Methodist minister in Clarendon County, South Carolina, led the charge to end public school segregation. This crusade initiated the civil rights movement to break down barriers of segregation in public schools. Reverend DeLaine believed and wrote that, "A person who hates another because of looks is just as bad as one who stupidly hates another's faith in the church of his choice." His opinion was that segregation in South Carolina was unconstitutional. This case was known in the U.S. Supreme Court as Briggs V. Elliot. It was heard as one of the five cases under the name of Brown V. Board of Education. This man stayed the course even after death threats made him leave his home State. He said the world needed to know, "I am not running from justice, but injustice."

Chapter One - Setting the Context

Reverend DeLaine's indelible spirit calls for us to run to justice in this generation.

Approximately 10 years later, the Civil Rights Movement built upon Reverend DeLaine's progress. Extended issues of labor and the moral obligation to include equal rights under the law in the United States were also part of the movement. Dr. Martin Luther King, Jr., became the national leader of the phase that moved us into the democratic process of this nation for a second time. MLK Jr. Among the civil rights leaders who made significant contributions during this era were Fred Shuttleworth, Ella Baker, Ralph Abernathy, Rosa Parks, Jesse Jackson, Fannie Lou Hamer, Andrew Young, Septima Poinsette Clark, Wyatt T. Walker, Jo Ann Robinson, The Honorable John Lewis, Bayard Rustin, and A. Philip Randolph.

Dr. King: The "Drum Major for Justice"

Our ancestors increased human mobilization and courageously met the challenges history records in the Civil Rights Movement, including ending the Jim Crow Era in 1965. Despite the violence — the beatings, bombings, jails, dogs, water hoses, and murder — the Movement continued. Many of us who kept boycotting, sitting, praying, preaching, meeting, marching, singing, and planning until the Civil Rights Act of 1965 was passed are still alive today.

During the Civil Rights Movement of the sixties, our courage to succeed was not deterred by raging violence, men, or dogs

Relay to Liberty and Justice

Through The Eyes of This Black Woman

Inhumane Control

Years after moving from authoritarian to democratic governance, White supremacy continues, as evidenced in the story of three Black men called the Angolan Three. White supremacists targeted these men as members of the Black Panther Party in the 1970s. For over 40 years, Albert Woodfox, Robert King, and Herman Wallace were exposed to segregation and violence in Angola Prison, Louisiana, USA. Collectively, they spent over 114 years in solitary confinement in a 6x9 cell for a crime that they did not commit. Two of these men decided that the story of their indecent sentencing of Black people continues to be one of the mechanisms that Jim Crow and slavery have kept in place.

The Angolan Three: From left to right are: Robert King, Herman Wallace, and Albert Woodfox

The justice system of this nation continues to practice systemic racism, illegal discrimination, and human rights violations. Today, Black people receive longer sentences for the same crimes as their White counterparts. Black men are given harsher sentences. Black men wait in jails before getting to court much longer than their White counterparts. Furthermore, like their ancestors, they are more likely to receive felony charges, which makes them ineligible to vote. Performing unpaid labor while incarcerated is another form of injustice that they suffer.

History reveals that anger, ignorance, control, and hate breed violence. However, our love for humanity and commitment to change must breed healing and accountability. Each of us must make our own decisions. Some of our ancestors chose to fight back with weapons, but most of our ancestors chose the path of non-violent, peaceful protests. They showed us a different way that is consistent with true Christianity's teachings.

Many Black people, especially young men, are incarcerated, placed in privately owned prisons, and given long unfair sentences.

Chapter One - Setting the Context

Never Again

It is imperative that we remember our history. Current social injustices must be met with the same dedication, genius, and leadership we experienced during slavery, Jim Crow, and the Civil Rights Movement. The more we exercise our constitutional rights, the more we remove Jim Crow from our lives. Black people must receive equitable compensation, treatment, access, protection, and justice.

Today, in the homes of Black people, access to affordable health care, access to affordable childcare, good schools, and safe neighborhoods continue to be issues we must solve. These are some reasons why Black people must create and support programs that improve our living conditions. Black people must build communities that do not have high crime rates. Our interactions with police must be healthy and non- combative. While life has changed in many ways for our community, we must still improve living conditions that provide a good education for our children, accessible healthcare, affordable housing, crime-free neighborhoods, and healthy activities for our children. We must be excellent, not perfect. We must look to our ancestors for examples of how we can improve things for ourselves and not rely solely on others.

Our history shows that we can effectuate the changes needed for our people. The cycle of injustices and the proliferation of crime demand that those of us who live with these Jim Crow Era realities are not blindsided. We must not be deceived by the different reasons that violence exists in our community. Everyone must be held accountable, and we cannot accept excuses. We must always recognize the impact that Jim Crow continues to have on Black people.

The day will come when Jim Crow does not exist.
"Never Again!"

This conversation about Systemic Racism compels us to be gravely concerned about the ever-evolving cycle of social unrest. We must remember our history as told by our fore parents. They cannot allow the mis- education and lies told by White supremacists, media, politicians, judges, and corporations to keep us disorganized and fighting each other.

Even with what may be a sad situation, our ancestors continue to whisper that we must come together as a unified community to "make a way out of no way." This is the America that our ancestors built. We must protect it for the next generation.

The fight to fully transition Black people from a White supremacist Authoritarian governance into an equitable Democracy is still a dream and a goal. The eradication of slavery and Jim Crow was an American triumph that was the result of Black and White people working together. Throughout American history, many Black and White people have stood hand in hand, calling out the abuse of inequality and inequity. Many White people gave their lives to end slavery and Jim Crow. Others still carry the physical scars and emotional trauma associated with being isolated and ostracized from their biological families who denounced their decision to stand for justice and exhibit true Christian principles.

James Peck, fought for human rights during the Freedom Riders fiasco in Mississippi.

After all these years, gerrymandering, redlining, and voter suppression still negatively impact our community. The persistent fight to keep segregation alive continues. We are the portrait of a people who continue to choose to view life in America through the lenses of change, not just timelines. We must break insist that on a history that includes the truth of all American ethnic communities. Ignorance keeps us vulnerable and weak. We are the portrait of a people who continue to choose viewing life in America through the lenses of change not just timelines. This is an urgent matter if we are to stand tall in the public square demanding our rights.

Image 1: White Freedom Riders beaten, too.

Image 2: In 1961, E. P. Ellis, a former KKK leader joined Ann Atwater and became best friends as they worked together to desegregate schools in Durham, NC, 197

Black Lives Matter

Black lives have always mattered to us, although they have not always mattered to all Americans. Black lives only mattered to White supremacists when we were their property. Black lives didn't matter to American autocracy between 1619 and 1965. Black lives didn't matter to the U.S. Supreme Court in the Dredd Scott case. Black lives didn't matter to American politicians when we were being lynched, raped, beaten, and segregated. Black lives didn't matter to White historians lied about us in the history books. The slogan "Black Lives Matter" never intended to dismiss the humanity of all people. It is used to declare the validity of who we are and what experiences are unique to us when it relates to police brutality, racism, slavery, disenfranchisement, oppression, mis-education, torture, lynchings, and unjust laws. Nevertheless, we do single out White supremacy's determination to commit genocide against us. We have chosen to tell the accurate and full history of this country.

For us, the term, Woke, means knowing the truth. It means being aware. It means we will not be lulled into a false sense of security. It means that people must be exposed and held accountable for the atrocities that have been committed against innocent Black people. We must build coalitions with other groups and leverage our voices to demand change. Woke means knowing that White Supremacy is still very prevalent in the branches of the American government, from Main Street to Wall Street. Politicians, Judges, and Corporations are still hard at work trying to maintain their privilege and oppress the Black community. Woke means populating the local, state, and federal branches of government with people who believe in justice, equity, and liberty. Woke means electing officials who care about all Americans, including our children, elderly, veterans, and disabled. It means electing leaders who understand that all Americans deserve the right to be treated with dignity.

Woke means having conversations in parks, playgrounds, barbershops, banks, and on campuses about the future of this country. Our fraternal organizations must answer the call and lead their members. We cannot be afraid to take a stance against White supremacy. Women's organizations, The Links, Jack and Jill, Social organizations, Black health organizations, various media outlets, publications, places of worship, and everywhere we congregate need to remind us of the work left undone.

Black Lives Matter

From the grave, our ancestors call to remind us to stand firm and face life with courage, knowing that America belongs to all of us. The fact that truth will never die provides us to focus. We must never give up, quit, or surrender. Every citizen of this nation is human and deserves to be treated as one.

There has never been a time in American history that Black people have not been indispensable to this nation's growth and development. We have been here from the beginning. There has never been a time when the economic machine that built this nation has not needed us to invent, educate, build, engineer, create, destroy, grow, harvest, invest, vote, fight, die, or pray. Our fore parents knew this. Every Black person must know what role they must play to ensure that the nation our fore parents built is not destroyed by a few traitors and fanatics. They must know how vital they are to the economic development of this nation.

Since the principal judicial and legislative offices were founded in 1776, White people still hold most of these federal elected offices. As of 2024, there has been one Black U.S. President, one Black U.S. Vice President, and one Black U.S. Attorney General. Of the 50 U.S. Senators, three are members of our community. Out of the 435 U.S. House of Representatives members, only 58 belong to our community.

Through The Eyes of This Black Woman

There are over 47 million Black Americans. We are approximately 14% of America's population. White supremacists are predictable. They have made their intentions clear. We must keep them from destroying our nation. Our ancestors showed us to fight them and win, and to prevent any forms of invisibility for our children. We must act in the best interest of humanity and the planet. This is what our ancestors left us as a legacy.

Our children must not remain invisible.

Our requisite on the next leg of this Relay to Justice and Freedom is to dispel the misnomer that the few representatives in our legislative and judicial men and women can do it alone. They represent the capabilities of our community at large, but they are not superheroes. They need our money, votes, and visible support. This applies to all levels of government.

Black men and women continue to be trailblazers. We continue to pave the way so that more of us are involved and serving in leadership positions. Unfortunately, many of us have been mis-educated or under- educated as a result of systemic racism. We rely too heavily on others to educate our youth. We must remain focused on setting goals that remedy the historical wrongs and injustices that prevent us from realizing our potential.

"If we do not act, we shall be dragged down the long, dark, and shameful corridors of time reserved for those who possess power without compassion, might without morality, and strength without sight."

Dr. Martin Luther King, Jr

CHAPTER TWO

A True Pledge of Allegiance

"A lie doesn't become right, and an evil doesn't become good just because it's accepted by the majority."

Booker T. Washington

Though slavery had been abolished, every evil attempt possible was made to keep us intimidated and subservient. Our daughters were raped, and our sons were pulled out during the course of the night and hanged, bludgeoned, beaten, or shot. There was no such thing as White America's respect for the Black family. The immediacy of physical and social dangers and degradation overrode any notion of good for the Black community during the Jim Crow Era. The intent was to recreate another form of enslavement through fear and intimidation.

I submit that White supremacist tactics of intimidation will never stop in America if there are no significant reforms to the judicial and legislative branches of government. In 2024, there is anxiety forming around who will be our next U.S. President. The Civil Rights Movement demanded America to pay attention to us, but it did not unlock its economic system for us.

Not all people are equal in a capitalist society when financial solvency is required to achieve equity in our quality of life. The abolishment of slavery led to physical freedom but not economic freedom. Our entry into mainstream society did not give our community equal opportunities. Even the right to vote has had limited benefits. In fact, many advances that were made for Black people and women are being systematically stripped away by both the legislature and the courts. We are at a crossroads in 2024. Our young yet great nation is the leader of the free world.

I am grateful to our ancestors for their tenacity. They did not allow cruelty and brutality to keep them from making progress. It is imperative that we understand how and why they were able to make a way out of no way. While the three branches of government were created for the purposes of checks and balances, interpreting the Constitution is the responsibility of the United States Supreme Court (SCOTUS). The court is supposed to be impartial, neutral, and above any political influence. However, over the years, we have seen that the Supreme Court cannot be trusted. Many justices were appointed because of politics, and their rulings have been unduly influenced by special interests, lobbyists, and political agendas.

We are faced with the real possibility of being relegated to secondary status that will be sanctioned by our Supreme Court. This will not be a gift to Black people in this country. At this stage in our history, we must become more vigilant. This demands that we have more of a presence in the judicial and legislative branches of government. We must write and interpret laws without bias or malice. We took leaps toward liberty and justice when our actions were centered on "We" and "Us," not "I" and "Me." We did not expect others to make things happen for us. We did it ourselves. No handouts, just hands up.

I suggest that we recognize our responsibility and do more to elect honorable local, state, and federal officials. Democracy is fluid, not stagnant. Changes in this society require flexibility, not stagnation. "We shall overcome someday" does not mean that we have arrived. It means that in this generation, we must remain open and watchful.

Separate and Unequal

Let me tell you what I remember about living "separate and unequal." Racial segregation in public schools was prevalent in the South. Unemployment and unfair wages were common. Poor housing and poor health were insidious plagues in our community. I remember when White people fought to keep us in separate public schools. I remember the stench in the restrooms and rust in the running water at fountains designated for "Colored Only." I remember being unable to try on clothes in department stores or to eat at food lunch counters. I remember boycotting and walking in the heat of the day while the hot sun beamed down. I remember walking down the street, being jailed in Orangeburg, South Carolina, in a jail that had not been opened since 1925. I remember being grouped into cells with young ladies who urinated and vomited out of anger and fear. Still, we sang "We shall Not be Moved," until our throats were sore, with the resolve that "before I am a slave, I'll be buried in my grave and go home to my Lord and be free."

I remember a White beggar coughing up phlegm from his throat and spitting it directly into my face. He had one leg and one crutch. When I refused to stop moving around during the boycotting stores in my hometown of Sumter, SC, he commanded me to move. He started shouting, "Move own you Black nappy head N r." When I would "not be moved," he burned my left arm with his cigar. The scar is still visible on my arm

At the time that I was being burned in front of Kress Five and Dime Store, my first cousin, the late Benjamin F.(Benji) Canty, III, was being thrown out of the Drug Store across the street from me. He chose to sit at the "For Whites Only" Lunch Counter. Benji took an awful blow to his head from a pipe

I remember sitting double on hand-me-down seats at Rafting Creek School in Rembert, South Carolina, until I was twelve years old and went away to boarding school at Mather Academy in Camden, South Carolina. At "The Creek" I sat next to my best friend, Esther Waiters Gardner from first through seventh grades. We were handed down frayed books, we sat on splintered benches, and we looked at dilapidated Blackboards that were sent to us from White public schools.

The Distress of Being Principal of a Black School in South Carolina During Segregation

My daddy was a school Principal. I remember watching him and five uncles agonize when they were commanded to honor the quota for Special Education and required to put the highest-ranking young men in their separate and unequal schools. The intent was to stigmatize these young men by placing them in Special Education classes. I remember how my grandmother, whom I called "Mama" talked about the way that she was treated when she was a Principal at "The Creek" and the kinds of inhumane demands she was expected to conduct with the Black young men.

I remember seeing White children riding buses as Black children walked several miles each day to school. I remember parents not getting paid for their labor. I remember the horrors of the Ku Klux Klan as they terrorized our communities, hanged our loved ones, and castrated others. I remember courts that sentenced innocent people without trial or due process.

Table Talk History

It took me years to digest that our table talk, and vicarious history lessons were the impetus for our Civil Rights Movement. Black History was not a part of the American literary culture until after we entered mainstream America in the late 1960s. "I ain't gonna study war no more" was a song that our ancestors sang, knowing that their rebellions might cause them their lives. The song meant that if they had to die for us to have a better life, they would. That was one of the vicarious history lessons we learned and followed during the '60s. In this Era can we become stagnant and determine that someone else must do for us what we can do for ourselves?

A Chronicle of Racism in America.

A reiteration of the plight of Black people in America became a Public Broadcast System (PBS) documentary called "Who We Are: A Chronicle of Racism in America." It was narrated by Jeffrey Robinson, a Harvard Professor. Dr. Robinson shared that the White European men who came to America between 1492 and 1619 declared that the natives, who had been here for centuries, did not have official proof of ownership of the land they had occupied for centuries before the Europeans arrived. These intruders gave themselves self-imposed authority and then took away millions of acreages from the Native Americans. Their arrogance overrode their competence. These White invaders lacked the ability to tend the millions of acres of land they took. They needed help. Cheap labor was what they knew of the English indentured servant concept.

By 1607, White and Black indentured servants collaborated with the early settlers. They worked side by side and became vital to the colonial economy. Typically, these servants worked four to seven years in exchange for passage, room, board, lodging, and freedom. While there were laws to protect their rights, they still endured much hardship. There were punishments imposed that could legally extend their service beyond seven years if they ran away or if women became pregnant. When these indentured servants were eventually freed. The contract may have included 25 acres of land, a year's worth of corn, arms, a cow, and new clothes.

By 1619, this land's new owners brought more of our ancestors here. Initially, they, too, were indentured servants because there were no slave laws in place. These ancestors were given the same privileges for freedom as the White European indentured slaves. But, in Massachusetts in 1641 and 1961 in Virginia, the small freedoms that Black people may have experienced were taken away. Slavery was profitable and a renewable resource. The White indentured servants became their overseers.

Enslaved people before and after our Emancipation Proclamation

Our Story Continued

We withstood struggles and continued to rise in this nation despite the serious fomenting violent courses of action undertaken by the White supremacists. In 1787, Democracy was established in America for the White men who were generations removed from the original settlers. In 1920, White women fought for and earned the right to vote; however, the cycle of keeping Black people "in their place" continued. Black women were excluded, although many of them were contributors to the cause of women's right to vote. Family, we people must be clear that this climb to freedom and justice is an uphill battle. It is neither on a timeline nor based on fairness or unfairness.

Our Call to Action

The preposterous fabrication that there is more than one race of people in the universe may be the reason for the fanaticism of racial superiority. The social reality of many ethnicities and cultures is about multi-ethnicities; people are the only ones that exist.

It cannot be said often enough: Black people lived as enslaved people from 1619 until the signing of The Emancipation in 1868. Over 212 years and 20.6 generations later, all Black people born on these shores or who become naturalized are citizens and are eligible to vote.

The move into mainstream America after 1965 gave rise to opportunities for our people. We could sit in the halls of educational institutions alongside our White counterparts and learn what they had been taught. This brought our people closer to understanding the structure of this democratic way of life but not its economic process. We are adaptive people; therefore, it is conceivable that conspiracies had to surface to break the cycle of what may have led to forming "a more perfect union" in America. What we have learned is that this democratic process, with all its flaws, is far more promising than our prior years of enslavement and Jim Crow.

Moreover, the effects of moving into classism with our children blending in the same schools, raised the issues of commingling and becoming a browner society from within. The migration of other members of ethnic groups, who are also brown, led to significant consternation from the children of the Jim Crow leaders.

There is a lot to unpack. It starts with the duality of behavior between what the founding writers penned and their lives. They wrote human equality—democracy—for White men while demanding sub-human separation for the enslaved Africans.

White women began to vote in 1920. However, these women did not extend this right to Black women during the Women's Suffrage Movement. It was not until 1965, when President Lyndon B. Johnson signed the Voting Rights Act that the full right to vote was granted to our entire community. Only then did all Black people move from the horrific dangers of Jim Crow, which was the engine of the American Authoritarian governance. Even with this progress, the roots of inequality and inequity remained unmovable and morphed into other ways to support their divisive control. This control prevails through the tentacles of Systemic Racism.

Black people moved from autocratic to democratic governance in America in 1965.

Lives in America are governed, in great measure, by "Laws and Acts." In 1965 President Lyndon Johnson signed the Civil Rights Act that gave all Black eligible citizens the right to vote. The U.S. Constitution says that all American citizens have equal rights and privileges. Historically, the judicial and legislative systems did not include Black people's rights to legal citizenship and fair practices. However, acts of "Conspiracy," or plotting to keep us "in our place," is not new to us. We live amid a perpetual conspiracy that fights to keep our community in a state of human confusion and nullification. The political arms of inhumane behavior still prevail.

Chapter Two - A True Pledge of Allegiance

It is important to distinguish a "law" from an "act" in order to bring clarity to our later discussion on the need for us to understand that Democracy is led by the voice of the people in America. That voice is heard through our voting rights. 'Laws" and "acts" are responses to the will of the people. This reality makes it imperative for our community to ensure that as we progress in mainstream America that we vote understand that there is never a time when we abdicate our responsibility to remain civil oriented and make it our obligation as American citizens to use our voice, i.e., vote. Maintaining vigilance to the politics that impact our lives means that we learn the relationship of the "law" and an "act" to our rights as citizens.

A "law" is a system of rules recognized by a nation to regulate the activities of its citizens. "Acts" are created as a new "law," or it amends an existing one. "Acts" are situation-specific and me provisions to a specific issue over an allotted time limit. For example, the "law" says that all eligible American citizens can vote. This became law before our enslaved ancestors were freed. The "law" also said that people born in America were citizens. With the exception of our fore parents who were brought over in the ships, those born here were eligible for citizenship after The Emancipation Proclamation was signed.

Much has been written about the trepidation Black people's right to vote has caused. A reason is due to numbers. The fear of the Black vote made many White supremacists resort to hanging and imposing felony charges with long sentences on our ancestors. The vote also caused "acts" that amended the original "law" that give Black people who were born in America limited voting rights. You may have heard of the Voting Rights Act. It was designed to allow Black people temporary voting rights. The John Lewis Voting Rights request is another "Act" and it, too, will be temporary. In 2024, Black citizens still do not have the right to vote as the "law" provides this as a permanent reality for White citizens.

In her book, The Fight of Our Lives, Iluilla Mendel voices the sentiment of our indelible spirit. She writes, "Through intense pain and sacrifice, it has brought back our understanding of our own value, made us see the good that we can create from unwavering unity and courage and from caring for one another. We have seen the immense power that we derive from learning to work together as a people and a nation…. We are facing the greatest test and are determined to show our strength. If some of us die in this struggle, others will be born and will defend with the same honor. We are always at the point of beginning. We will never give up to terror or any other evil."

Regardless of our age, class, or experiences, Black people must know the "elephant in the room." Our vote speaks for us, it says that "we will never give up to terror or any other evil." Our fore parents were not afraid of the White supremacist's whip. They were determined to prevail in pursuit of "liberty and justice for all," as the Pledge of Allegiance declares.

"Love and compassion are necessities, not luxuries. Without them, humanity cannot survive."

Dalai Lama

Legalized Inequities

This conversation has been incubating in my "experience womb" for years. I felt its movement when the jury in Los Angeles, California, acquitted the group of policemen who beat Rodney King mercilessly. I remember this time so vividly because I was lecturing out West at a university. My late daughter Tamarinice (Margi) was in college in the North. Her phone call to me came in at 4:00a.m. She was sobbing relentlessly. Her questions flooded so profusely that I could not respond. Some of Margi's questions are still permanently etched in my mind. She asked, "Mommie, how can this be possible? What kind of law makes it suitable to acquit police officers

Through The Eyes of This Black Woman

who violently beat a Black man almost to death? Mommie, they put Black people in jail for most of their lives on fabricated charges.

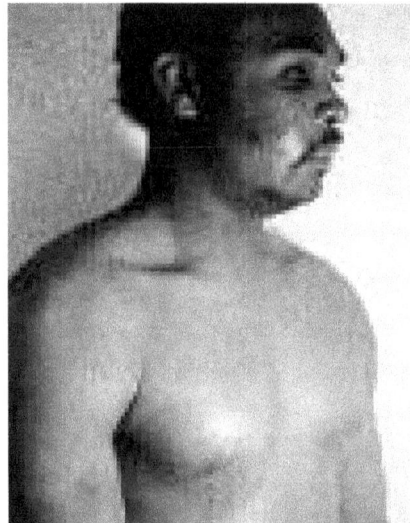

A Los Angeles police team beat Rodney King in 1991.

Where is Justice? Where is God in this?"

The more she questioned, the more loudly she exclaimed and sobbed. I listened as I tried to string together a sentence or two that might make some sense. But I could not. I could not get rid of the lump in my throat that would not digest. Rodney King's incident reminded me of the massacre at South Carolina State University in 1968.

This "crucifixion" convinced me that I must always take part in our Relay to Liberty and Justice for the rest of my life, if necessary. My resolve deepened even more when I recognized Margi's conversation being the same at this time as mine had been almost so many years earlier.

The massacred L to R: Delano Middleton, Samuel Hammond, Jr., and Henry Smith

This "crucifixion convinced me that I must always take part in our Relay to Liberty and Justice for the rest of my life, if necessary. My resolve deepened even more when I recognized that Margi's conversation was the same Cas mine had been when I, too, was in undergraduate.

Relay to Liberty and Justice

Our Relay to Liberty and Justice Must Continue

In 1952, Charlotta Amanda Spears Bass became the first Black woman to run for the office of Vice President of the United States. She paved the way for Kamala Harris.

On January 1955, at 15 years old, Claudette Colvin refused to sit in the back of the bus in Birmingham, AL. She paved the way for Rosa Parks

In December 1955, Rosa Parks was the Civil Rights Activist who refused to sit in the back of the bus in Montgomery, AL. She paved the way for the Civil Rights Movement of the 50s and 60s.

Through The Eyes of This Black Woman

In 1957, James T. McCain, Sr., became the Field Secretary and Director of the Organization for the Congress of Racial Equality (CORE). This great educator paved the way for other educators to join the ranks of Black clergy as leaders for justice

In 1967 Attorney Thurgood Marshall became the first Black Judge on the United States Supreme Court. He paved the way for Supreme Court Judge Ketanji Brown Jackson.

In 1972 Shirley Chisholm ran for U.S. President. She paved the way for Jesse Jackson.

In 1984, Rev. Jesse Jackson, a renowned orator, led the justice with Dr. King and Operation Breadbasket. Ran for U.S. President. He paved the way for Al Sharpton.

Relay to Liberty and Justice

Chapter Two - A True Pledge of Allegiance

In 2004 In 1993 The great Poet Laureate Maya Angelou shared her Poem called "On the Pulse of Morning" in the inauguration of the 42nd US President, William Clinton. She passed the Baton of Liberty and Justice to Amanda Gorman who in 2020 shared her poem called "The Hill We Climb " in the inauguration of the US 46th President Joseph R. Biden.

Today, Reverend Al Sharpton, renowned preacher, Civil Rights Leader, President of National Action Network (NAN), and, National News Commentator for MSNBC, ran for US President, in 2003. He passed the baton to the man who became the First Black US 44th President, Barack Obama.

In 2013 Cory Booker received the Baton of Freedom and Justice from Edwin Brooke. Senator Booker paved the way for Rafael Warnock to join him in the U.S. Senate.

Demonstration of Strength

It is safe to conclude that our ancestors understood the power, presence, and protection of the indelible spirit and used it as a standard for their intrinsic guiding principle. They understood that their way of effecting changes could not mirror the heinous practices of their slave owners. Kindness and courage, coupled with intellect and ingenuity, became their modus operandi. Learning how to live inside the deeper meaning of humanity became their power. Working to achieve excellence became their presence.

Our ancestors were strong-willed warriors. Their courage was not aborted because of their circumstances. Of course, our people got angry; they were also shocked. They also became tired and disappointed along the way. Nevertheless, these realities did not alter their determination to struggle for freedom and equality.

Although we are in a post-physically enslaved era, we must resist the psychological, economic, moral, and social slavery of today.

Frederick Douglass contended, "if there is no struggle, there is no progress. The struggle may be moral, psychological, or spiritual. Power concedes nothing without a demand. It never has, and it never will." We have never been people who give up.

Loyalty, love, justice, and righteousness are the major attributes of courage. Our fore parents showed courage that led our community from cotton fields into boardrooms across this country. We still have the responsibility to uphold the ingenuity of our ancestor's indelible spirit and prove that this society can be a better place for our children and all children.

"Where you see wrong or inequality or injustice, speak out, because this is your nation. This is your Democracy. Make it. Protect it. Pass it on."

Justice Thurgood Marshall

Randy and Dee's children Anthony, Laila, and Anissa

CHAPTER THREE

Making Our Lives Better

"The 'Truth' is not altered by the question, 'Whose truth?'"

Thomasina M. Portis

In the Prologue, I talked about the intent V. the content of the U.S. Constitution. The fact that we were omitted by enslavers like Jefferson and other framers of the Constitution does not negate the fact that we have always been among the "we." One of the most fallacious misnomers has been that we are not human beings. The reason I tell everybody that physiologically there is, but one race is because it is true. We are all breathing and living human beings regardless of ethnicity or complexion. This society has not had the ability to disprove us as human beings as White supremacists perpetually fight to extract our humanity.

The determination to make America a Christian Nation was not the intent of the agnostics, stoics, or the philosophers who wrote the Constitution. They believed in the universal consciousness that shows up in every culture by different names. Universal consciousness gives rise to the people's Universal truths we all have.

These writers created a faith document; a testament of not just who we are today, but who we become in the future. Their initial hope was that generations would take this Constitution based upon the Universal belief that things become right. The intention of the writers was never to subscribe to any religious faith. The real intention was to form a financial lifeline through Capitalism.

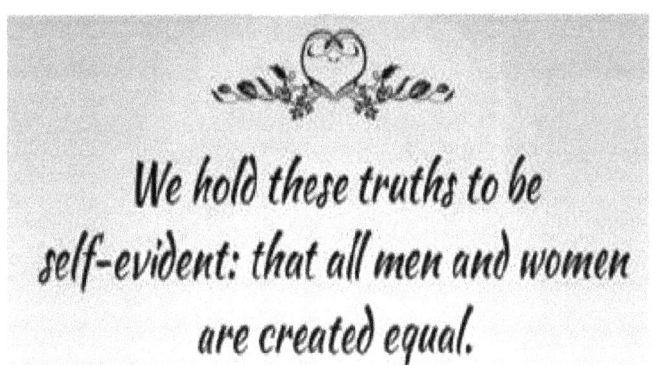

Creative and Intellectual Geniuses

As we continue having our conversation, I acknowledge that there are several ways to tell this story. It would be far more expansive than I shall explore. Great people like Marcus Garvey, Malcolm X, Minister Farrakhan, Wade Nobles, Asa Hilliard, Molefi Asante, Medgar Evers, and so many other great men could be explored. Women such as Afeni Shakur, Dr. Betty Shabazz, Dr. Angela Davis, Dr. Coretta Scott King, Maya Angelou, Merlie Evers Williams, and Toni Morrison could be explored as well.

Chronicling the Lie

Understanding the persistent efforts to undermine the origins and rights of various ethnicities is crucial for all of us. The ideology of White supremacy posits that Black people are inherently inferior to their White counterparts, asserting that Black people are destined to live and die in a state of dehumanization.

Proponents of racial segregation between Black and White communities ensure that regardless of the political party in power—whether Democratic or Republican—the laws and regulations enacted perpetuate lower standards of living for Black people through Systemic Racism. This ideology elucidates why our social positions and working conditions have historically confined many Black people to low-wage, essential worker roles. Advocates of this pernicious belief system are aware that the progress of this nation has been significantly driven by the contributions of Black people as they continue to find ways of chronicling the lie, through Systemic Racism tactics about us being inferior to them.

People With Purpose

When I listen to some of the scholars of the first generation of Black people in mainstream America, they pose a provocative inquiry regarding this present-day Democracy and its relationship to our community. When I say, "Democracy, as fragile as it is still worth us fighting for it," the antagonistic retort from them is "How can we fight for something that was never for us and turn it into great?" This gave me reason to pause. Then I began to realize the fairness of this question.

I grew-up in the South in the last of the Jim Crow Era and in the midst of people who believed in non- violence as the better way to evoke change. In 1949 Rev. DeLaine began the Civil Rights Movement fight for equal rights in education for Black children in Clarendon County, South Carolina. By 1965, education and labor continued and expanded the need for better education. The requests also included better jobs and wages for the Black community. Upsurgences toward freedom began as far back as 1822 and continued. -

- Denmark Vesey in 1822 and Nate Turner in 1831. These ancestors made attempts that were more aligned with violence against their slave owners.

- From 1850-1860. She "conducted" 11 trips from Maryland to Ontario, Canada, I was called the underground railroad to freedom. Though Harriet was never afraid to fire her gun, her success was a human "railroad that led over 300 people to freedom. Her model has provided much more success.

- By 1920 Marcus Garvey a Black nationalist believed in racial separation and made attempts to move Black people back to Africa. His organization was called the Universal Negro Improvement Association (UNIA). It represented the largest mass movement I African American history. The nationalist message was "Back to Africa."

- By 1931 Elijah Muhammed had established the Nation of Islam with a message that mixed racial pride, hatred of the White Devil, and the need for economic self- sufficiency.

- By 1964 Malcolm X broke from the Nation of Islam and became a member of Islam. His message became "an ultimatum between voting or violence."

- In the 1950s Dr. Martin Luther King became the main voice for the Civil Rights Movement of that Era. The call was for freedom and liberty for all people. It was this movement that many of us chose to risk our lives for a better America that includes equality for all citizens.

- From the 1960s-1970s Black Power began a revolutionary movement. It emphasized racial pride, economic empowerment, and the creation of political and cultural institutions.

- In 1966 The Black Panther Party for Self-Defense was founded. It was a revolutionary organization with an ideology of Black nationalism, socialism, and armed self-defense, especially against police brutality.

We Make Beauty Out of Ashes

Our ancestors knew that the sum total of humanity rests in each of us. As our people led these insurrection charges and freedom marches from the 1800s through the 1900s, the purpose was the same. They were working for us to have a better life, and the sum total of each contribution was the same.

Each move was an attempt to get us closer to freedom and liberty. I call them all Civil Rights Movements. Contributions from our great leaders led Dr. King and others in the White House in 1965 to witness the signing of the Civil Rights Act by President Lindon B. Johnson. We remained on each other's shoulders until the proverbial wall of separation was torn, and we marched with high expectations and hope into the future as citizens of the United States of America. Our concerted efforts of thousands and thousands+ of us had chased away the Jim Crow Era.

When that Act was signed and we moved into mainstream America, we knew that we were going to have educational, housing, work, and other experiences never before afforded to us. Oh, what a time!! We understood that we had gained a new life and had chased away the weight of poor education. The other things like work and housing would come to most of us through our preparation, we thought.

I do know that my thought-base may seem foreign and unattainable in this Era, but I am convinced that the educational experiences and successes of our first, second, and third generations in mainstream America "make beauty out of ashes." Ashes are the inequities and inequalities this of this American White Democratic process. Beauty represents the strides we continue to make while continuing to rise to make this the American DEI Democratic process in America today. After all, the intent of the writers of the Constitution was for generations to come to capture and be guided by the ideals of a Universal Creator, not by any religion.

Now, Family, I make my case as I suggest ways to make life even better for our community. We must resolve to work diligently to save our Democracy today. I do not lay claim that my suggestion is the only route to freedom and liberty, but I do maintain that the higher probability to move forward is through our ingenuity not violence, not apathy, no silence. I know autocracy, and I do not want you to ever have to experience it. Please listen!

Believers of Black and White ethnic separation ensure that regardless of the political party in power – Democratic or Republican – the legislations translate into lower standards of living for Black people through *Systemic Racism*. This ideology explains why our social positions and working conditions historically keep so many of us, every decade, as essential workers in lower-paying positions.

Chronicling the determination to abort the origin and rights of other ethnicities is imperative for each of us to understand. The White Supremacy Ideology espouses that Black ethnicity is subservient to White ethnicity. It contends that from birth Black people are to live and die dehumanized.

Believers of Black and White ethnic separation ensure that regardless of the political party in power- -Democratic or Republican--, rules and regulations legislated translate into lower standards of living for Black people through *Systemic Racism*. This ideology explains why our social positions and working conditions historically keep so many of us, in every decade, as essential workers in low-wage positions.

Through The Eyes of This Black Woman

Every human being has certain inalienable rights. Reasons for separation was negotiated for some reason or another. These writers believed that the Universal Creator would never say that any group of people is better than another. They created a faith document; a testament of not just who we are today, but who we become in the future. Their initial hope was that generations would take this Constitution based upon the Universal belief that things become right. The intention of the Creator is not religion. The real issue is on a lifeline is Capitalism. The rich are the ones who benefit, and the alternative is the modification of violence.

The subscribers of this heinous ideology know that the advancement of this nation had to include the genius of Black people. Here are three examples.

Astronomer Neil Tyson   Scientist Kizzmekia Corbitt   Governor Wes Moore

Benjamin Banneker - a Freed Man

The Freedman

"For to be free is not merely to cast off one's chains, but to live in a way that respects and enhances the freedom of others."

Nelson Mandela

Throughout the history of Black people in America, there has been a persistent portrayal depicting us as an illiterate and intellectually incompetent ethnic group. This stratagem is employed to perpetuate the White ideological denial of, and indifference to, the innate intelligence of Black people. This denial began when our forebears were chained in ships and brought to America against their will for the express purpose of free labor.

The repudiation of Black intelligence is evident throughout American history, manifesting from the cotton fields to sports arenas, from public school classrooms to private higher education institutions, and from golf courses to boardrooms where policies are formulated. These strategies

Relay to Liberty and Justice

of repudiation have perpetuated the legal marginalization of our ancestors, who were never considered immigrants. They were denied work permits and funding for small businesses and were dictated on how to behave to ensure their intellectual abilities were never acknowledged. This systemic suppression continues, albeit in more subtle forms. A few Black individuals may ascend to positions of policymaking, while even fewer become decision-makers who shape the policies that guide the nation. Presently, some state and national leaders believe it is their prerogative to revert America to an era of yesteryear.

A careful reading of Mr. Banneker's letter to Thomas Jefferson offers insight into the tenacity that has coursed through the veins of Black people then and now.

Since the 1400s, when Columbus arrived on these shores, records show that Black people lived among Native Americans, prospering, and never being enslaved. Many of them in the South were recorded as successful farmers.

Benjamin Banneker was born in Baltimore County, Maryland. His mother was never enslaved, and his fat$her was freed from slavery. His parents sent him to privately integrated schools where he received an eighth- grade education. The young intellect became a mathematician, astronomer, inventor, and writer who took over his parents' farm and became a successful farmer.

In August 1791, Mr. Banneker wrote a letter to Thomas Jefferson challenging his ideology about Black intellectual inferiority and his racial convictions. He implored Jefferson to help end the "unjustifiable cruelty and barbarism" prevalent within the institution of slavery in America. The composition of this letter and the gift of his Almanac underscore Mr. Banneker's intellectual aptitude and courage as he demonstrated how to live in a manner that respects and enhances the freedom of all humanity.

Thomas Jefferson, 19 August 1791

Sir, I am fully sensible of the greatness of that freedom which I take with you on the present occasion: a liberty which Seemed to me scarcely allowable, when I reflected on that distinguished, and dignifyed station in which you Stand; and the almost general prejudice and prepossession which is so prevalent in the world against those of my complexion.

I suppose it is a truth too well attested to you, to need a proof here, that we are a race of human beings who have long laboured under the abuse and censure of the world, that we have long been looked upon with an eye of contempt, and that we have long been considered rather as brutish than human, and scarcely capable of mental endowments.

Sir I hope I may Safely admit, in consequence of that report which hath reached me, that you are a man far less inflexible in Sentiments of this nature, than many others, that you are measurably friendly and well disposed toward us, and that you are willing and ready to Lend your aid and assistance to our relief from those many distresses and numerous calamities to which we are reduced.

Now Sir if this is founded in truth, I apprehend you will readily embrace every opportunity to eradicate that train of absurd and false ideas and opinions which so generally prevails with respect to us, and that your Sentiments are concurrent with mine, which are that one universal Father hath given being to us all, and that he hath not only made us all of one flesh, but that he hath also without partiality afforded us all the Same Sensations, and endued us all with the same faculties, and that however variable we may be in Society or religion, however diversified in Situation or colour, we are all of the Same Family, and Stand in the Same relation to him.

Sir, if these are Sentiments of which you are fully persuaded, I hope you cannot but acknowledge, that it is the indispensable duty of those who maintain for themselves the rights of human nature, and who profess the obligations of Christianity, to extend their power and influence to the relief of every part of the human race, from whatever burden or oppression they may unjustly labour under, and this I apprehend a full conviction of the truth and obligation of these principles should lead all to.

Sir, I have long been convinced, that if your love for yourselves, and for those inestimable laws which preserve to you the rights of human nature, was founded on Sincerity, you could not But be Solicitous, that every Individual of whatsoever rank or distinction, might with you equally enjoy the blessings thereof, neither could you rest Satisfyed, Short of the most active diffusion of your exertions, in order to their promotion from any State of degradation, to which the unjustifiable cruelty and barbarism of men may have reduced them.

Sir, I freely and cheerfully acknowledge, that I am of the African race, and in that colour which is natural to them of the deepest dye, and it is under a Sense of the most profound gratitude to the Supreme Ruler of the universe, that I now confess to you, that I am not under that State of tyrannical thralldom [i.e., the state of being in someone's power], and inhuman captivity, to which too many of my brethren are doomed; But that I have abundantly tasted of the fruition of those blessings which proceed from that free and unequalled liberty with which you are favoured and which I hope you will willingly allow you to have received from the immediate hand of that Being, from whom proceedeth every good and perfect gift.

Sir, Suffer me to recall to your mind that time in which the Arms and tyranny of the British Crown were exerted with every powerful effort in order to reduce you to a State of Servitude, look back I intreat you on the variety of dangers to which you were exposed, reflect on that time in which every human aid appeared unavailable, and in which even hope and fortitude wore the aspect of inability to the Conflict, and you cannot but be led to a serious and grateful sense of your miraculous and providential preservation; you cannot but acknowledge, that the present freedom and tranquility which you enjoy you have mercifully received, and that it is the peculiar blessing of Heaven.

This, Sir, was a time in when you clearly saw into the injustice of a State of Slavery, and in which you had just apprehensions of the horrors of its condition, it was now Sir, that your abhorrence thereof was so excited, that you publicly held forth this true and invaluable doctrine, which is worthy to be recorded and remember'd in all Succeeding ages: "We hold these truths to be Self-evident, that all men are created equal; and they are endowed by their creator with certain unalienable rights, and that among these are, life, liberty, and the pursuit of happiness."

Here was a time in which your tender feelings for yourselves had engaged you thus to declare, that you were then impressed with proper ideas of the great valuation of liberty, and the free possession of those blessings, to which you were entitled by nature; but, Sir, how pitiable is it to reflect, that although you were so fully convinced of the benevolence of the Father of Mankind, and of his equal and impartial distribution of these rights and privileges, which he had conferred upon them, that you should at the same time counteract his mercies, in detaining by fraud and violence so numerous a part of my brethren, under groaning captivity and cruel oppression, that you should at the same time be found guilty of that most criminal act, which you professedly detested in others, with respect to yourselves.

I suppose that your knowledge of the situation of my brethren, is too extensive to need a recital here; neither shall I presume to prescribe methods by which they may be relieved, otherwise than by recommending to you and all others, to wean yourselves from these narrow prejudices which you have imbibed with respect to them, and as Job proposed to his friends, "Put your Souls in their Souls stead;" Thus shall your hearts be enlarged with kindness and benevolence toward them; and thus shall you need neither the direction of myself or others, in what manner to proceed herein.

And now, Sir, although my sympathy and affection for my brethren hath caused my enlargement thus far, I ardently hope, that your candour and generosity will plead with you on my behalf, when I make known to you, that it was not originally my design; But that having taken up my pen to direct to you, as a present, a copy of an Almanack which I have calculated for the Succeeding year, I was unexpectedly and unavoidably led thereto.

This calculation, Sir, is the production of my arduous study, in this my advanced stage of life; for having long had unbounded desires to become acquainted with the secrets of nature, I have had to gratify my curiosity herein, through my own assiduous application to Astronomical Study, in which I need not recount to you the many difficulties and disadvantages, which I have had to encounter.

And although I had almost declined to make my calculation for the ensuing year, in consequence of that time which I had allotted therefore, being taken up at the Federal Territory, by the request of Mr. Andrew Ellicott, yet finding myself under Several engagements to Printers of this state to whom I had communicated my design, on my return to my place of residence, I industriously applied myself thereto, which I hope I have accomplished with correctness and accuracy; A copy of which I have taken the liberty to direct to you, and which I humbly request you will favourably receive; and although you may have the opportunity of perusing it after its publication, yet I chose to send it to you in a manuscript previous thereto, that thereby you might not only have an earlier inspection, but that you might also view it in my own handwriting.

And now, Sir, I shall conclude and subscribe my Self, with the most profound respect, your most Obedient humble Servant,

Frederick Douglass: the Courage of a Statesman

Frederick Douglass was a former slave who became a fearless orator and Abolitionist.

"You may shoot me with your words, you may cut me with your hatefulness, But still, I'll rise."

Dr. Maya Angelou

Frederick Douglass was born into slavery and endured profound physical and social abuses. On July 5, 1852, this remarkable orator, who had become a freed slave and a fervent abolitionist, delivered the keynote address at an all-White abolitionists' Fourth of July celebration. In his speech, he eloquently conveyed his perspective on the Independence Day holiday.

Through The Eyes of This Black Woman

The insights of a man who experienced the brutality of slavery and then achieved freedom are essential reading for this discussion. I present some notable aspects of his life to enhance your understanding and reflection on his experiences and oration. Recognize the parallels between the social injustices of Douglass's time and those that persist today. Let his determination to overcome adversity inspire your own journey.

As you delve into this information and then read Douglass's oration, I hope you are inspired to share your story and become as resolute in your pursuit of success as he was. I firmly believe that we can dismantle the legacy of White supremacy when our local, state, and national legislative and judicial branches are more representative of Black American citizens.

In 2021, Luke Tomes wrote 10 Facts About Frederick Douglass:

1. He taught himself how to read and write. Throughout his childhood, Douglass remained illiterate. He was not allowed to read and write on the plantation because the plantation owner considered education dangerous and a threat to their power. Douglass took matters into his own hands. He used his time running errands for his owners to fit in reading lessons. He would carry a book while running errands and trade small pieces of bread to the White children in his neighborhood, asking them to help him learn to read his book in exchange.

2. He helped other slaves to become literate. Being able to read and write and later producing three autobiographies, Douglass taught his fellow slaves to read the New Testament of the Bible. His lessons, which sometimes included 40 people, were broken up by local mobs who felt threatened by his work to enlighten and educate his fellow slaves.

3. He fought a "slave breaker." When Douglass was 16, he fought Edward Covey, a farmer with the reputation of being a 'slave breaker,' When any farmer had a troublesome slave, they sent for Covey. Douglass' fierce resistance for Covey to Covey's violent abuse resulted in a scuffle that changed Douglass' life. Douglass said: "This battle with Mr. Covey was the turning point of my career as a slave. It rekindled the expiring embers of freedom and revived within me a sense of my own manhood. It recalled the departed self-confidence and inspired me again with a determination to be free."

4. He escaped from slavery in disguise. In 1838, with the help and money from the freeborn Black woman, Anna Murray, his future wife, Douglass escaped from slavery dressed as a sailor in a suit procured by Anna; he had money from her savings in his pocket alongside papers from a sailor friend. About 24 hours later, he arrived in Manhattan as a free man. He said, "I felt as one might feel upon escape from a den of hungry lions. Anguish and grief, like darkness and rain, may be depicted, but gladness and joy, like the rainbow, defy the skill of pen or pencil."

5. He took his name from a famous poem. Arriving in NYC as Bailey, Frederick took the surname Douglass after asking fellow abolitionist Nathaniel Johnson for a suggestion. Johnson, inspired by Sir Walter Scott's 'Lady in the Lake,' suggested that of one of the poem's protagonists continuing the Scottish literation connection, Douglass was a fan of Robet Burns, visiting Burns' Cottage and writing about.

6. He traveled to Britain to avoid re-enslavement. Becoming an anti-slavery lecturer in the years after 1838, Douglass suffered a broken hand in 1843 when he was attacked in Indiana during the 'Hundred Conventions' Tour. To avoid re-enslavement because his exposure grew with publications of his first autobiography in 1845, Douglass travelled to Britain and Ireland, giving abolitionist speeches. While there, his freedom was bought, allowing him to return to the U.S. as a free man in 1847.

7. He advocated for women's rights. Douglass attended the Seneca Falls Convention in 1848, speaking to say it was self-evident that everyone should have the vote. He was an ardent defender of women's rights and would spend much of his time promoting electoral equality across America.

8. He Met Abraham Lincoln. Douglass argued both for post-Civil War emancipation and the vote and recruited Black soldier from the Union army; in 1863, Douglass met with Lincoln, a fellow Burns admirer, to seek equal terms for Black soldiers but would remain ambivalent about the President's attitude to race relations, even after Lincoln's assassination.

9. He was the most photographed man of the 19th century. There are 150 separate portraits of Douglass, more than Abraham Lincoln or Walt Whitman, two other heroes of the 19th century. Douglass wrote extensively on the subject during the Civil War, calling photography a "democratic art" that could finally represent Black people as humans rather than "things." He gave his portraits away at talks and lectures, hoping his image could change the common perceptions of Black men.

10. He was nominated for Vice President of the United States. As part of the Equal Right Party ticket in 1872. Douglass was nominated as the VP candidate, with Victoria Woodhull as the Presidential candidate, (Woodhull was the first-ever female presidential candidate, which is why Hillary Clinton was called "the first female presidential candidate from a major party" during the 2016 election.) However, the nomination was made without his consent, and Douglass never acknowledged it. Although he was never officially a presidential candidate, he did receive one vote on each of two nomination conventions.

Why tell Douglass' Story?

I share this story about Frederick Douglass because he exemplifies our collective identity. His narrative helps us recognize the parallels in our experiences across different eras. His life is emblematic of the many unsung heroes who came before and after him. In every era, our ancestors displayed remarkable genius and courage. These qualities continue to empower the fight for liberty and freedom in America.

The determination and stamina of Douglass serve as a source of encouragement today. The indelible spirit that led him to become such an articulate and courageous Statesman resides within each of us. Hardship can only lead to resignation if we succumb to passivity and wait for external salvation. We succeed by working, hoping, and believing in the change we can affect. In every generation, there have been people who embody the spirit of Frederick Douglass. Believe in the indelible spirit within you and forge ahead into greatness, just as Douglass did.

Frederick Douglass delivered a speech titled "What to the Slave is the Fourth of July" on July 2, 1852. I hope you feel the excitement to read it in its entirety (see Appendix Two). I encourage you to absorb the various lessons it imparts. As you read his oration, envision a once enslaved young man show his transformation as this majestic, articulate, and courageous Black man addressing an all-White abolitionist group on Independence Day. He boldly offers his perspective on the nation's Fourth of July celebration. Douglass juxtaposes his power, presence, and progress with the possibility of being dismissed by White men who had welcomed him as an Abolitionist. His courage to speak truth to power signified his

willingness to face backlash for the cause of truth. As you read Mr. Douglass's speech, I hope you appreciate his courage and celebrate his intellect.

CHAPTER FOUR

Christianity V. White Nationalism

"For such people are not serving our Lord Christ, but their own appetites."

Romans 16:18 King James Version

White supremacists misrepresented our motherland and the humanity of our ancestors. Lies were used to negatively describe Africa and enslaved Africans. The political and governmental expertise of our fore parents became outdated. Their educational and work experiences were exploited through the oppressive practices of free labor, heinous punishment, and attempts at intellectual denigration. Our absence in the mainstream of this nation was deliberate.

Mr. Frederick Douglass said,

> But the church of this nation is not only indifferent to the wrongs of the slave, but it also actually takes sides with the oppressors. It has made itself the bulwark of American slavery, and the shield of American slave-hunters. Many of its most eloquent Divines who stand as the very lights of the church, have shamelessly given the sanction of religion and the Bible to the whole slave system. They have taught that man may, properly, be a slave; that the relation of master and slave is ordained of God; that to send back an escaped bondman to his master is clearly the duty of all the followers of the Lord Jesus Christ; and this *horrible blasphemy* is palmed off upon the world for Christianity.

The White Supremacy Ideology reveals itself as immoral and as a socio-pathic repugnance that demands to be authenticated. This may be the reason for the distortion of the Bible and the origination of an American religion that remains a facsimile of Christianity and a moral code of conduct apropos to the need for power, profit, and privilege. This social religion continues to support the White supremacists' War on Ethnic separation and power.

Christianity

Christianity is based on love, joy, peace, long-suffering, gentleness, goodness, faith, meekness, and temperance Galatians 5:22-23 King James Version. The foundation of Christianity is that Jesus lives, saves, loves, and forgives. We believe that He absorbed humankind's sins when He asked God to forgive the people who had any part in condemning Him to death as well as those who actually crucified Him. Jesus said, "Father, forgive them, for they know not what they are doing" Luke 23:32 King James Version.

Historically, the mainstream society of America has believed in violence as the way to show strength. The idea of forgiving those who torture and murder us seems to challenge more and more people. Today, the idea of honest elections is suspect to White supremacists and justified as an act of insurrection after the 2020 presidential election.

Chapter Four - Christianity V. White Nationalism

Could this domestic insurrection be a result of the Christian Nationalists' religion?

Many of us view stories of our ancestors as meek or weak because they did not always fight physical violence with physical violence. Yet, the ability to forgive someone who does not want to be forgiven, especially when that person performs acts of pure evil, is one of our ancestors' gifts to us.

Fundamental to Christianity is its foundation rooted in the concept of love. It is characterized as tough, romantic, forgiving, respecting, benevolence, and timeless. This concept of love extends beyond family structures, ethnicities, and social injustices. It is the strongest and most lasting force within human beings. This foundation of Christianity is the basis of our ancestors' benevolent and the root of their indelible spirit that we were taught to engage.

If I speak in the tongues of men or of angels, but do not have love, I am only a resounding gong or clanging cymbal. If I have the gift of prophecy and can fathom all mysteries and all knowledge, and if I have the faith that can move mountains, but do not have love, I am nothing. If I give all I possess to the poor and give over my body to hardship that I may boast, but do not have love, I am gaining nothing. Love is patient, love is kind. It does not envy, it does not boast, it is not proud. It does not dishonor others, it is not self-seeking, it is not easily angered, it keeps no delight in evil but rejoices with the truth. It always protects, always trusts, always hopes, always preserves. Love never fails. But where there are prophecies, they will cease; where there are tongues, they will be stilled; where there is knowledge, it will pass away. For we know in part, and we prophesy in part, but when completeness comes what is in part disappears. When I was a child, I talked like a child, I thought like a child, I reasoned like a child. When I became [an adult], I put the ways of childhood behind me. For now, we see only a reflection as in a mirror, then we shall see face to face. Now I know in part; then I shall know fully, even as I am fully known. And now these three remain: faith, hope, and love. But the greatest of these is love. 1 Corinthians: Chapter 13 (New International Version).

Altruism, Christianity, and Democracy

Altruism is a basis for our human relational core. Understanding human goodness and imperfections is made possible by the empathetic and sympathetic qualities of altruism, regardless of ethnicity or class. Unfortunately, altruism, a formidable force of nature, is often perceived as a weakness in our society.

People distort Christianity. The social conditions and culture of people in Biblical teachings are oftentimes used to validate ethnic cleansing, engage in genocide, and perpetuate White supremacy. Nationalism is a concept of social privilege and power that declares White people superior.

Through The Eyes of This Black Woman

The attributes of Christianity, as previously described, and altruisms—i.e., the intrinsic standards of morality such as integrity, determination, etc., may be considered as co-partners for human equality and equity. These two attributes from the ideal template for Democracy. They provide a guide for human beings to relate to each other on a plane of commonality that transcends social norms.

There may be people who share the joy of parenting. I know that joy oh, so well. There may be people willing to share with me the hurt, pain, and turmoil endured by the unexpected death of their only daughter. I live with this wound of loss and memory of love; and I feel both deeply. This is an example of a devastating reality that commingles love and loss. This dynamic duo can reach into one's soul (humanity) as it moves in the sanctuary of one's spirit and fellowships in committed relationship with God.

"Never underestimate the power of intrinsic values. They inspire every struggle for a better world."

George Monbiot

Black Americans demonstrate altruism's ability to transcend ethnicities, and Christian Nationalism

The empathetic and sympathetic qualities of altruism put us on a leveling field of understanding human goodness, and imperfections regardless of ethnicity or class. Unfortunately, altruism, a formidable force of nature, is often perceived as a weakness in our society.

As I have this conversation with you my Family, I am reminded of my childhood. I recall that this passage of Scripture may have been my first long recitation at around six years old. At Rafting Creek Baptist Church, each Easter Sunday the Church would be filled with children in their Easter outfits prepared to give their Easter speeches. Immediately after Sunday School, we were placed on the front pews of the church waiting for Mrs. Alice Dinkins, our Sunday school teacher or Moma, the secretary of the Sunday School, to call our names. We would gallantly march up front, as we had practiced weeks ahead. Then, without microphones, we spoke loudly to be heard as we modeled out outfits. That was one of the highlights of the year. OH! We could rely on our 350-membership Church having every seat filled on Easter Sunday.

Rafting Creek Baptist Church – Rembert, SC. My undying love remains with my first church home.

Relay to Liberty and Justice

William Lloyd Garrison, a White Abolitionist, wrote,

> "A slaveholder's profession of Christianity is a palpable imposture. He is a felon of the highest grade. He is a man-stealer. It is of no importance what you put on the other side of the scale."

Evangelical Racism

In her book White Evangelical Racism – The Politics of Morality in America, Dr. Anthea Butler gives a compelling explanation of what she espouses as the politics of morality. She describes it as being the axis that evolves Evangelical Racism. I term this movement's behavior as a socio-political religious movement that uses Biblical rationale to support its need to be a superior person. In America, those of us who are Christians believe that the Bible is a message that describes God's intention for our lives. It has a spiritual message of hope and love that overrides the social conditions of despair that continue to plague humankind because of sin. Both of these themes run concurrently showing the good and evil of human nature.

Dr. Butler's introduction opens with a very concise rationale that provides and provocative and concise explanation of the despairing behavior of members of a religious order who use Scripture to validate the insidious and ugly behaviors that justify racism. She says:

> White Evangelical Racism tells a concise history of the evangelical movement and – here is the hard part – the racist and racial elements that imbue its beliefs, practices, and social and political activism. It is racism that binds and blinds many White American evangelicals to the vilification of Muslims, Latino, and African Americans. It is racism that impels many evangelicals to oppose immigration and turn a blind eye to children in cages at the border. It is racism that fuels evangelical Islamophobia. It was evangelical acceptance of biblically sanctioned racism that motivated believers to separate and sell families during slavery and to march with the Klan. Racist evangelicals shielded cross burners, protected church burners, and participated in lynchings. Racism is a feature, not a bug, of American evangelicalism.

White Nationalism

White Nationalism in America is an ideology that promotes the belief that White people constitute a distinct nation and seeks to develop and maintain a White racial and national identity. It often involves advocating for policies and social structures that prioritize the interests of White people, at the expense of other ethnic and cultural groups. A key component of White Nationalism is the belief that White people are racially superior to other ethnicities.

Many White Nationalists believe in the superiority of White ethnicity and advocate for the separation of different ethnic and cultural groups. This can manifest in calls for the creation of a White-only nation or the exclusion of non-White individuals from certain areas or roles within society. They have an anti- immigration stance. White Nationalists often oppose immigration, especially from non-European countries, fearing that it will dilute the White population and culture.

White Nationalists frequently reinterpret history to emphasize the achievements of White people while minimizing or ignoring the contributions and suffering of non-White groups. This can include downplaying the atrocities of slavery, colonialism, and other forms of racial oppression. While nationalism is a broader concept that involves a strong identification with one's nation and culture, White Nationalism specifically ties this sense of identity of ethnicity. White Nationalists may co-opt patriotic symbols and rhetoric to promote their agenda.

White Nationalists typically view multiculturalism and diversity as threats to their vision of a homogenous White society. They may oppose policies and practices that promote inclusion and equality for all ethnic and cultural groups. White Nationalism has been associated with various movements and organizations, some of which have been involved in violent acts or have been labeled as hate groups by organizations like the Southern Poverty Law Center (SPLC) and the Anti-Defamation League (ADL).

In recent years, White Nationalism has gained more visibility in American politics and society, often through social media and online communities. This has led to increased concerns about hate speech, violence, and the erosion of social cohesion. The ideology is widely condemned for promoting racism, intolerance, and division.

White Christian Evangelical Nationalism

White Christian Evangelical Nationalism is an ideology that combines elements of White Nationalism, Evangelical Christianity, and American Nationalism. This belief system advocates for a society structured around both a specific ethnic identity (White) and a particular religious identity (Christian Evangelical).

White Christian Evangelical Nationalists see their White ethnic identity and Evangelical Christian faith as central to their sense of self and community. They believe that the United States was founded as a Christian nation and should remain one. They seek to influence politics and policy to reflect their religious and ethnic beliefs. This includes advocating for laws and policies that align with their interpretation of Christian values, such as opposition to abortion and LGBTQ+ rights, as well as support for religious displays in public spaces.

Proponents view their culture as superior and under threat from increasing diversity and secularism. They advocate for policies that they believe will preserve their cultural and religious heritage, such as immigration restrictions and promoting Christian education. White Christian Evangelical Nationalists often express a strong sense of American patriotism, intertwining their religious beliefs with national identity. They may view the United States as having a special divine mandate or mission.

This ideology typically opposes the secularization of society, promoting the integration of Christian principles into public life and government. This includes advocating prayer in schools, religious-based laws, and other forms of public religious expression. Similar to White Nationalism, White Christian Evangelical Nationalists engage in historical revisionism and theological revisionism, portraying American history as fundamentally Christian and downplaying or ignoring the contributions and experiences of non-White and non-Christian groups.

White Christian Evangelical Nationalists see multiculturalism and diversity as threats to their vision of a homogenous White Christian society. They resist efforts to promote inclusivity and equality for all other ethnic and religious groups. This ideology has gained more visibility in recent years, often manifesting in political rhetoric and movements that advocate for a return to what they see as traditional American values. Make America Great Again is widely criticized for promoting exclusionary and discriminatory practices that undermine the principles of pluralism, religious freedom, and equality.

Worthy of note is the long-standing reality of White Christian Nationalists' role in endorsing hate crimes or even performing hate crimes. These Nationalists were instrumental in justifying slavery, Jim Crow, and passing laws that legalized segregation. Their stance on separatism seems maniacal. Many of them, such as the Ku Klux, Klan and The Proud Boys are either directly or indirectly responsible for acts of domestic terrorism. Many White Supremacists declare themselves to be Christians who are determined to set a moral nation under their Christian values.

During the 1600s, many White Christian Nationalists were slave traders and enslavers. They negatively described Africa and disavowed the intellect of our people as they attempted to rewrite the history of Africa. They deliberately misrepresented our motherland and the richness of its culture.

There were Nationalists in Ghana who built beautiful sanctuaries for Christian church services. They were also members of the slave trade whose buildings were ornate and beautiful inside their sanctuaries. White congregational services were held there. Our parents were chained in urine, feces, and vomit in their churches' dungeons. Sometimes, our people were held there without food or water until the arrival of the slave traders. Those who died while waiting were thrown into the sea. Today, the Christian Nationalist resurgence in our nation is serious. The militancy that has occurred in recent years must not be taken lightly.

Democracy V. Christianity

A Democracy is a system of government in which power is vested in the people, who rule either directly or through freely elected representatives. In a Democracy, the authority of the government is created and sustained by the consent of its people, typically expressed through regular, free, and fair elections. All citizens have equal access to power and can participate equally in the political process, often through the right to vote and run for office. Laws are applied equally to all citizens, including those who govern. There is a legal framework that ensures justice and protects the rights of individuals.

Democracies uphold fundamental rights such as freedom of speech, assembly, and religion. Citizens have the right to express their opinions, form associations, and seek redress for grievances. Elected officials are accountable to the people and must act in the public interest. Government actions and decisions are open to scrutiny and subject to checks and balances.

While decisions are often made based on majority rule, the rights of minority groups are protected to ensure that they are not oppressed or marginalized. These principles work together to create a system where governance is based on the will and participation of the people, promoting fairness, justice, and equality.

White Christian Nationalism V. Democracy

White Christian Nationalism is harmful to Democracy for several reasons. White Christian nationalism often promotes the idea that the country should be defined by a specific racial and religious identity, excluding, or marginalizing those who do not fit this identity. This goes against the democratic principles of equality and inclusivity. Democracy thrives on diversity, equity, and pluralism, where different viewpoints and cultures are respected and represented. White Christian Nationalism undermines this by promoting a homogenous culture and suppressing diversity.

By privileging one group over others, White Christian Nationalism can lead to policies and practices that discriminate against minorities, whether based on ethnicity, religion, or other characteristics. This threatens the democratic principle of equal rights for all citizens. In addition, a key aspect of Democracy is the separation of church and state, ensuring that government remains neutral on matters of religion. White Christian nationalism blurs this line, pushing for policies that align with a specific religious doctrine, which can alienate and disenfranchise those of different religions or no religious beliefs.

White Christian Nationalism can increase social and political polarization by fostering an "us versus them" mentality. This division can lead to conflict and weaken the social cohesion necessary for a stable and functioning Democracy. Nationalist movements, including White Christian Nationalism, often have authoritarian tendencies, promoting strongman leaders and undermining democratic institutions and norms. This can lead to the erosion of democratic checks and balances, concentration of power, and suppression of dissent.

Historical examples show that nationalist movements often lead to undemocratic outcomes, including the rise of authoritarian regimes, persecution of minorities, and suppression of freedoms. White Christian nationalism is no different in its potential to lead to similar outcomes. Overall, White Christian nationalism poses a threat to the founding principles of Democracy by promoting exclusion, undermining pluralism, and fostering division and authoritarianism.

Social Development Through American Religion

White Supremacists are perpetrators of Christian Nationalism under the guise of Christianity. These believers declare human inequality as godly. Their social disciplines and teachings posture as spiritual development. For generations, this dogma has misconstrued Christian principles through socio-political Biblical lenses. Its aim continues to focus on validating human separation.

Here are three examples of lies told by Christian Nationalists to advance and promote evil:

1. In 1832 Albert Raboteau, an Episcopal Priest from South Carolina wrote a pamphlet called Slave Religion. He said that it was for the deliberate purpose of "showing from Scriptures in the Old and New Testaments, that slavery is not forbidden by the Divine Law: and at the same time to prove the necessity of giving religious instruction to the Negroes."

2. The false biblical story of Ham. Ham was one of Noah's four sons sharing the same biological parents. The fact that Ham's skin was Black did not change his genetic reality. The Bible says that the curse was on Ham's son Canaan, not Ham. White supremacists continued the Ham lie. In the mid-1800s--240 years slave owner Thomas R. R. Cobb, a leading Confederate, wrote, "The great Architect (God) had framed them both (enslaved people) physically and mentally to fill the sphere in which they were thrown. His wisdom and mercy combined in constituting them thus suited to the degraded position they were destined to occupy. The Curse of Ham is now being executed upon his descendants."

3. The Insurrectionists who committed treason on January 6, 2021, lied and continue to lie about the 2020 presidential elections being stolen and widespread voter fraud. Christian Nationalists fueled the flame of deceit and treason. Their behavior was the direct cause of over 150 law enforcement officers being injured and four deaths. Their behavior was supported by the Christian Nationalist political leaders. This treacherous act was endorsed by Christian Nationalist pastors and churches. There was a blatant disregard for the Constitution, the rule of law, and the doctrine of separation of church and state.

Democracy and Christian Nationalism cannot coexist. While Democracy is not a religion, it is an ideology based upon fair validation of all humanity. Christian Nationalism continues to distort Biblical instructions and social disciplines that condone the White Supremacy Ideology.

The Black Church

Left: Bishop Richard Allen was the organizer and first pastor of the African American Methodist Episcopal Church. Right: Bishop Vashti M. McKenzie, is the first woman Bishop of the A.M.E. Church

The social indoctrinations of Christian Nationalism, the abuse of Scripture, and the mistreatment of Black congregants persuaded Richard Allen to break away from the Methodist Episcopal Church. Consequently, Allen formed the first organized Black church and named it the African Methodist Episcopal Church (A.M.E.). In 1794 this church was recognized as the first organized Black denomination in the United States and was officially incorporated in 1816.

Like White Christian Nationalism, Black American Christianity also has socio-political realities at play. The following represent some characteristics that are distinctly different from the White Christian Nationalists experiences during slavery:

1. Historically, Black preachers had to preach the sermon approved by the slave master, which touted getting to heaven for a reward while accepting slavery as an assignment from God.

2. Poverty was preached more as a spiritual condition of acceptance rather than as a social condition.

3. Financial solvency was non-existent, which implied an exclusive feat instead of the basis for human survival.

4. "God will provide" was the Black Christian mantra for overcoming adversities.

5. Black people's relationship with God provided protection from the societal injustices we experience and gave them the courage to "go through" and "overcome" with the guidance of the Holy Spirit.

The concept of being rewarded in heaven was the rationale given to the enslaved, for enduring suffering, poverty, and hardship on earth. However, the concept of faith, hope and anticipation became the hallmark that gave Black Christians courage to persevere. Their belief that Jesus Christ provided all things gave them the courage to continue the relay toward a better life on earth and after death. Faith is the evidence of our relationship with Christ that transcends the dogma of doctrines and socio-political inequities.

"Now, faith is the substance of things hoped for, the evidence of things not seen."

Hebrews 11:1 King James Version

The Black Church in America had the most significant influence on the Black community. In the Church, God and people commingle. Historically, it was a place where all-day Sunday services were held. Politically conscious meetings about the state of our community occurred in our places of worship. Black education was first taught in our Churches. Socially, many people would come to Church on Sundays with the specific expectation of finding a future spouse. Our Church was a spiritual and social part of the Black Americans Experience. These acts of "community," were in-part, reasons our Churches were bombed during the Civil Rights Movement and why they continue being bombed and burned today.

The Black Church

The Black Church is still a fundamental source of funding for Black education. This funding occurred long before America allowed our community to have school buildings. However, there is never enough information about the outstanding contributions the Black Church has made and continues to make for our people.

Historically, Black people's Biblical analysis of Christianity revolves around the sustaining power of God's love and forgiveness. Based upon this concept of Christianity, love is believed to be a strength. It does not require being reciprocal. Love also represents the possibilities of a better life on earth and teaches us a guaranteed full life after death. "

Our old folk understood clearly that unforgiveness was a negative, dark, and heavy emotional overload. It suppressed their creativity and ingenuity so they would not hold on to or belabor such weights. Their ingenuity gave them the ability to forgive and trust less. They also understood that trust is something that has to be earned. In other words, they practiced the Scripture that says, "Wherefore seeing we also are compassed about with so great a cloud of witnesses, let us lay aside every weight, and the sin which doth so easily beset us, and let us run with patience the race that is set before us" Hebrews 12:1.

They taught us that ingenuity and creativity are weapons that save lives and moves our agenda ahead. These concepts befuddled White Supremacists, who deemed us unintelligent, as our fore parents forge ahead Continuing to Rise. Ingenuity and creativity remain the strength our fore parents gained from the indelible spirit. This spirit remains available to each one of us. It remains the core of Black people's strength as we Relay to Liberty and Justice.

The attributes of Christianity, as previously described, and altruisms—i.e., the intrinsic standards of morality such as integrity, determination, etc., may be considered as co-partners for human equality and equity. These two attributes formulate the ideal template for Democracy. They provide a guide for human beings to relate to each other on a plane of commonality that transcends social norms and religions.

There may be people who share the joy of parenting. I know that joy oh, so well. There may be people willing to share with me the hurt, pain, and turmoil endured by the unexpected death of their only daughter. I live with this wound of loss and memory of love; and I feel both deeply. This is an example of a devastating reality that commingles love and loss yet remains timeless. This dynamic duo can reach into one's soul (humanity) as it moves in the sanctuary of one's spirit and fellowships in committed relationship with God.

Preachers, we must not allow ourselves to become reticent. Our ancestors created ways to engage their congregations in social and political matters. They, too, were faced with White supremacists such as the Ku Klux Klansmen raiding their meetings. They did not let such behaviors stop them, and they did not retaliate. They prayed for their oppressor.

What is Lacking?

Mr. Frederick Douglass said,

> "But the church of this nation is not only indifferent to the wrongs of the slave, but it also actually takes sides with the oppressors. It has made itself the bulwark of American slavery, and the shield of American slave-hunters. Many of its most eloquent Divines who stand as the very lights of the church, have shamelessly given the sanction of religion and the Bible to the whole slave system. They have taught that man may, properly, be a slave; that the relation of master and slave is ordained of God; that to send back an escaped bondman to his master is clearly the duty of all the followers of the Lord Jesus Christ; and this horrible blasphemy is palmed off upon the world for Christianity."

William Lloyd Garrison, a White Abolitionist, wrote,

> "A slaveholder's profession of Christianity is a palpable imposture. He is a felon of the highest grade. He is a man-stealer. It is of no importance what you put on the other side of the scale." We carried over the lie from White Christian Nationalism that taught our ancestors to believe that "Money is the root of all evil." This is an excellent example of twisting Scripture so that it keeps our community from being socially and financially prosperous. The Scripture specifically states that "the love of money is the root of all evil." Thus, The Bible teaches that it is the LOVE of money, not the money itself. However, because of the misinterpretation, many church folks have unrealistic views about money. For instance, many parishioners continue to resent requests for funds in church and refuse to honor the Biblical request to "tithe." Also, these realities were tied to the literal meaning of the quote, "God will provide.," such that the financial health of some Black churches suffered.

The imperative need today is to teach clearly and to treat financial solvency as a gift from God and a tool to be used to advance our human lives. Nevertheless, The Bible specifically says, "The LOVE of money is the root of all evil." How many times do you think slave owners twisted this Scripture to suit their own social purposes? More importantly, how often did slave owners twist Scripture to promote their own political agendas?

This challenge from the Late Dr. Samuel Proctor's declaration to Black preachers is apropos today. He said, "Preachers are the most intimidated in the areas of social, political, and economic issues, but God's people live in the real world – as Jesus did- with armies, taxes, poor beggars, rich farmers, clever political leaders' with problems of ethnic separation, class discrimination, and gender inequality. There is neither a way to preach "The Good News" of God or to teach equity and justice for all people without addressing these social, political, and economic areas."

CHAPTER FIVE

Two Roads Diverge

"The student is not above the teacher, but everyone who is fully trained will be like their teacher."

Luke 6:40

My Parents
Reynolds, Edward "Chick" and Dr. Margaret Wright Davis

Two Roads Diverged Inside the Systemic Racism System

My mother was beautiful. She was an outstanding leader and trailblazer in her professional, social, civic, and Christian life. She believed in fighting to ensure that no one was being discriminated against. Her various positions of leadership gave her a voice that was recognized by both the White and Black communities in Sumter, South Carolina and beyond.

Momma taught Moya to understand that the way for our community to continue to rise would be through learning that two diverging roads also represent one's choice in every situation. The two roads were in front of her. One was called REACT and RETALIATE. The land marker read, "An Eye for an eye. The other road was called RESPOND. That land marker read, "Get the job done while respecting all human beings." To travel either of these roads meant learning how to be a warrior. My matriarch and my mother chose the second road.

On that road called RESPOND, the lesson they learned and taught by example was how to face and respond justly to injustice rather than reacting to it. This was the road less traveled, so it was their wilderness experience. Their lives were not lived as passive warriors. Their life's epitaphs bespeak their leadership, determination, and courage despite the costs. Like their ancestors, they paved the way for their generations to continue to rise.

My mother, as was her mother, was courageous; she was the daughter who never lived anywhere but in Sumter County. These determined warriors would scratch their way, if need be, to higher ground. They chose to be change agents for the cause of humanity.

Moya did not follow her sisters to Mather Academy boarding school, Camden, SC or to Bennett College in Greensboro, NC for her undergraduate degree. Instead, she went to day school at Lincoln High School and on to Morris College, both in Sumter, SC during the week. She came home on weekends to work on the farm with mama and her brother Hamp. When he returned home from The Army, Vorhees College in Denmark, SC was his next educational venture.

Relay to Liberty and Justice

Unlike her sisters, my mother received the actual and subliminal teachings from her mother and, as an adult, volunteered as a woman of service to her community and church in many of the same capacities. While her personality was quieter than Moma's, whose demeanor was more vibrant and curious, she was also a beautiful woman of substance.

My mother, Dr. Margaret "Moya" (pronounced "Muh yuh") W. Davis, was a retired teacher and administrator in public education and an assistant professor at Morris College, Sumter, South Carolina. While at Morris, Moya recognized a need for academic support for some students who were being left behind, so she ascertained permission from the college president and chaired the committee that designed a General Studies Division. She subsequently became the first chairperson of that Division.

In her church, Moya became the first woman Trustee. She also blazed the path for other women to join local, state, and National Baptist Associations.

As President of an International Reading Collaborative, my mother was the first woman from South Carolina to present at an International Convention held in Stockholm, Sweden. She took a coalition of Black and White women and men to share the experience with her. Moya was the trailblazer in the former School District #2. She was the district's first administrator and Director of Reading and the first Black woman chair of the former Sumter School Board, District # 17. I remember coming home for a visit and having an experience of a lifetime.

An Eye-opening Experience

Having lived away from my hometown for more than twenty years, thanks to this trip I realized that I knew only the Black section of the town I still called "home." Socially mingling with White people in Sumter, South Carolina, had not been my experience. Yet, during one of my visits, I became aware of a socialization between Black and White ethnicities that I could not have imagined in my early life. I met White people who did not believe in the White Supremacist Ideology and was amazed.

On this visit with her, Moya told me that we were going to lunch with two of her friends from the school board, and when they came to pick us up, I was amazed—being both cautious and observant. She had not told me they were White, and when I went out to get into the car, I noticed the back seat was available for us. I hesitated. The back seat? Were we riding in the back seat of a car behind two White ladies? I asked myself, "… did my mother say they are her friends?"

Do you get this message? Had they been two Black ladies, I would never have given getting in the back seat a second thought. My history caused my problem. In my childhood, Black people sat in the back seats of vehicles driven by White people or vice-versa; it was not customary for White and Black people to ride in the same seat. Riding in the back seat with two White women in the front was etched in my brain as something I would never do in this town. After all, I marched and went to jail, protesting this very matter.

My mother referred to these two ladies as her friends. That notion was just as foreign as riding in the back seat of their car. The level of my suspicion was high. The women shared how glad they were to meet me. They had asked Moya to let them know when I was in town so they could take us to lunch and get to know me. I was cordial yet reticent as I looked for a "slip-up" moment.

These women took us to a restaurant that I never knew existed in our city and informed me of the many years they had eaten great food there. I watched my mother to see if she was comfortable with the restaurant. The three of them talked about how much the menu changed from week to week. AH, my mom had been here before; she had become a frequent customer!

Through The Eyes of This Black Woman

Wow! Sumter really was a foreign place for me. I saw that these three women were indeed friends. They took Vacations together in the mountains and went bird watching. What? My mother? Bird watching? As it turned out, she loved doing it as much as she enjoyed the authentic relationship she shared with these ladies. Over the years, I got to know them better. When Moya died in 2018, at 93 years of age, they were a comfort to me as they openly shared the pain of her death, the authenticity of their friendship, and the value of the three of them serving their Black and White Sumter community together.

Social relationships are a human reality. These relationships are not relegated to ethnicity. Unfortunately, discrimination and bigotry make it problematic for many people. Some multi-ethnic families are still ostracized. I believe that the pain of White supremacy continues to create social disconnects as well as generational moral, social, and emotional imbalances in all life.

I share this story because it is a representation of the way that our ancestors believed that life perpetuates itself through the deeds we leave behind. Doing our best to make life better means doing so wherever and whenever we can. My grandmother lived most of her life while Moya lived all of her life in Sumter County SC. From 1895- 2018 — a total of 123 years and five generations — their contributions to the people of their State afforded them the honor of being inducted into the South Carolina State Black Hall of Fame, and I am so honored to know of their trailblazing experiences.

These two women have had a tremendous impact on my life. Consequently, I continue learning the road less traveled. I have discovered that the road less traveled is the road that breaks down barriers and supplies room for others to tread. Herein is the evidence of the indelible spirit at work to build better human relations with people — with God's creation--regardless of ethnicity or the color of their skin.

In Memory of Moya. This brilliant and beautiful woman lived to be the ripe old age of ninety-three. I suspect that if her life had not been ravaged by Alzheimer's, she may have asked God for a few more productive years; at least as long as her mother lived. She was 99.7 years old when she died.

When Moya was unable to speak as she was accustomed to it, there were times that she would look over at the chimney in her family room. It appeared that she was trying to read her favorite poem called "Hold High The Torch". Once she told me that the unknown author blessed her soul by penning what she would love to leave as a legacy to us.

In the loving memory of both of my parents, I share the life of service each rendered and would want us to continue. Their torches burned brightly in education and as trailblazers in Sumter County School for a composite of 75 years. She was the first Black official administrator in their district. She was The Director of Reading, and my dad was the first Black Assistant Superintendent in their District. When they were active, Sumter County was divided into two districts.

My father died at 62 from Emphysema. Had he lived, I imagine that after retiring from the District, he might have joined Moya in higher education at their Alma Mater Morris College.

Moya's Favorite Poem and Final Charge to Us...

Hold High the Torch
(Author unknown)

Hold high the torch!
You did not light its glow-
"T'was given you by other hands, you know.

'Tis yours to keep it burning bright,
Yours to pass on when you no more need light;
For there are other feet we must guide,
And other forms go marching by our side;

Their eyes are watching
Every smile and tear and efforts which we think are not worthwhile
are sometimes just the very help they need,
Actions to which their souls would give more heed;
So that in turn they'll hold it high!
And say, "I watched someone else carry it this way."
If brighter paths should beckon you to choose,
Would your small gain compare with all you'd lose?

Hold high the torch!
You did not light its glow-
T'was given to you by other hands, you know.

It started down its pathway bright, the day the Maker said:
"Let there be light."
And He once said, who hung on Calvary's tree —
"Ye are the light of the world...
Go! Shine for me."

CHAPTER SIX

Race and Racism

"Peace cannot exist where justice is not served."

Congressman John R. Lewis

Race

Race is a social construct used to categorize humans based on physical characteristics such as skin color, facial features, and hair texture. These categories have no consistent biological basis and do not represent distinct genetic groupings. All humans are members of the same species. We are called Homo Sapiens. This name is derived from Latin, where "Homo" means "man" and "sapiens" means "wise" or "knowing," reflecting our capacity for thought and intelligence.

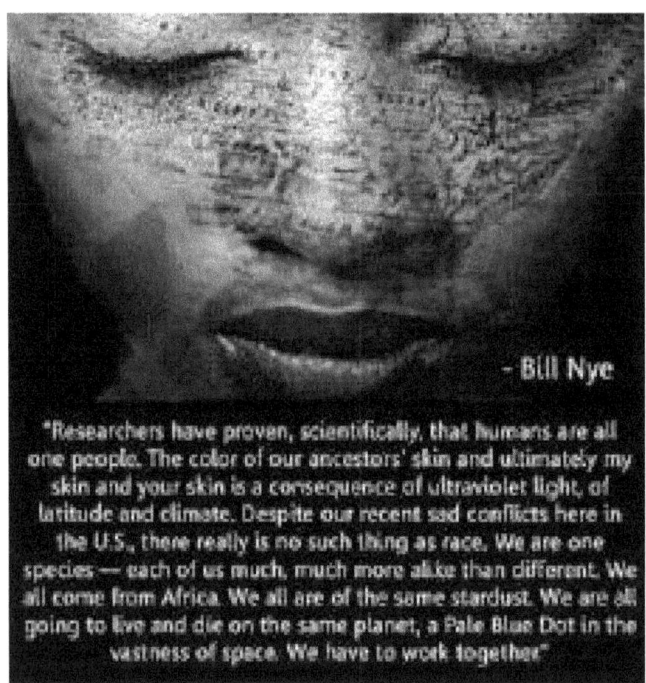

Scientifically, human genetic diversity does not support the concept of distinct biological races. The genetic differences within any given population group are greater than those between different groups. Human beings are 99.9% genetically identical, and the variations that do exist do not align with traditional racial categories. Anthropologists and biologists largely agree that race is not a biologically valid classification. The concept of race does not correspond to clear, distinct genetic groupings or subspecies within the human species. Modern humans share a common ancestry, and our evolutionary history does not support the idea of separate races. Traits associated with race, such as skin color, are adaptations to specific environmental conditions and do not indicate deeper biological differences.

The idea of race has been used historically to justify social hierarchies, colonialism, slavery, and systemic discrimination. It emerged during European colonial expansion as a way to rationalize the exploitation and oppression of non-European peoples. Race is a social construct that has real and significant consequences. Society categorizes people based on perceived physical differences, and

These categorizations impact individuals' social, economic, and political experiences. Race influences policies and practices in areas such as law, education, employment, housing, and healthcare. It also shapes personal and group identity, cultural practices, and social interactions. The concept of race has been used to create and maintain power structures and inequalities. Racism and racial discrimination are rooted in these constructed categories and continue to affect people globally.

Race lacks a solid basis in biological science. It is a powerful social and political construct with significant implications for individuals and societies. Understanding race as a social construct helps in addressing the inequalities and injustices associated with it.

Racism

Racism is a belief system and set of practices that perpetuate the idea that certain races are inherently superior or inferior to others. It is grounded in the social and political construct of race and manifests in various ways.

While race is not a scientifically valid concept, it involves a range of beliefs, behaviors, and institutional practices that are discriminated against, and harm people based on their perceived race.

Individual Racism is personal beliefs, attitudes, and actions that reflect prejudiced views and discriminatory behavior towards people based on their race. This can include overt acts of hate and violence, as well as more subtle forms of bias and microaggressions.

Institutional Racism is policies, practices, and procedures of institutions that disproportionately affect certain racial groups negatively. This includes disparities in criminal justice, education, healthcare, housing, and employment.

Structural Racism and/or Systemic Racism is the overall system in which public policies, institutional practices, cultural representations, and other norms work in ways that perpetuate racial group inequity. It involves the cumulative and compounding effects of an array of factors that systematically disadvantage certain racial groups.

Cultural Racism is the societal belief that cultural practices and values of one race are superior to those of another. This can include stereotypes, media representations, and cultural norms that marginalize and devalue certain racial groups.

Manifestations of Racism:

1. Prejudice: Preconceived opinions or attitudes about individuals based on their race without factual basis or experience.

2. Discrimination: Unjust or prejudicial treatment of different categories of people, especially on the grounds of race.

3. Stereotyping: Oversimplified and fixed ideas about a group of people, often leading to expectations and assumptions about individuals based on their race.

4. Violence and Hate Crimes: Physical attacks, threats, and other forms of violence Directed at individuals or groups based on their race.

5. Segregation: The enforced separation of different racial groups in daily life, such as in housing, education, and employment.

Impact of Racism:

Racism has profound negative effects on individuals and society, including:

1. Economic Inequality: Disparities in income, wealth, and access to resources and opportunities.

2. Health Disparities: Differences in health outcomes and access to healthcare services.

3. Social Inequity: Limited access to quality education, safe housing, and fair treatment within the justice system.

4. Psychological Effects: Stress, trauma, and a diminished sense of self-worth and belonging for those subjected to racism.

Addressing Racism

Combating racism requires a multifaceted approach, including:

1. Education and Awareness: Increasing understanding of the historical and social contexts of race and racism.

2. Policy Reform: Implementing policies that promote equity and dismantle institutional and structural racism.

3. Cultural Change: Challenging and changing cultural norms, media representations, and societal attitudes that perpetuate racism.

4. Advocacy and Activism: Supporting movements and organizations that fight for racial justice and equality.

Remember that the American story of our ancestors extends long before the slave ships deported them to these shores. They were brought from the shores of Africa; they were chained; piled on top of one another; placed into the bottom of filthy and diseased sea-faring vessels; subject to all types of illnesses. Our people—our ancestors—were forced on an unsolicited trip. They were raped and ravaged; their native tongues were stripped from their psychic.

The Slave Ship: La Amistad

To be taken from their familiar surroundings and to have their socialization demolished, was more than inhumane. This act will always be considered one of the darkest, if not the darkest period in American history. To come to an unrecognizable land and to hear a foreign language while simultaneously starving and sick, as one is shoved, beaten, and then physically examined in the public square describes inhumanity beyond horrific.

Chapter Six - Race and Racism

Enslaved people on the deck of the ship called the Wildfire.

Pay Attention

Family, do you notice myriads of ways White supremacists have had to employ race and racism in order to justify the types of racism described in this chapter? Do you realize that these matters are executed to prove that race is a biological rather than a social matter? Imagine this. Since 1619 they have exhausted numberless unsuccessful attempts to prove that we are an inferior people.

The Our enslaved ancestors endured much torture, and many gave their lives for us.

A careful review of the many ways in which the White supremacists have had to go as they endeavor to authenticate their claim of our inferiority is astounding. To say that they are persistent is an understatement. To say that they are determined seems true. However, the fact is that their consistent attempts, since 1619, on these shores prove that their attempts must continue.

Relay to Liberty and Justice

From cotton fields to Congress

The perpetual attempts to keep us segregated and less fortunate show in today's public schools, public housing, and in the sub-cultures that arise due to poverty. While the proportions of people in poverty are far too many, our Black brothers and sisters began proving upon their arrival on these shores that the no physical brands or segregation in any form would keep us from Continuing to Rise.

300 Year Guarantee to Suppress Black People: Their Disgrace!

The Willie Lynch Syndrome was devised to explain the psychological problems and disunity among our community. He purported that is White supremacists would "Plant seeds of distrust and envy within the Black community to ensure they never fore strong bonds." Well, family, we can attest to the fact that that discourse failed.

Since they could not successfully divide the majority of us, the only way White slave owners thought they could suppress or scare our ancestors was to kill us. Hanging Black people was attributed to Willie Lynch. He declared lynching to be one of the most effective methods for keeping Africans enslaved for at least three hundred years. In 1712, this man stood on the banks of the James River in Virginia and presented a letter of instructions to some slave owners. Some framers of the U.S. Constitution as well as Clergy attended. Lynch's intention was to teach the slave owners how to reduce their African captives to a sub-human status—to kill their spirits, trouble their souls, and dismantle their culture.

Isn't it interesting? Slave owners were more than aware that these enslaved human beings were already civilized. To think of White men in America enslaving African Kings and Queens and highly skilled people is unconscionable. They needed and used these Africans to cultivate their land because they had no idea how to do so themselves. It must have been intimidating to these slave owners to attempt to make a person inferior while also needing to learn from these people and depending on them for survival.

The need to denigrate people, by default, implies their intelligence. Although the African socialization process may have been contrary to the slave masters' it was apparent that socialization existed among the enslaved. Notice that the British slave owner, William "Willie" Lynch, came from the West Indies to the United States to teach slaves owners how to "restrain" not "train" enslaved people. The intent of his teaching to kill our ancestor's spirits was impossible! Christian Nationalists continue this plight.

They Keep Coming!

The message was that even killing Black people could not stop their move to keep coming to America. The interesting thing about his message speaks to the dichotomy White supremacist has to face. Their determination to kill, denigrate, and suppress us keep them busy. Why? Because we keep coming! We show up in their halls of higher education. We show up in the medical and scientific rooms. We show up in their Boardrooms. We keep coming. The fear of us showing up and judges and politicians has them perplexed. They know that when we show up in numbers that we show the difference in environmental advantages and raw intellect.

How Does this Happen?

After many generations of mistreatment and probably no formal American education, some of our ancestors became national leaders. They moved from slavery after their emancipation into Congress as Senators and members of the House of Representatives during The Period of Reconstruction, 1863- 1877. Note that the Period of Reconstruction came immediately after the Emancipation Proclamation was signed. Has it ever made you wonder how our ancestors prepared to take such a gigantic leap of progress? I remain amazed and energized by these men who most likely remembered their ancestors who were civilized leaders for many centuries in Africa.

The tenacity of a man who upon immediate freedom from slavery steals a ship that he may never have commanded, sailed it using maps he may never have seen before, and takes a Confederate ship and surrenders it to a Union fleet. Does this sound like the work of an unintelligent person? Does this story sound like the determination of a coward? Here is the story.

A Sail to Freedom

Robert Smalls - a S.C. State was a congressman served from 1875 to 1887, was self-educated.

In 1862, the second year after the Civil War, Robert Smalls stole a ship from the harbor in Charleston, South Carolina and sailed it disguised as a confederate ship captain. When he was outside of confederate waters, he ordered his crew to raise a White flag and to surrender this confederate ship to the Union fleet. In 1895 Mr. Smalls became the first-generation Black politician to serve in the South Carolina State assembly. Nothing beats our ingenuity and creativity.

Never Forget

Dr. Martin Luther King, Jr., shared his dream. He said, "I have a dream my four little children will one day live in a nation where they will not be judged by the color of their skin but by the content of their character." A statement like this seems a bit disconcerting for White supremacists. In 2024 they are full steam ahead with dismantling the US Constitution and fighting to make their America great. Well, Family, we have the opportunity to really give them their wish. We have the opportunity to keeping filling the poles in 2024 and render to Dr. King his dream. That would make America great.

> *" Our ancestors are an ever widening circle of hope."*
>
> **Toni Morrison**

CHAPTER SEVEN

The Fearlessness of Hope

"I was trying to raise myself to be a Black man in America, and beyond the quiver of appearance, no one was around me seemed to know exactly what that meant."

President Barack Obama

Barack Obama was America's First Black President, 2009-2018

A Moral Compass: Competence, Compassion, and Kindness

Barack Hussein Obama was this nation's 44th President. His leadership for eight years supplied the ray of hope and optimism in some corridors of this nation. On the other hand, the reality of being in America and led by a Black man, whose name was not Christian American, infuriated the White supremacists. They began a "full- court press" to ensure that he would not succeed. And yet, he won two terms. How could a Black man become President in a White European-run nation? What did he see that would have him say, "I see what's possible when we recognize that we are one American family, all deserving of equal treatment. All deserving of equal respect?"

An American Intercultural Reality

President Obama was born into the beauty and the perils of human unity and ethnic separation. He was conceived during the marriage of a Black African man and a White American Mid-Western woman, then, basically raised by White maternal grandparents who were raised in Kansas and living in Hawaii. His blood siblings include five Black Africans consisting of one sister and four brothers; one Black/White brother; and one White/Indonesian sister. This Black American man experienced Hawaiian and Indonesian cultures during his formative years.

In President Obama's young-adult life, he chose Black acculturation instead of what Cole Brown describes as a "grey boy." Imagine what President Obama's very presence must be to the White supremacists. His uniqueness includes the richness and a positive perspective toward the unity of humanity. His heredity, his upbringing, his life is an American paradox that is not received well by the people who have governed this country since its beginning. Many White legislative and judicial leaders continue to be outraged because a Black man represented this country successfully and effectively as the great intellectual World leader of the free world, and the Commander-in-Chief of this country.

From the tainted perspective that White people have of Black Americans, President Obama perplexed them. How could this Black man possibly be an American citizen? There is no recorded history of a Black citizen rising to the pinnacle of American political success.

Through The Eyes of This Black Woman

The hysteria that arose after President Obama was elected was incredulous but understandable Through The Eyes Of This Back Woman. Obama's election evoked the reality of what can happen to a country whose history is slanted to include the value of only one segment of humanity. Moreover, it grows as evidenced by the violence that continues to ensue, and the polarization that we are currently experiencing. This is a crystal- clear example of what happens when vital historical information regarding all humanity is omitted from the education of its citizens.

My third grandbaby Ayden was just learning to talk when President Obama was elected. When Ayden heard our rejoicing over Obama's win, my baby would yell, "Yeah! Rock-a- Bahma!" This kid might have had the wisdom to describe our Black President's moral compass: competence, compassion, and kindness at their best.

American History denied: Racism grows Tentacles

The courage it took for President Obama to come out of what most of us thought was obscurity and speak at the Democratic Convention with such force and fierce energy, was a "wow!" Moment for many of us around the U.S! We asked, "Who is this articulate young man who dares to speak with such vigor?"

Many of our ancestors were sold that he would go far "someday." His audacity to leave the Senate after one term and declare his run for President of the United States was something that reverberated for a long time in our communities. The apprehension that arose about whether he was ready to become a Presidential candidate was not nearly as much of our conversation as, "Who is this brilliant, scholarly politician who dares to stand tall among the flock of leaders?" And "Is he Black enough?" The community asked. "Does he know us well enough?" "Will the nation embrace him because he is half White and looks Black?" And we asked, "How can a Black man from Hawaii possibly know how to embrace the Black culture?" Yet, Mr. Obama kept coming on strong and impressing us with his daring drive and intellect. Thus, when he was elected President, there was rejoicing in our community! For those of us who were members of the Civil Rights Movement who had seen several attempts before him, there was not a dry eye amongst us.

As with every other leader, history records their strengths and their weaknesses. For this discussion, I will celebrate this Black man who became the first Black President. Obama came to become a politician when he served in the Illinois and U.S. Senate. Yet until he spoke at the Democratic Convention of 2008, if one was not from the Mid-West, most Black Americans did not know him. Oh! When Senator Obama spoke that night Black America held fist and wiped tears of joy. It is no wonder that a seemingly introverted Black man who had lived where no one around him knew what he was searching to become in the America, led as our national leader. His critics will never override his leadership or his accomplishments while in office. They include:

1. The economy and labor markets experienced long periods of stable growth.
2. Job growth had its largest expansion on record in early 2017, dating back to 1939. It provided a solid economy after years of improvement.
3. Economic growth accelerated over time:
4. Job growth logged its longest winning streak
5. Employment opportunities increased.
6. Wages and incomes were on the upswing.

7. Household debts were dwindling.
8. Government finances improved; and,
9. The passage of The Affordable Care Act (Obamacare) was initiated.

Cheering Greatness

A careful read of the Obama quote at the beginning of this chapter speaks volumes about our nation. For anyone to be in an environment where he or she must look for examples of their identity is distressing. And yet, this might be another person's truth in this democratic nation. There must be ways that we can build to strengthen relationships and increase our presence across this nation. I argue that criticisms from even among our community will not override the elation the masses in communities felt when he was elected. Not only was he the President of the United States he was also the leader of the Free World. It cannot override the goodwill of his and First Lady Michelle's tenure as the first Black family in to live in the White house for eight years.

The Reality of Who We Are

I believe that President Barack H. Obama is a great icon. He is the enigma that bred a lot of intrigue. I think the fact that he appears inured by the unpleasant things that might have made him quit the race for the presidency was astounding. He set his course, and then he moved with energy, vigor, and tenacity. He sat with the fireside chatters and left them in awe with his poise and intellect. The way he and his wife Michelle conduct themselves makes Harvard look pretty good.

The conversations about people being disappointed because of their anticipation of what he would do for Black people have never resonated with me. His orientation was not Black, yet he was Black. His experiences of Blackness were commingled in the culture of his White grandparents from Kansas and with his parents and sister in Indonesia. Who among us knows a Black person with such an orientation? At his core, he has the indelible spirit that resides in each of us.

I also suspect that during his tenure as our 44th President, he may have had to realize that his blackness was under scrutiny and at other times he had to understand blackness as a culture from Michelle and others close to him. She has learned the nuances of the White world and more prejudices because of her being a brilliant and beautiful Black woman. Yet, I can only imagine the social and political situations both Obamas incurred while being the First Family of America and the Leading Family of the Free World.

The irony of his tenure in office is that he was able to institute what was officially named The Affordable Care Act (ACA). With the eroding of the middle-class and lower middle-class, millions of people need health insurance. History will show that under the leadership of Barack Obama, the Affordable Care Act was initiated. The White supremacists who dared to speak against this landmark, attempted to block it by referring to it and declaring it a socialist enactment and nicknamed The Affordable Care Act, "Obamacare." But they could not change the power of this legacy.

There were those who would take insurance away from many people who need it most, to ensure that credit for such a national accomplishment would not be credited to a Black US President. It appeared that a segment of this nation, including national politicians denounced it and State politicians refused to allow this insurance in their jurisdictions. They would rather millions of people suffer without healthcare than allow a Black man to be credited with instituting something of such magnitude for the first time in American history. Yet, despite the insulting way Congress treated him, i.e., their every effort to ensure that nothing would be done in the U.S. Senate or Congress during The Obama tenure, health care for millions of Americans was instituted.

A Black U.S. President for eight years stirred the White supremacists into action. These ideologists were outraged. Some of them got together as early as the morning of his first inauguration to begin plotting his demise. The rage led to the antithesis of where the country was headed. Systemic Racism raised its ugly tentacles, and here we are now with wars and rumors of wars with a President who continues working amid the trauma this country faces today. Divine Intervention Prevailed.

Under the current administration Affordable Health Care has expanded by lowering health care costs and by taking on Big Pharma. It is making a difference for millions more Americans. I must repeat… All White men of European descent are not White supremacists. America must take courage and learn to withstand criticism. Black Americans must learn to celebrate the fact that we have intellectual prowess. We dare not be defined by someone else. We are resilient. We are creative. We are unmovable when we set our minds to the situation before us.

"Won't it be wonderful when Black history and Native American history and Jewish history and all about U.S. history are taught from one book. Just U.S. history."

Maya Angelou

National Action Network: led by Rev. Al Sharpton and Martin L. King, III

CHAPTER EIGHT

The Mania

"Never Forget that intelligence rules the world and ignorance carries the burden. Therefore, move yourself as far as possible from ignorance and seek as far as possible to be intelligent."

Marcus Garvey

The Black Intellect Saga

Belief is defined as the acceptance that something invisible is true and/or that something literally exists. Today, in the White Supremacist Ideology, there is evidence that some people believe Black inferiority and lack of intelligence exist. Legalized *Systemic Racism* legitimizes this erroneous thinking through judicial and legislative practices that manifest support of this inhumane rationale through the following:

- Educational realities for the masses. There are increasing numbers and members of our community who attend what were originally White educational institutions, but the rate of attrition is still staggering. Public education in America still suffers greatly while private education is too costly for most Black families.

- Black higher education institutions are perceived as marginalized institutions of learning when compared to the "Ivy League" schools. The numbers of Black people who matriculate and graduate from White, private, and other educational institutions may not exceed 10% of Black ethnicity.

- A workforce where the majority of its managers and administrators in businesses and corporations are White men.

- Housing in most American cities shows disparity based upon economic classism.

- A healthcare system exists that marginalizes comparable health care due to the disparity in the economic realities of most Black families.

In each of these instances, there is an argument to be made about the *Systemic Racism* system that supports their theory that Black people lack intellectual ability. This untruth is baked into the policies that govern the distribution of equal and fair opportunities.

Meritocracy is a Fallacy

It is important for us to attune ourselves to "buzz words" that are coined to deceive us. In education, one such word remains, "meritocracy." It is legitimized through standardized test that is based upon the educational and environmental experiences of most White children. It has everything to do with lack of knowledge, but absolutely nothing to do with innate intelligence. In the third generation of Black people in the mainstream of America since 1965, the SAT, ACT, and GED tests are likely to show higher rates of success in their test scores.

This matter of standardized testing is both subject content and vocabulary driven. This same matter is true with the IQ test. These three standardized tests have played into some very disappointing and anguishing moments for Black people. For years, many members of our community have been left out of great American opportunities because of test scores in these types of standardized tests.

Systemic Racism through Meritocracy

In September 1971, Richard Herrnstein explained that "meritocracy" is the holding of power by people selected based on their ability, not because of their money or social position. Meritocracy marginalizes our community in every area of the American government. Is meritocracy inherited? His argument concluded that meritocracy is the same as "heredity." He further wrote, "When people can freely take their natural label in society, the upper classes will, virtually by definition, have greater capacity than the lower, i.e., meritocracy."

Richard Herrnstein also wrote about IQ. This skewed research included in intelligence quotient (IQ) testing. He concluded that the IQ testing was the premiere test. The contradiction is clear. Many students move "into another world" when they enter school environments that do not relate to their environment. The IQ test is standardized according to the socio-economic structure of this society. As other ethnic communities other than White are showing strides in closing the academic achievement gaps, most of the Black community and some members of the Brown community continue to close the achievement gap. The correlation between classism and education is apparent. In the public school system where there is the startling reality of generational economic deprivation, the curriculum continues to have little or no relevance to the lives of many of its students.

Gift to U.S. President Richard Nixon

Four years before becoming a U.S. Senator representing the State of New York, Daniel Moynihan shared with U.S. President Richard Nixon, Mr. Herrnstein's findings on the IQ and the "hereditary" meritocracy theory. This president's disdain for Black people was no secret. According to Moynihan, Herrnstein put his findings together with the exact goal in mind of influencing Nixon's legislative purposes related to Black progress during his presidency.

Black Intelligence is Innate

The following indicator of Black intelligence is not a phenomenon. The societal factors that we discuss continue to distinguish a disproportionate number of Black people from the dominant White American academic, social, and cultural experiences.

It is very important to reiterate that the ability of Black people to rise amid the factors that are intended to prove us to be "intellectually different has never, nor will they ever keep us from rising. Were it not for our inclusions in the building of this nation, it could not be the young, advanced nation that it is. The myriads of excellences that could not be aborted have contributed greatly to America - greatest nation in the World.

History proves that our community does not lack innate intellectual ability. Here are some examples. We celebrate them.

(L) Ramarni Wilfred, IQof162; (M) Anala Beevers, IQ of over145; and (R) Alannah George, IQ of 140

(L & M) Caleb Anderson, a twelve-year-old genius, is studying towards an aerospace engineering degree at The Georgia State University and (R) Joshua Beckford is child protégé who attended Oxford at the age of six.

The Art of Oration

When I was a little girl, I remember marveling at a girl who memorized all of Mr. Douglass's July 4th address. She recited it at an annual oratorical contest that was held nationwide for local school winners. Many of us who attended all- Black schools remember this contest.

CHAPTER NINE

Blueprints

"Schools are social institutions where academic acquisitions take place."

Thomasina M. Portis

My world in my early years was an all-Black one. All school staff were members of my community. Many teachers who lived outside of the community boarded with families in the school community. We lived, shopped, took part in recreational activities, and worshiped together.

Textbooks were hand-downs from the White schools. Each year our first responsibility was to sand them down, clean them, then cover their backs. In some cases, we had to glue cardboard together to make backs for them. Many of the pages were missing. Our teachers knew what poor condition the books were in, yet they had us manage these books as though they were pieces of precious gemstones. These caring educators were preparing us for opportunities beyond our circumstances. They were aware of our social issues.

I will never forget my teaching, Mrs. Wilhelmina D. Scott. She taught me in the first grade after the first teacher died and again in the sixth and seventh grades. She loved us. Little did I know that she would become one of my most incredible role models.

Mrs. Wilhelmina D. Scott

I became a lover of reading because of Moma and Mrs. Scott. One day, while teaching, she had me reading aloud from our sixth-grade South Carolina history book. As I read, I recognized that some pages were missing. The last page I read was twenty-six. The following page was forty-seven. Since after page 26, there has been no page 27, I stopped reading. She instructed me to read. I informed her that I could not. She asked why. I told her because the next page was forty-seven. Mrs. Scott came over to my desk and looked me straight in my eyes of nine years. She said, "Look, young lady, when I said read, I did not tell you to follow page numbers. I told you to read. Until I say next or stop, you read what you see. Do you understand me? Now, read on.

Then, this lady became a bigger example of a human being who understood her responsibility to prepare us for the unknown life situation awaiting us. She spoke about my upcoming life so, her words hid in the recess of my being and resonated with me much later in life. She said, "Tommy, the important thing is to appreciate what YOU DO HAVE while not allowing what YOU DON'T HAVE to stop you." I listened, and even as I recall that day, I still get chills when I think about her statement.

Mrs. Scott, along with my family, school, and community, taught me that giving up is never a possibility. I must always do excellent work while remembering those who blazed trails for us. Mrs. Scott would tell us that nothing is perfect, but excellence is attainable. She was pouring gems of wisdom that took time to become a part of my life. Each of us leaves blueprints for others to follow. Our assignment is to show an active "sermon," to others, whenever we could.

School

I reminisce with excitement about the school community collaboration of my early childhood. I began reading English and music notations, as well as playing the piano at the age of three. Mrs. Mary Lou Goodman Dickey, who boarded with us, was a teacher at Rafting Creek School. She became my music teacher because every time she began to play our piano, I banged on it. So, she taught me to play it instead of breaking my fingers. What a gift!

The Home Demonstration Agent, Mrs. Helen Walker Nelson, made it my assignment to read to our community members about all upcoming county events. So, she had me read patterns to the ladies who made beautiful quilts and clothes at age four. My church had a piano with no one to play it; therefore, I got that task. At Rafting Creek Baptist Church, I played for Sunday School at age five and became the church's first musician at age seven. I made a whopping five dollars a month when I graduated to play for the full church services. I was on my way to being rich!

Our reading, mathematics, home economics, science, social studies, and community service increased as young girls collaborated with the older ladies during harvest time in an organization called the 4-H Club. We learned how to check the pressure on the pressure cookers as we canned food. We made clothes, sheets, and pillowcases from the farmers' colorful fertilizer and soda sacks, then gave them to families who could not afford school clothing. We also gave many of the canning goods away to the elderly and indigent of our community, for their children. Were it not for this community service, many children would not have gotten their education. We learned to cook for the elderly and to clean houses through our assignments of helping the sick in our community.

Through 4-H Club activities, I learned how to measure quilting pieces, read sewing patterns for the older ladies, run errands, and how to measure walls and floors. Hence, our community was a major part of our educational experience.

In addition to reading, mathematics, social science including weather and topography, the young men in our elementary school collaborated with the older men on the farms—harvesting or planting veggies, cotton, and sugarcane. They joined the Future Farmers of America Club (FFA) and learned to read weather patterns for planting, as well. Appropriate measurements for building, curing foods, and dividing the right quantities of fertilizer and soda for crops were oh so real among their training.

The Future Farmers of America for boys

We all learned to harvest. We canned vegetables and grew pigs as well as chickens to win prizes at the Annual County Fair. Our organized physical education development was through sports and chores; it was not through a daily class inside classrooms. Can you guess why? During the fall and spring, memorization of poems and plays helped our retention in many courses. Sports were especially important to us. Our favorites were basketball, football, track, and baseball. We had oratorical contests, plays, banquets, and school choirs. Our community service skills included tasks that required multi-generations to work together. We learned etiquette and other social graces for young men and women when we became appropriately dressed to fit the occasion.

The relationship between the school and community meshed into our formal acquisition of academic and social skills as well as community service. Chores at home, homework, and recreation were our everyday engagements for successful academic achievements and service to others. In the afternoons ladies would come to the school to can food and to make quilts. Schools are indeed social institutions where the acquisition of academics takes place.

Desegregation forged Many Changes

Desegregation in the 50s and early 60s happened to a "select few" Black children who attended formally all- White schools. These young children reported how they were mistreated. Some of them were unable to ride the White buses and were unwelcome on Black buses. Others were hung suspended between two worlds at an incredibly early age, and some were traumatized.

Black students who integrated White schools were unwelcome on Black buses and separated in former all-White classes

The innate desire of any teacher who is dedicated to teaching is to help others develop intellectual advancement that will improve life for themselves, their families, their communities, and their nation. In doing so, the apprehensions that the difference in ethnicities present often paled in the school environment. People are people with the opportunities to create sub-cultures that make life better and different for everyone.

Even in school systems fraught with the devastation of being relationally unprepared to accept these two cultures commingling in the same environment initially, the forces of relationship and love broke down many barriers. Today, from townships to mega metropolitan cities, many Black and White people are bonded in authentic friendships. Yet, there is always a breakthrough that will cause Black and White people love each other. They become friends intentionally to build families together. (See the Movie Freedom Riders)

A Different Culture - Relationship and Love

The innate desire of any teacher who is dedicated to teaching is to help others develop intellectual advancement that will improve life for themselves, their families, their communities, and their nation. In doing so, the apprehensions that the difference in ethnicities present often paled in the school environment. People are people, with the opportunities to create sub-cultures that make life better and different for everyone.

Even in school systems fraught with the devastation of being relationally unprepared to accept these two cultures commingling in the same environment initially, the forces of relationship and love broke down many barriers. Today, from townships to mega metropolitan cities, many Black and White people are bonded in authentic friendships. Yet, there is always a breakthrough that will cause Black and White people love each other. They become friends intentionally to build families together. (See the Movie Freedom Riders

Fast Forward a Few Years - There is a Great Value in Listening.

In Proverbs 19:20 of The King James Version it says, "Listen to advice and accept instruction, that you may gain wisdom in the future." I imagine that one of the best lessons in life is learning how to listen to others. Many times, what is said may differ significantly from what we carry in our life experiences. Our ancestors knew this every well. Many of them lived because they learned to listen. I imagine that our first enslaved parents may have learned that their lives depended on it. They must have had to listen to the inflections of the slave owners' voices to follow instructions, long before they understood this foreign language. Here is one of my life changing experiences.

Relay to Liberty and Justice

Family, we must continue our Relay to Freedom and Liberty through formal and vicarious indelible spirit experiences from generation to generation.

Challenging Conversations

My most challenging conversations on Systemic Racism were more through experiential learning than formal academic instruction. As an Assistant Superintendent, one of my assignments was to develop and implement a Multiculturalism Plan over a five-year period around five multi-centric ethnicities for a school population of almost 90,000 students. This plan included training the teachers, local administrators, central administrators, and staff for schools to include transportation and food service employees. This was a population of approximately 120,000. The centric committee that was assembled to implement this Plan were Euro- American, African American, Native American, Asian/Pacific-American, Hispanic/American, and a person who was legally blind.

In her book Nice Racism, Robin Diangelo shares what must have been a frustration for The Reverend Angel Kyodo Williams. Reverend Williams said exactly what I felt many days during preparation for our Multicultural Plan process. While addressing the urgency to keep racialized people in a room during anti- racism work, she said:

"People who have always been entitled to space and to place have no idea what it's like to have never been entitled to space. I'm entitled to gather to determine the way and the path to my freedom. You will let me do that and not obstruct it. You will not put your needs and your desire for some kind of picture above my necessity. Doing so obstructs my ability to understand what it is to first be with myself. To be with people that I have not been allowed to be with, just as I am. Put aside your urgency- we've been separated for 400 years, kept from one another, for this to just be over."

Lord knows, Reverend Williams voiced my sentiments! I remain unsure that any of us would have signed up for this task had we known the depth, width, and height of the walls of stone that insulated us. My responsibility was to guide these members of my staff that I had selected for this assignment. I was not charged to judge them. At times I was frustrated having to face private walls I needed to chisel away. I traveled through my personal, mental, and emotional mindsets of differences and predispositions. This reality was a blood, sweat, and tears adventure.

The enormous task of building trust and respect, then learning how to listen to a different ethnic perspective without judging, was, at first, very intimidating. Our entire group was guilty of dismissing and judging each other's experiences. It became clear that there were also common emotions that we each could name, i.e., pain, love, hurt, anger, etc. It took almost a year to get our group prepared to face the work of writing the Multiculturalism Plan for that school system. After about eight long and tedious months of harrowing experiences in a room with professional educators, things finally began to gel for us.

A teacher in our group began to cry one day when we were discussing immigration and deportation. This woman dug into her pocketbook, pulled out her wallet, took out a card, and held it high in the air for us to see. In a tiny voice, she said, "If a policeman stops me and I do not show this card, I am b-i-g trouble. I could be ordered back to the reservation."

She continued by saying, "I am Native American, and I am required to always carry an identification card." She also said that she probably would not be welcomed back on her reservation because her tribe did not believe their children would get a fair shake in the mainstream. For what was considered their protection from hurt, the powers-that- be in the tribe would discourage them from leaving home. If they left, they may not have received a warm welcome back. Many of us cried with her. We are in America. She belongs to the only indigenous people in this nation! We felt her hurt and the ugly weight Systemic Racism continues to wield.

In that breakthrough emoting session, members of our group who were unclear on how we would get this work done got a clearer perspective. Our trust and acceptance levels of each other blossomed. We began to listen Without judgement and to fade our judgmental hearing, from this lady's experience. Trusting us with her pain about this ugly truth resonated with us in a place deeper than our profession. It made the way much easier for us to respect the rights and cultural norms of each other.

We acknowledged leaving this experience with a broader understanding of the differences between respect Tolerance. We knew that we all bled, ate, slept, loved. Once the first step of interpersonal work was accepted, we learned easier routes to take for writing the guidelines for our Multiculturalism Plan.

I have told this story several times. Many people who do not like to discuss how much all people are alike and different suggested that this must have been a psychology class. I would argue that it might have also included sociology.

My Belief about Human Beings

It is from experiences of this kind that I formulated a set of beliefs about human beings. I believe the following: that…

- Human beings are born with the divine spirit of goodness.

- Human beings are created equal with strengths and weaknesses.

- Human beings are imperfect with the potential for excellence.

- Human beings have opinions that deserve respect.

- Human beings initially decide their value based upon classism, ethnicity, religion, and non- religion.

- Human beings miss the most significant value of relationship and community when our differences are more important than our respect for humanity.

CHAPTER TEN

Economics

"Dishonest money dwindles away, but whoever gathers money little by little makes it grow."

Proverbs 13:11 New International Version

A Place called "Lack"

"My people are destroyed for the lack of knowledge" Hosea 4:6 (king James Version), is a sentiment that is expressed whether one does or does not know it as a Biblical truth. Do we really understand that it might be this lack of knowledge that brings people who experience poverty in a place of commonality? That place is called "lack." If not corrected, its residual effects form a disenfranchised culture or sub-culture. When acknowledging the myriads of issues of inequality and inequity in this country, for this conversation it is purported that a way to combat this problem is for public education in America to teach Economics and the American Capitalism process to all students.

The Bartering System

Our ancestors got off the boats from Africa and went straight to work without any pay. Therefore, they did not have money to live. They lived on the land of their slave masters. After 1865 they worked, were given "pennies" compared to their labor, and then came the Jim Crow Era. How did they live? They brought from their homeland a system called Bartering. It was simply an exchange of goods and services without using money. We are a people who were not introduced to money or the economic system of mainstream America. Therefore, our way of living included bartering. It became common in our community, so when we got a few pennies, we became once a month paycheck consumer. Even when we came into the mainstream in1965, we got more formally educated, began to receive mainstream employment, but we spent money in the form of consumption. Today, most Black Americans do not understand the economic system and capitalism as its catalyst. It was never taught to us as was English and math.

Bartering goods for immediate consumption.

Relay to Liberty and Justice

The Power of Economics

While there are more and more Black economists in our ethnicity who can help us make financial solvency our reality, our community, by-in-large, has never been formally educated about the American Economic system. As ingenious as we are, how did we not know that economics should be taught alongside English on every grade level? How else could we know, in our ethnic community, that Economics is the fundamental financial process of our livelihood; not money in isolation of it?

Two Systems of Exchange for Goods and Services

Wall Street became the hub of investments, in the 1700s, then America's system of Economics through a Capitalism process flourished. In 1852 public schools became compulsory in some areas of the country. Since the capitalistic process began in this country, training in this discipline was provided to predominately White students.

In that era, Black Freedmen children attended elite schools. Benjamin Banneker may be an example of a Black child who learned the basics of this American economic system. Today's public education system does provide a course which teaches about the American inequality snippets which show that a mere two percent of Black children do not go to White schools 10 years after Brown V. Board of Education was rendered. Common knowledge and application investing became a norm in many of their lives.

When public-colored schools grew rapidly after 1954, Economics was never in the curriculum. Most of our people continued to use money through the consumption process. The process of exchange used by the enslaved was called the bartering System. Even today our people continue to barter money and goods. They also live in a sub-culture in the ghettos of big cities, in sub- standard housing clusters, or on the streets.

In 1964, ten years after the Brown decision, only two percent of Black children in the south attended schools with White children. By 1972 nearly half was doing so. Even if Economics had been provided to all students, 52% of our Black students may have received training in Economics who live in communities where the concept remained foreign.

I believe when every student in this country's education system learns the value of economics, it will help to clarify the relevance of an education--vocational and/or academic and it will bring the poverty- rate down substantially. It also helps us understand how to get out of poverty when we use this American economic system properly. It gives us the tools to raise the number of our ethnic community who live in a sub-culture lifestyle, into middle and upper classism. I suspect that the perpetrators of *Systemic Racism* may have known that the study of Economics would have kept them from having financial control over our community.

It is of note that our ancestors who were brought to America in 1619 through the enslavement period were not users of this economic process. They were the ones who produced the product that made the process lucrative for the White European men and their families. After Emancipation, even if the formerly enslaved may have made money (currency), they still did not know currency's relationship to the Economic process. During the Jim Crow Era some of our fore parents may have learned the value of each form of currency they had, but never its use in relationship to Capitalism and this American Economics process.

The norms of investing rather than just the concept of saving money were more inherent in the White community regardless of their economic status. This rang true to me in the bank one day. A mother had bargained with her daughter to choose to go to school or to take care of are of her ailing granddad. A part of this daughter's responsibility was to bank and invest in her granddad's pension.

After the initial banking matters were completed, the daughter started to get up from her chair. Her mother told her to sit down because they were not done. Then, she explained to the banker that her daughter wasn't going to learn economics in school, but she had to learn it. She said that her family had been investors in stocks and bonds for generations and that her daughter had to learn that there is more to getting streams of income that the interest on savings in the bank. She also said over and over again, "When I was in school, we learned about this in our Economics class. Every student had to take it, too.

To be sure that we had it right, our people would quiz us. It seemed that that class was more important than learning how to talk properly." I sat there listening in amazement! Then, the mother asked the banker how much of the monthly pension of $780.00 per month would he suggest her daughter use for investing and how much for saving.

Their conversation drifted in investing in a particular company that made farming and building equipment since the demands for this equipment would become very high when the infrastructure for America's roads and bridges got underway. From that point on, I sat in my cubicle thinking about what was being revealed to me. Wow, I thought! This is a powerful revelation of how System Racism impacted the education system during segregation, especially. I would wager that less than ten percent of Black students were able to take an Economics course, since formal education became available to our community. I also realized that this conversation could not have been a common practice during our table talks because at best, the majority of our families knew that we should "save for a rainy day." Investment and Economics were not part of our conversations.

Classism

This is another true story of what happens when classism and the acculturated consciousness of bartering collide. From 1619–1865, our enslaved ancestors had no money to use, so they used a bartering system for consumption of goods and services and lived the segregated life. In 2008 there was an integrated community of middle- class White and Black families. For the most part, their professions and salaries were compatible. Their household incomes ranged from $120,000.00 to $180,000.00.

During the housing crisis, the Washington Post reported that more Black people lost their homes than their White counterparts. The residual incomes from multiple streams through investments, that the White families had, helped them to save their homes. The bank savings of the Black families was not enough to help them to save theirs. In this 21st century, President Kennedy's statement that says, "… Economics has made us partners, and necessity has made us allies…" was not true in the masses of Black Americans. Necessity did not make Black families allies because we live in a country where the White supremacy ideology kept us from becoming economic partners unless the ratio of Black students taking Economics has exponentially improved since the late 20th Century.

The Nemesis called Debt

Debt is still a nemesis. Our lack of knowledge about the way this financial system works breeds monumental financial, social, and health barriers for our people. One of the reasons so many of us live under the bondage of interest rates is because we do not understand the correlation between debt and the other nemesis called the impact of the credit report.

At a minimum, Black people take eight years longer to pay off debts than our White counterparts. This is because we did not shift from the bartering consciousness. The time is now for our community to see the value in this economic system and master it. We can begin in small increments until it is mastered. Nothing ventured; nothing gained.

Financial Bondage

Our poor credit rotation is another version of Jim Crow as we live beside our White contemporaries in the American mainstream today. Poor credit remains a way to keep our community at large out of the middle class. Even in Black colleges, this course is not a requirement for all students. It must become a required course. It should be introduced as early as fifth grade.

Perspectives Navigate Our Lives

I believe there is hope for our community to move from the economic disparity we face daily. Educational aid is needed to begin the process toward economic solvency. The ploy to keep us financially ignorant will succeed only if we ignore becoming aggressive pursuers of a positive financial shift. We must become active in Parent and community interest in schools, go to the School Board and demand that economics is taught to every student. Remember, our perspectives navigate our lives.

Wealth Relay Runners

In 2024, we have financially solvent and professional investments role models!!! Reading the success stories of so many Black people who learned this financial system, is amazing. Except members of the wealthy freemen who escaped slavery, most of us are downline generations of Americans in poverty. So are most of our present-day wealthy Black sisters and brothers. They are the runners of economic success of our Relay to Liberty and Justice. White supremacy is alive and well. So are the wealthy members of our community.

There is an opportunity now for more of us to fit into this capitalistic reality. At least we have learned that the first step to gaining a modicum of privilege requires the arduous work and sacrifices of operating the economic system and becoming financially capable of gaining some degree of private profitable streams of income. They worked hard, practiced the principles of economics, and have gained another rung of success. This is available to us. It is a fair conjecture to conclude that public education must include courses in Economics for every student, but it is also a system that some members of our community-at-large learned the system and did the work.

Begin with Small Investment Endeavors

Financial solvency happens at all ages. Some of us might take the entrepreneurial route toward eliminating low wages and/or a single income. Social media await your genius. It is a platform waiting to get your ideas and to help you realize them. Here are a few stories of interest, I hope.

In the 70s, as a retired bus driver, Andrew Starks, now 96 years old, noticed houses on his block were vacant. He started buying them. This entrepreneur bought and rented houses out for decades at rates below the market value. He empowered others to attain financial solvency as he rented and sold several homes at affordable rates. Just as our ancestors fought for a better life for us, we must not falter.

Read Dr. Lonnie Johnson's story of patience and entrepreneurial success. In high school, he was the only Black person to enter a science fair. He continued his education and earned a Ph.D., at Tuskegee and worked for NASA. In 1988 while experimenting at home he had an idea of a pressurized water gun and built the prototype with PVC and a soda bottle. His invention eventually became the Super Soaker. In 2013, he won a dispute with Hasbro and was awarded $73 million in unpaid royalties.

Dr. Lonnie Johnson, Inventor

True Eden Sneed is a little girl who became an official entrepreneur on her ninth birthday. She has included her brothers and cousins as members of her endeavor. Her beautiful parents get it. They are teaching their children how to rely on their innate ingenuity as they become spiritually, socially, and educationally prepared to build multiple revenue streams. This helps ensure financial solvency and community outreach.

"Train a child in the way they should go, and when they are old, they will not turn from it"

Proverbs 22:6 "King James Version

The rich rule over the poor and the borrower servant to the lender. "Proverbs 22:7-9 Go to True's website. www.trueedenbeauty.com Purchase her products. Help her succeed.

True and siblings giving back to the community; True diligently at work; True's parents Ken and LeLe Sneed

CHAPTER ELEVEN

The Birth of The Jim Crow Era

"In the absence of justice, what is sovereignty but organized crime?"

St. Augustine, 354 A.D.

Fasten Your Seat Belts

White Supremacy is perpetuated, for Black people, through the proverbial "arms" of Systemic Racism. It is so interwoven into our present-day American fabric that, for a great segment of this country, White Supremacy is probably invisible. The effect of Systemic Racism is evil. People who are insulated from its proverbial "arms" may disavow its existence. Despite the differences in our realities, each of us must see the value of telling our story. It weaves the tapestry of the complete American way of life. Destroying the invasive arms of Systemic Racism, after the Jim Crow Era may be a reason for the returning quest to overthrow this fragile set of Democratic practices. As St. Augustine asked, "In the absence of justice, what is sovereignty but organized crime?" This is a provocative question.

As we engage in this conversation, our nation may be headed for another form of the Jim Crow Era to include the elimination of women's rights and the right to choose whom you love. There is also the possibility of a government shutdown. It is probable that the U.S. economic situation will deteriorate. The shutdown will be lucrative for 10% of the wealthiest people in this country. Millions of us, however, will be negatively affected.

Why is this happening? Some members of legislative aggregates across America are being led by a comparatively small, militant, and antisemitic group who identify as Qannaz and White Nationalists. They are referred to as the Right Wing of our country. Our civil and human rights are secondary agendas to these dissenting legislators. These legislators are presently our majority rulers in The U.S. House of Representatives and some State legislative branches across this country. Their quest is to form an autocratic form of government in America.

Denigrating Cycles Continue

The majority leader of the U.S. House of Representatives and some members of our State Legislative bodies are frantically reformulating rules and regulations through what appears to be the same White Supremacy Ideology that supported slavery, peonage, and the Jim Crow atrocities. They do not agree that our present Constitution is a vehicle to use for democratic purposes. Their emphasis, in the final analysis, seems to be power for the wealthy at the expense of the masses of people. Senator Mitt Romney of Utah has decided that we are in moral turmoil. As a U.S. Senator, he saw, firsthand, that the agenda set inside the halls of Congress is running contrary to Democratic policies. A frenzy to destroy much of the multicentric progress made since 1964 is clear. The insurgency for power has moved our legislative institutions away from the vows they made to uphold the office they now hold.

This news sounds the alarm for us to become more diligent and pro-active in our choice of legislators. The discomfort of this reality is a reminder of the task that confronts us. As with all past encounters with the perils of White Supremacy, our present assignment is to follow the guiding light of our indelible spirit. We cannot afford fear or anger. This is a call to forge a democratic process that respects the rights of all American citizens. Our mantra is coupled with the spirit of our ancestors. It declares… "Before I'll be a slave, I'll be buried in my grave. Then, go home to my Lord and be free."

An Urgent Reality

Historically, our ancestors became legislators on the state and national levels after the Emancipation Proclamation was signed in 1863. According to the Howard University Law Library, https: library.law.library.edu, The Jim Crow Era was another form of enslavement for our people. It began 14 years after the Emancipation Proclamation was signed and lasted from 1877 until 1965. This was the year that all eligible members of our community gained full voting rights. This time, 67 years have passed, and America is, again, on the precipice of being ruled through the White Supremacy Ideology.

White people who do not believe in the white Supremacy Ideology must join arms with Black, and Brown people. We must be consistent and active participants in reversing the status of our Union. We must insist that the laws made and operationalized, support the equal rights of all American citizens. Yes, this is the conversation we are having in 2024.

Voting and Decoding

Voting is imperative. Decoding the rhetoric hand down from the Whit Systemic Ideology is equally imperative. Changes in housing, the economy, education, health, policing, employment, and climate change can only happen when we change the constituency of our legislative bodies. People who are going into politics need to proportionally be Black, White, and Brown. The objective is to hear the needs of ethnic groups and to uphold the will of American citizens who desire to solidify a democratic process.

We, the American citizens, must know something about the people we place into legislative offices. We also become watchdogs who flood our leaders with phone calls, mailings, or presence. Inequality and unfair practices have led us to decode messages that convey dissonance. This current 2024 revolt works only to reverse the progress made toward advancing human equality in all areas of our American life.

A Recap of White Supremacy's Injustices

In the Prologue, we shared a brief synopsis of this reality that plunged us into our second enslavement called Jim Crow. We must not miss the fact that there might never have been this historical reality about our ancestors' contributions that led to the birth of this American economic system and its continuous intentions to suppress Black people. This is an account of our integrity to allow our genius to produce what became the original commodity on the first Stock Exchange.

Never forget that our ancestors had an indelible spirit that forged them beyond fear into some courage that was built on the integrity of the civilization from whence they came. It was not predicated upon the ill-intent of the White supremacists of this nation. Despite the Jim Crow Laws, the original collaborative effort included Convict Leasing, Policing, Jim Crow Laws, and Sharecropping. We are the people who provided the commodity needed for America to develop its economic process.

Now, let's be sure that we understand the inferences and the deliberate acts of humanity that were initiated during the enslavement and imposed upon our community during the Jim Crow Era. In 1820, it was the name of a black minstrel show where White folk became famous performing in black face makeup. They also highly exaggerated the stereotypical Black character. This term was considered as not offensive as "N…. R, coon "or " darkie."

Picking cotton

This conversation is also about a brief reality check for us as we find how laws are still in place to keep us on as major contributors to this economic system. Are today's laws far removed from the White supremacists' antics of the 1800s? The First Southern Commodities on Wall Street Originated on the Backs of Our Ancestors.

Please understand that in 1792 the first major economic transaction on the New York Stock Exchange came from the old and the industrial South. The items from the old South were cotton, tobacco, sugarcane, and corn. From the industrial South the commodities were iron, steel, bricks, and mining camps. Some economists estimated that New York received 40 percent of U.S. finance from the cotton revenue from its financial firms, shipping businesses, and insurance companies. (How much of this 40% was shared with the Black and Brown communities of that era?) Cotton, picked by our ancestors' hands, was the first commodity sold on the stock market. The stock market is the economic engine in America. These are important issues that we must tell our generations!

Policing to Protect Free Labor

My dear Family, take note of the origin of policing and compare its progression into today's reality. Do you remember in the Prologue when I talked about the U.S. Penal System? Please read this section very carefully, I think it will help you to see just how cyclical Systemic Racism is. The White Supremacists never stop. You will see the resemblances of their behavior as you read on if you haven't already done so.

Policing in Southern States was originally organized for the specific purpose of "containing" Black people in an enslaved social and mental state to supply economic solvency to White people. One might argue that the fundamental intent of policing after 1865 has never been eradicated from the reason for policing's fundamental origination. The 13th Amendment legitimized legal policing through what became known as Black Codes. Before this Amendment became active, Black people made up 1% of the U.S. penal population. After Black Codes were legalized, the Black incarcerated population went up 85%. Masses of Black people incarcerated after the 13thAmendment gave rise to the Black Code.

Chapter Eleven - The Birth of The Jim Crow Era

Masses of Black people incarcerated after the 13th Amendment gave rise to the Black Code.

Systemic Racism is Fertilized

As far back as this era, we can see how the legislative body designs the political system so that White supremacy's determination for economic and social separation remain the dominant reality of our present- day democratic process. In this case of Black people, legislators' rules and regulations in the United States Congress displayed the racism process called "Peonage." This piece of American history is rarely presented in public education. It fertilized Systemic Racism.

In 1866, one year after the 13th Amendment was ratified--the amendment that Supposedly ended slavery-- Alabama, Texas, Mississippi, Florida, Tennessee, and South Carolina developed a way to legally lease our ancestors for free labor (Peonage). Hundreds of White men were hired in these States as police officers, and the penal system, became important in this society. This legalized behavior made the business of arresting Black people very lucrative.

Today, as police reform continues to weigh in the balance, remember that at the inception of policing as an official job, the Southern officers' primary responsibility was to search out and arrest Blacks who violated Black Codes. Once captured, these men, women, and children were leased plantations to tend cotton, tobacco, and sugar cane. Or they would be contracted to work in coal mines or railroad companies.

False Penalties Never End

Here is the clause in the 13th Amendment that every Black person should know and understand. The 13th Amendment declared that "Neither slavery nor involuntary servitude, except as a punishment for crime whereof the party shall have been duly convicted, shall exist within the United States, or any place subject to their jurisdiction." This was ratified in 1835. Reading the clause again, it is revealing. After the passage of the 13th Amendment, more than 800, 000 Black people became a part of the judicial and penal system. False penalties never ended. Peonage was supposed to decrease. However, after World War II, fallacious crime charges, long jail sentences, and the myriads of Black people killed by policemen continued. This process is still financially lucrative to the powers-that-be.

Laws to keep psychological suppression alive for Black people are a stimulus for White supremacy. Policing connects with Systemic Racism and oppression still exists as an absolute economic necessity for economic success at the expense of our people. Let's follow the systematized collaboration with the Convict Leasing Plan and the judicial and legislative systems then and how that plan pays into the consternation of the low wages that plague so many Black and Brown people today.

Relay to Liberty and Justice

Southern policing at its finest

Systematized Collaboration

The Civil War of 1861-1865 left the White South broken. Multi millions of dollars made on the backs of enslaved people were used to finance that war. The lavish lifestyles born from the backs of enslaved people were gone. White supremacists devised a plan called "Convict Leasing" to regain it. This newly devised Plan needed legal support. Therefore, laws were formulated to give slave owners opportunities to use formerly enslaved people for free labor again. To make it work, the Convict Plan used policing procedures from the Black Codes.

Specifically, the Convict Leasing Plan required systematized collaboration between slaveholders, members of the judicial system, police officers, and former slave owners who were farmers and industrial owners. This may be when Autocracy was folded into the Democracy of White men to clarify the intent of the Declaration of Independence and the U.S. Constitution.

The police arrested formerly enslaved people based upon charges such as walking on railroads, being loud in public, and not having jobs. The judicial system handed out felony convictions. The former slave owners paid all court fees then received custody of the convicted man or woman in a place of jailing. These slave owners rented out fraudulently convicted felons to farmers and industry owners. The farmers and industry owners paid the former slave owners, who in-turn paid judges $10 for each case, and paid police officers as well. The only people not paid even a penny were former enslaved people. Here is how formerly enslaved people became free laborers. Does this sound familiar?

The first step of Convict Leasing was jailing on felony charges. Formerly enslaved people worked six days a week for more than 16 hours per day. The felony charge stripped them of their American citizenship. They were no longer able to vote or to hold government offices as they did after the Emancipation Proclamation was enacted. Their new former slave masters and bosses were allowed to beat or to kill them at will.

The second step of Convict Leasing placed the felons in chain gangs. They had to build roads and Southern railroads. Their workdays were the same as the farmers. ' The new bosses were allowed to beat or to kill them, at will.

The third step of Convict Leasing was called sharecropping. After The Emancipation Proclamation, the Old South needed people to tend and harvest their crops. The industrial South needed people to run their plants and to build railroads. Formerly enslaved people needed homes. Centuries of White ownership had stripped them of owning anything of their own to manage.

Black people were allowed to work a parcel of land on former slave owners' property under the pretense of renting for board and food. The sharecroppers had to buy tools and supplies for whatever they farmed, and they had to buy food and clothing. Without funds, they were provided these things "on credit" from the landowners. When the harvest was gathered and sold, the sharecroppers' debt absorbed their promised earnings; and the workers could not leave the property owing the landowners. This became a recurring cycle.

The Jim Crow Laws: 1887-1967

"Jim Crow Laws" were structured to legally convict formerly enslaved people and to speed up the Southern Convict Leasing Plan. These Laws separated Black and White people. In addition to separation, these Laws allowed the following.

1. They kept Black people and poor Whites from working together and forming unions.

2. They gave the best jobs to poor White employees while all Black employees got the worst jobs and lower wages, if any wages at all.

3. They endorsed economic separation through lower income and higher joblessness to Black people. They increased racial segregation and education discrimination.

4. They forbade Interracial marriage.

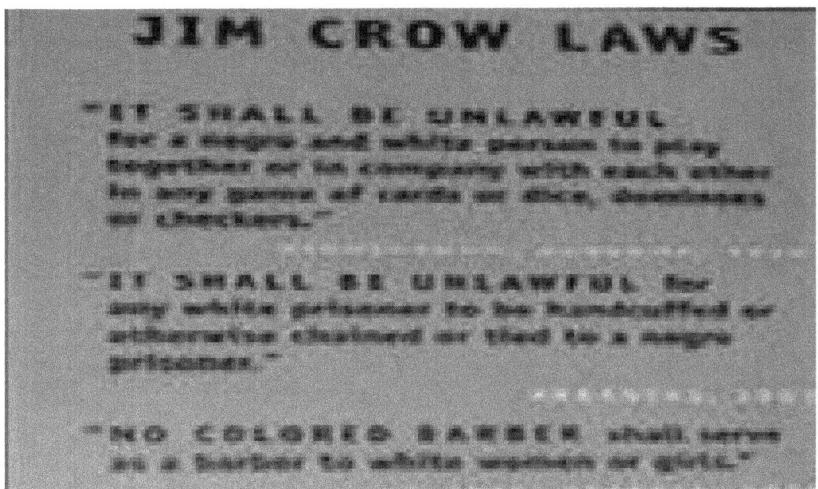

Sharecropping

The "thing-I-fycation" of our people continued. Our Ancestors moved from building farms to building railroads. They became sharecroppers because The Convict Leasing Plan remained prohibitive. Most of them still did not have money and could not secure permanent residences. American money itself may have been foreign to the majority of them. From 1619–1865, these formerly enslaved people had no use for it and had never learned the value of American currency or its relational usage in this Economic and capitalist society. Even after being emancipated, without being educated, their reality was poverty. Consequently, many sharecroppers died never owning anything.

Relay to Liberty and Justice

After The Civil War, The Convict Leasing Plan made leasing a major undertaking in Jim Crow Laws and netted the lucrative financial aid southern White men needed to rebuild their wealth. Slavery by any other name is still slavery.

In the 1930s, the Jim Crow Laws remained in place long after President Franklin D. Roosevelt outlawed any forms of Peonage. These Laws prohibited discrimination based upon race, color, religion, sex, or national origin.

Money is most effectively used for capital gain and consumption, not just consumption.

Variations in Convict Leasing

A historical look into how the Convict Leasing Plan continues to affect a segment of our community is easily traced. I am familiar with the situation of Black workers being paid hourly wages. At any time of the day, their supervisors may pull them "off the clock" for as long as six out of an eight-hour stint.

Many of these Black workers may need to travel a minimum of 30 miles per-day to their worksite, but the money they are paid is used for gas and food for lunch and is consumed by the end of every week. The next week, the cycle starts all over again. If something happens to their cars and no public transportation is available, the routine is to fire these employees and hire others. The new workers are paid hourly wages; therefore, building tenure is impossible.

Modern-day Sharecropping

While speaking with one of my dearest friends, she told me that as late as the mid'40s, her family of ten people, and sometimes eleven, lived in a two-bedroom, one-bath house with a living room, kitchen, and an unfinished basement. She said that her dad was an entrepreneur who rented his shop from a landowner who agreed to buy his equipment and monthly supplies. In addition to the rent hikes, so went the prices of his needed monthly supplies. This man worked 12 hours a day, six days per week. He was never able to catch up on rent to the landlord. His wife and both of his parents helped to take care of the family. In other words, this husband-father- son was a victim of modern-day sharecropping.

There was no welfare, and no health care came from the neighborhood physician. Her paternal grandmother had to teach her White supervisor what was needed to be a supervisor, yet her grandmother was never a supervisor. Her maternal grandmother did domestic work for several White families. Her pay was about eight dollars a day, including carfare. She had no health insurance, and she died of ovarian cancer.

Having no money, this friend's daily task as a child was to go to the local Black-owned grocery store and ask the grocer or his wife to "please charge it." She dreaded the grocer's wife's loud question about when her parents would pay something down on the grocery bill—a question asked, especially when the store was full of people! To this day, the trauma of her grocery shopping experiences makes her avoid grocery shopping, if possible.

Nevertheless, despite challenges, this child's indelible spirit remained intact. The love bolstered by her family and strengthened by her Black teachers' encouragement became her motivational perspective. At a young age, she realized that the road to excellence is one you choose; and she chose the road to excellence! There are members of our community who have similar experiences today.

Historically, when we consider how the Convict Leasing Plan continues to impact a segment of our community, the plan's inception and purpose are easily traced. The examples are ever before us. For instance, during the height of the COVID-19 Pandemic, a penitentiary in California forced women inmates to work countless hours making masks. They were paid a penny per mask. As is the history of our penal system, most of these women were Black.

Decoding Information

The thought of considering present-day low wages and hourly employment without benefits as compared to free labor in the 1800's may seem far-fetched. Learning to decode the Convict Leasing Plan, Jim Crow Laws, and their relationship to low-wage jobs today is as educationally crucial as courses in Mathematics, Science, and English. The Plan, the Laws, sharecropping through former enslaved people' re-enslavement, and using the low wage without benefits continue to promote economic fractures. Hence, poverty for many, and generations of wealth for the few is this reality.

Tulsa, Oklahoma

Here is a classic example of our Relay to Freedom and Equality coupled with a demonstration of our people Continuing to Rise. This man understood the content of the Constitution and applied it to our people. At the turn of the 20th century, O.W. Gurley, a wealthy Black landowner purchased forty acres of land in Tulsa and named it Greenwood after his Mississippi hometown.

The district grew over the twenty or so years to become known as "Black Wall Street." This leader collaborated with other Black entrepreneurs and began a system where someone who wanted to own a business could get one, and with their cooperation, do well. They worked together. It is said that the money they made rotated within that community almost 10 times before leaving it.

O.W. Gurley Founder of Greenwood

Relay to Liberty and Justice

Through The Eyes of This Black Woman

In 1921, a lie was told and circulated that a young Black man insulted a White woman. The White men of Tulsa used that unsubstantiated lie as their reason for burning the entire Greenwood community to the ground. This Must Never Happen Again.

Before The Massacre

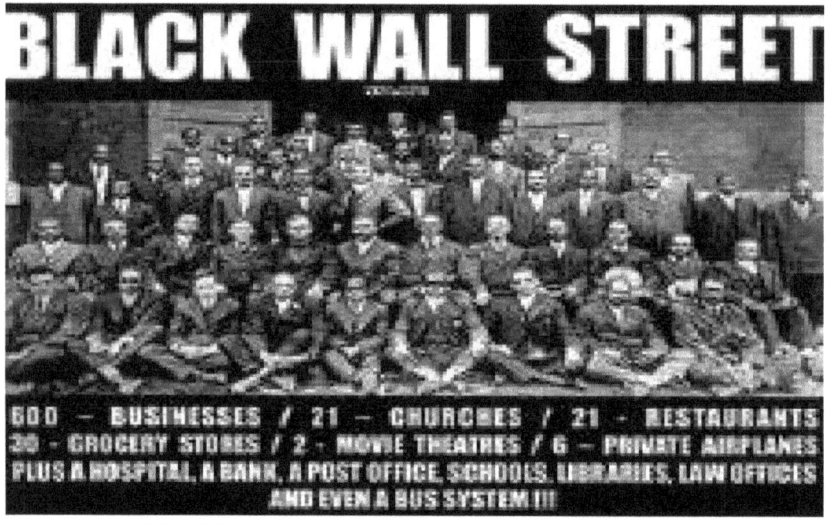

It was a massacre. Hundreds of Greenwood's residents died. Over 1000 homes were destroyed. The White Supremacists left bloodshed, looting, and the actual burning down of America's most affluent Black community in 1921 within two days!

After the Massacre

Chapter Eleven - The Birth of The Jim Crow Era

Remembering the 35-block district that boasted more than 300 Black businesses.

I continue to bring up economics because it is the foundation of our liberation from poverty and many other injustices rendered to our people. We must build the economic power to break the cycle of the injustices done in Greenwood so that nothing resembling this travesty ever happens again in America!

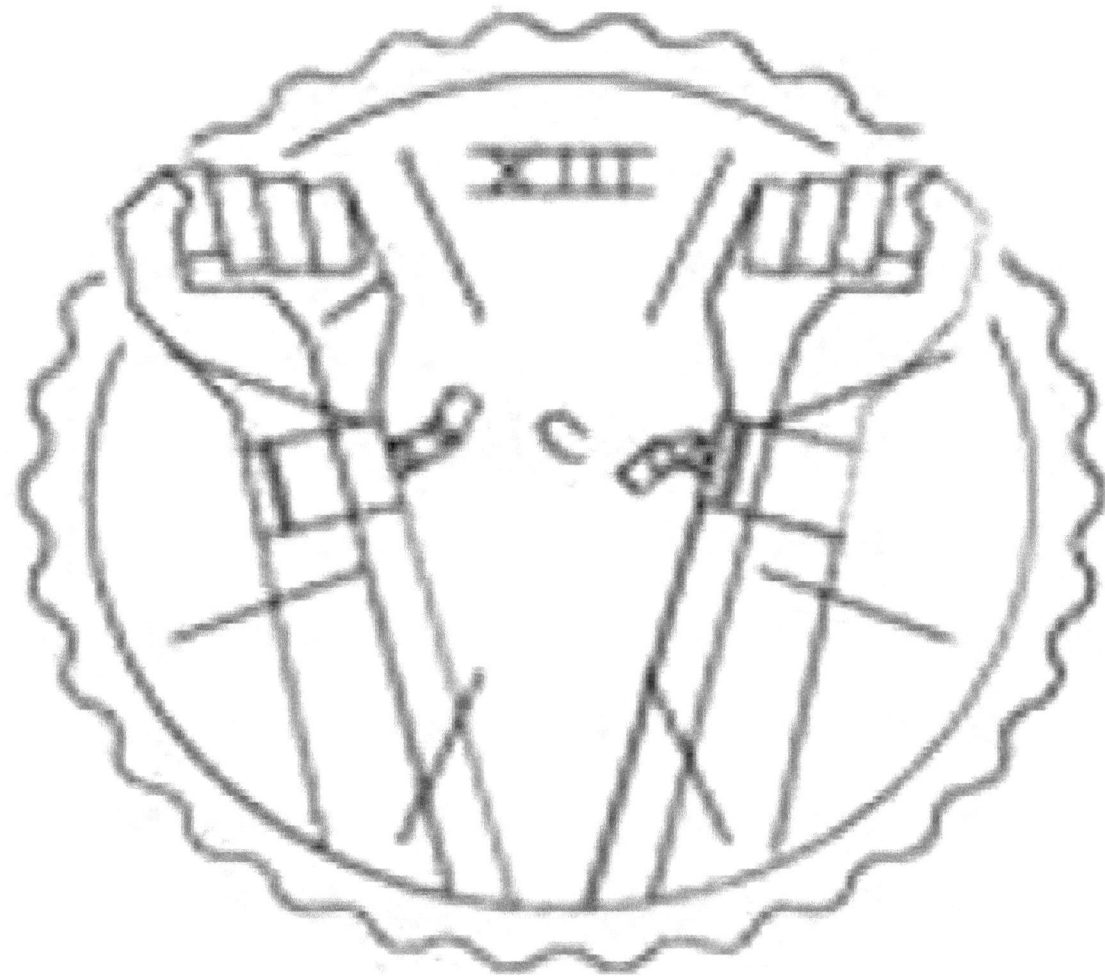

Our ancestors never allowed physical chains to change their focus. They kept on their Relay to Liberty and Justice.

Relay to Liberty and Justice

CHAPTER TWELVE

The Great Migration

"When a stranger resides with you in your land, you shall not wrong him. The stranger who resides with you shall be to you as one of your citizens; you shall love him as yourself, for you were strangers in the land of Egypt."

Lev. 19:33-34 King James Version

Migration is an expression of human aspiration for dignity, safety, and a better future. It is part of the social fabric, part of our very make-up as a human family.

Isabel Wilkerson chronicles untold stories of our history in her book entitled, The Warmth of Other Suns. She shares that our ancestors heard of "good jobs" and friendly neighborhoods in the North, Mid-West, and West. Between 1935 and 1970, they left the South in droves to get a better life. Yet, they were fraught with different examples of the same problem when they believed that moving from the South would solve it. Discrimination by any other name is still discrimination.

Migration from South to West, 1930s

Much to their chagrin, things were not as good in the cities as they had imagined. These southern migrants went to family members, or they found other overcrowded places to live. The proliferation of the migration caused cities and families much trepidation. The cities were not financially prepared to accommodate such an overflow. Therefore, there were not enough jobs, resources, or adequate subsidies to accommodate the influx of migrants.

Many family relationships were strained. The migrants became more like squatters with their families and friends. There were more mouths to feed and more people who needed a place to sleep in their already cramped quarters. Many families and friends slept in shifts to accommodate the new members of their households. Eventually, the economic and emotional strains became real for the migrants and their families. Unfortunately, they had no funds to move. The tensions that arose caused family disconnects.

Creative and Locked Out of Mainstream

Jobs were scarce for the migrants and their families, so they found creative ways to make ends meet. Many of them were not able to read or to write, so in their new homes "running numbers"

Chapter Twelve - The Great Migration

and house parties, where the person who lived there took a percentage from people who played poker or dominoes to make ends meet. These were not the passing times. They were broadening strategies used to feed their families.

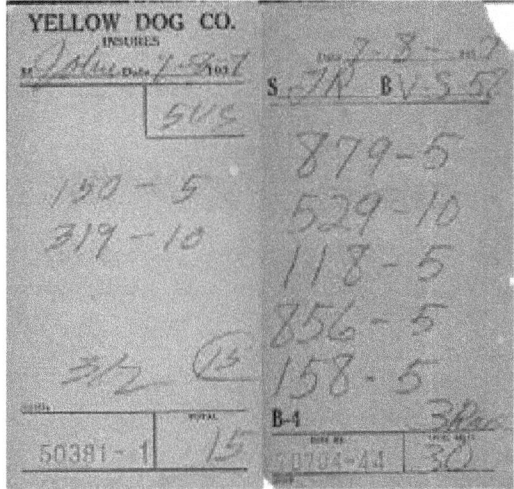

This is what the numbers keepers' sheet looked like in 1934.

The Art of Memorization

This was the beginning of the lottery system as we know it today. However, instead of going into stores to play numbers, in the early years of migration people, especially in the north and mid-west did what was known as "Running" numbers. It became a rather reliable means to survival. Jobs were scarce or wages so menial that people could not make enough money to accommodate their families. People who barely read or wrote could figure out the number combinations then commit them to memory.

Avid players got hunches on what number to play for the most inconceivable ways. A car tag number, dreams, or the number of times someone telephoned in a day are mere examples of their hunches. The fascinating thing about this was many of these 'Runners" could remember the numbers and the amounts of money each person gave them. The numbers were actual bets on horse races. Another stream of funding came from hosting what was known as "Rent Parties. " The house' person could remember who won what hands and how many times. Need-less-to-say, most "Then, there were the Bootleggers. Usually, they were not imbibers, so they knew who ran up tabs.

These were jobs! This was the means to an end for many people. The fascinating thing was the money circulated throughout the community as a way for each participant to have a round of winning. They bartered and borrowed from each other. And the cycle continued. Of course, these gambling games were illegal. There was a boss and the crooked officials who came for their "take."

I cannot say that these things did not go on in the South, I just never heard of the games. Of course, "Bootlegger" made Moonshine frequently. Back home, I had never heard of this very serious business called "Running Numbers." I thought that my relatives were going to go to jail for this infraction. A few times I actually saw people chew on the pages until police passed by them.

One of my favorite big cousins made her living playing numbers. It was interesting to watch the illegal game become the norm of so many people's lives. Many times, two or three people would pool their pennies to play a number. And oh when they "hit!" It was time for celebration.

Relay to Liberty and Justice

 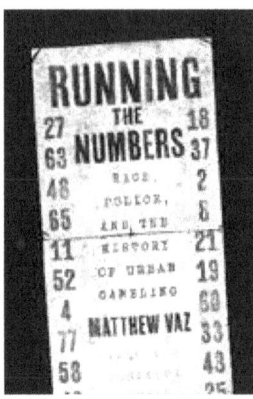

This was a more sophisticated way that "Running the Numbers" developed by Madam Stephanie St. Claire

Madam Stephanie St. Clair: Robin Hood, 1920

The art of the numbers game was perfected by Madame Stephanie St. Clair. This woman was beautiful, educated, bilingual, savvy, and a cunning entrepreneur. Her enterprise was racketeering. Many of her runners were migrants who needed work to take care of their families. She was well known in Harlem as Madam St. Claire, where she lived and commandeered her territory. Madame St. Claire never gave up interest in her people. She was a civic activist who denounced the corruption of police officers as she commanded the streets racketeering. Just think, this woman had built an empire in New York alongside Bumpy Johnson, Dutch Schultz, and Lucky Luciano.

Madam St. Claire invested $10,000 to develop a numbers racket and became a "policy banker." Her policy banking was a mixture of investing, gambling, and playing the lottery. This was a lottery system similar to the Hispanic and Italian communities, but it was especially designed for the Black community. She believed in keeping money in the community and did so with much success. Her accumulated personal wealth helped the Black community for most of the early 20th century. She acquired her money through racketing, but she took care of the needs of many people in her community and ensured that the money she was making circulated through the community.

This was a highly intelligent and industrious woman. She was an educated Black woman who could not get an appropriate job based on her education experiences. So, she became an entrepreneur to reckon with. For years she was the Madam of Harlen for everybody who wanted to be a runner of numbers. She took care of her people, and they made her a wealthy woman. She commanded her territory and was the civil rights voice for her people. Madam St. Clair resisted the mafia interests over the years of Prohibition. Finally, the entrepreneur passed her criminal business on to Bumpy Johnson. Her Gross net in cash was $500,000 in cash, which is equal to $8 million today.

The Cotton Club Bred Members of the Harlem Renaissance

Gangster Owney Madden, a Chicagoan, created the Cotton Club on 142 & Lenox Avenue to be a Whites- only club, except for the entertainers and staff. This club operated during the era of Prohibition and Jim Crow. While it had all black entertainers, it really was a White Only Club. White people wanted to enjoy the Harlen, New York nightlife, but some of them did not want to socialize with Black people.

The club featured our greatest Black entertainers of the era. Count Basie, Cab Calloway, Ella Fitzgerald, Fates Waller, Louis Armstrong, Dizzy Gillespie, Nat King Cole, Billie Holiday, and Ethel Waters. Poets like Paul Lawrence Dunbar and Langston Hughes.

Finding a Way to Get Ahead

Speaking of Langston Hughes, here is a tidbit the might be an incentive. Never frown on menial jobs as you are working your way to your specialty. Langston Hughes wanted to get into the Cotton Club to share his poetry. Much to his chagrin, the White folks wanted to hear music as they ate and danced. Undaunted, he applied for and got a job as a Busboy. As he cleared tables, he would recite poetry. Eventually, people would ask him to clear their tables and have him recite something he had written. Before long, Langston Hughes was a featured poet who opened up the music shows there. Today, in several states there is a restaurant chain called Busboy and Poets. They are named after Mr. Hughes. Our people have always known how to make a way out of no way. The ingenious ways our fore parents found to make their way through their migration period is incredible.

Mainstream Workforce Realities

Our people were driven by the notion that formal education would prepare them for a better life once they were in the mainstream workforce. Before 1960, a vast number of our people were trained to teach. In the migration process, most teaching positions were filled. When they were hired in city and government positions, many of our people became trainers for White employees who may have less work and educational experiences. They not only saw their White counterparts with less experience get promoted, but often they were the ones who trained them. During this era of migration, in addition to working the available jobs for pitifully low wages, house rent parties and running numbers became mainstay subsidies for their livelihood and their common social practices.

By the 1940s, there was an influx of formal education. Some of our community members were able to move away from these conditions. They began building a "Negro" class system. This further worsened the familial and social disconnects. Migration and classism caused our community to disconnect a second time. The first time was during slavery when the enslaved people who worked in their slave owners' houses were disconnected from those relegated to work in the fields.

Until the 1960s our Black community was a financially homogenous one with remarkably similar lifestyles. Since the mid-1960s, another phenomenon has taken place. Distinctly diverse cultures were born within our Black community. The decisions and experiences of our community divided us into three major segments based upon classism. We just explored the ethos of one segment of our community after migration that fractured family relationships and left us in social, emotional, and material poverty. W also shared information concerning those members who decided to become illegal drug entrepreneurs. That too fractured our community and broke hearts. There is a third group of community members who began to excel in the American Marketplace and "Moved on up to the eastside." By 1970, the general homogeneity we shared for generations in our once homogenous environment expanded to include classism on a much larger scale.

Black classism is now the generational reality that has divided what was once a community of survival. It was replete with stories of our ancestors told by the elders of the Community. There remain, however, some points of commonality that we share. Here are a few examples. We have stories of Black men's realities of being harassed by the police, our Black women being overlooked because of their names, and our children being fallaciously labeled in mass and treated differently

Through The Eyes of This Black Woman

by default. Most Black professionals are paid less than their White counterparts. We Are Our Black community!

Some of our daily experiences have become varied while others have remained intact. For instance, Black families continue to experience aspects of police improprieties. The difference in outcomes in the U.S. Courts may be based upon economic and social statuses rather than the color of our skin. Let's not forget that we cannot overlook the consistency of the White supremacists' desire to keep us fractured. When we realize that keeping us divided may be a ploy, then it gives us reason to unite our efforts to rise as we eradicate some of the ways in which the supremacists' ploys infiltrate our community. Regardless of our differences, what unites us is our ethnic experiences past and present.

Taking a "Chance" on Acquiring Funds

With the Ronald Reagan administration (1981-1989) came the addition of drugs for consumption and sales. Eventually, the legalized lottery system overpowered "running numbers" as a mainstay livelihood in these neighborhoods and in America. Unfortunately, many of our people thought selling drugs was a great means for jobs and employment. Little did they know what awaited our community.

Their decisions to drop out of mainstream jobs and education to begin a career in selling drugs caused long- term travesties. The repercussions had residual effects which continue to plague our community today. The number of those who flourish by this decision in our community pales in comparison to the many who continue to suffer. Drug addiction, long sentences for the possession of drugs, and the proliferation of gangs to protect their drug territories became the norm in the subcultures called "The Ghetto."

During this same period in the South, modern machinery took the place of day labor and farming. Black people's opportunities for better industrial and local jobs were almost impossible and non-existent. Southern life began to mirror that of the North and Midwest. Declining health conditions shortened life spans, more people jailed, and the inability to connect education experiences with the reality of life, became tenets of our sub-cultural norms.

When education and members of our community dropped out of mainstream employment to sell drugs, their decision played directly into the hands of the White supremacists' design. The White people who supplied the drugs to our community gained wealth at our expense. Life for some of our community in the south and those who migrated was the antithesis of Nayib Bukele theory, which says, "So, if people have an opportunity for a decent job, a decent education, a decent health care system, I know that migration will be reduced to zero."

Every day many Black people still "take a chance" as a source for getting funds. Running numbers were the order of the day. Now the lottery is it. Many of our siblings continue working on a "hunch" to make a "hit" to "make ends meet." Clergy, this is an exciting time to teach financial concepts to upcoming pastors in our seminaries and to find other ways to help our community learn the most helpful ways to engage financial solvency as a God-given right, I would argue. "On earth," economics builds financial solvency.

Change the religiosity of the lottery in our community.

Relay to Liberty and Justice

The cycle of incarceration began with the mass of our community again. Cheap labor awaited them in prisons that were privatized. These prison owners held multiple contracts to provide supplies and services to industries and governments through prisoner's cheap labor. Even with this reality, the cycle was evolving like this: sell drugs, receive disproportionate jail sentences to those of White people with exact infractions, and/or die for an early age. Slavery never truly ended, for some members of our community, it simply changed forms "The cost of liberty is less than the price of repression."

We, Too, are America

Systemic racist practices did not dissuade most Black people from concluding that America is our nation. However, disappointing our circumstances may be, we are resolved that this is our home. We were born here. We belong here. We continue to work to make this nation great. We own this truth. Our determination to make this a reality means that we still have not succumbed to the myriads of injustices we face. In most instances we stayed focused on making our lives better.

The fact that all public schools do not provide the same quality of education, employment still is inequitable, wages are not consistent with our counterparts, we continue to prove that intellectual ability and determination to succeed keeps us focused on moving forward. We do not have to like or respect behaviors that are inhumane. We cannot reach our goals while harboring hatred toward others. Our ancestors understood how much hatred fuels hatred and refused to allow that vile emotion to and Justice to be weighted by emotion. They demonstrated how to use adversity in ways that allow us to be a community who is Continuing to Rise.

The social, political, judicial, and educational inequities that continue to exist do not negate our intellectual ability to succeed. Continuing to Rise means that the only way we will not progress is if we stop ourselves. Injustice and inequality are and have always been our realities.

The Christian Nationalists in this country, forever carry the belief that this country belongs to them exclusively and that America is a Christian nation. These are false assertions. Aberrant contextualizing Christianity leads to a belief that the distinctions in humanity are based upon the color of our skin. This misnomer has become a learned behavior and the model for living in White supremacists way of life. Yet, they have never been able to annihilate our ethnic, emotional, or spiritual countenance.

There is a line in the poem Invictus by Ernest Henley that says, "My head is bloody, but unbowed." Our ancestors taught us that even when in the natural, their heads were bloody and bowed, their indelible spirit continued to stand tall. This is a lesson they taught. This is a lesson many of us born in the Jim Crow Era learned and so I pass it on to you. We, too, are America! I asked my second son to give me some examples where racism exists. Ronnie said, "Tell me somewhere racism doesn't exist." An example of the first generation to be born in the American mainstream are these my godsons in this photo. While their education opportunities were greater than most of us who moved into this phase of desegregation, there remained fragments of our stories. They have probably heard things such as, "You don't know what hard work feels like." "When I was your age, there were no buses to catch to go to school or to church. We walked."

These implications of hard times are not their stories, but, like those who paved the way for them, these young men have their stories. They are just as heart wrenching and real to them. Yet, they model excellence and the determination to succeed in their stations of development. The common denominator for each generation is the tactics that White supremacists use to keep us oppressed. These Black men represent scores of others whose resilience comes through their bellies from the souls of their ancestors and from the indelible spirit that has always kept us interested in equality for all humanity.

Some of my godsons of international and national prominence in Music, Technology, Commerce, and Physical Therapy

From Perception to Truth

We, the people of the United States, are great words to me. White American farmers were smart! They went to Africa to discover the ability to do for them what they did not know how to do for themselves. They did not know how to develop their land. Their specific concern was not just our ethnicity. The people they bought could have been purple! These farmers needed Agricultural ability. At that time, Southern landowners were rich in property but lacking in finances. They needed free laborers.

Our ancestors knew when to plant, how to be patient, and when to expect a yield from crops. They knew the signs and requirements for tilling the soil. They understood that changing vegetation in the soil yearly was significant. They knew how to calculate the harvest yields, based upon weather conditions. They understood the moon's relationship to the oceans.

Southern men knew their livelihood required the sharp minds of human beings who already understood the relationship of the astrological movement of the heavens to our climate. Africans were the authority who would become their free laborers—i.e., their enslaved people. Today, livelihood requires sharp minds, willingness to succeed, and gratitude for our opportunities to demonstrate that we are overcomers. Yes, we the people of the United States do form a more perfect union.

CHAPTER THIRTEEN

VOTE

"When the righteous are in authority, the people rejoice: but when the wicked beareth rule, the people mourn."

Proverbs 29:2 King James Version

John Lewis, Chairman of the Student Nonviolent Coordinating Committee (SNCC), is leading the charge in March 1965.

My son Randy and I were having a conversation regarding the information in this book when he said, "We were not taught to give a lot of thought to positions in the Public Service or politics when we were growing up." I was startled. While his statement was uncomfortable for me to accept immediately, it caused me to pause. Sadly, I concluded that his declaration had merit.

When we became displaced in the south after The Emancipation Proclamation was signed, our jobs were aligned with menial labor. Our employment most connected to mainstream America norms was teaching and small business ventures. Once we were in the mainstream, we were eligible for other types of employment, if we qualified. The fervor to become more educated became our focal point. In fact, many members of the southern branch of our community determined that education may have become a "mini-god" to our community. An assignment on a weeknight would mean missing a Prayer Meeting or weekly service to get it done.

Our years on the outside of this democratic process left us bereft of the importance of understanding how American Democracy included us. Our immediate focus was becoming prepared to qualify for the myriads of jobs we never knew existed. Unless our employment dictated the necessity, understanding the U.S. Constitution was more of an educational exercise than it was a connection to our daily.

We can no longer be oblivious of the guiding principles of our society. After 50 or more years of advancing into mainstream America, Randy's statement that made me pause is now my impetus to advocate for applying the relevance of the Constitution into our daily lives. When we were desegregated, learning about the Constitution either in history or as a subject may have seemed life information foreign to our lives. That is not true anymore. I submit that understanding the U.S. Constitution and its relationship to our daily lives as an imperative, is a no longer for just for our Talented 10%.

As we embrace the belief that our nation is moving more toward DEI as our reality, my request for our community-at-large to become adept in economics, is equally as necessary. What might be our position in 2024 as a community-at-large had we placed the importance of the Democratic principles into our daily life patterns? If the attention in our community-at-large, there is a possibility that we might have prevented the divisiveness our country faces in this phase of its history.

What projections can we make had we been more attuned to the importance of the wording of the Fifteenth Amendment of the United States Constitution? Would we be the fractured nation that exists today? Could DEI be more advanced in our culture as a norm? Read this carefully with these questions in mind. Would there be concerns about the outcomes of the 2024 U.S. Presidential, Congressional, State, and local elections?

There is a Civic Organization in the State of Georgia called Black Votes Matter who honor Section one of the Fifteenth Amendment. Though Atlanta is their base, the members of this group go throughout the State of Georgia organizing people to vote for DEMOCRACY in the upcoming 2024 Presidential election. This group has aligned themselves with a group whose expertise is grassroots organizers. Together they have formed a coalition that volunteers who are determined to increase the number of voters in all 156 counties in their State.

Democracy is a citizens' issue. It is much larger than any political party. The goal of this organization in Georgia is to move through all 156 counties, find the non-voter regardless of their ethnicity of culture, and register citizens regardless of their political preference.

This Civic coalition is making substantial progress getting people to vote. Wow! This sounds like the organized and clarion call from the March on Washington in 1963. They are excited and appear to be committed to Section One of The Fifteenth Amendment. What a tribute. Is there reason to surmise that if our numbers in Congress were greater that the enforcement of this article might be more highly probable.

I spend a lot of time listening intently to various Newscasters. It has become very evident to them that America's democratic process is being challenged and almost derailed by people who believe in the White supremacy ideology. It must be clarified that the White ideology is not just a belief of White people. It is the ideology of ethnic separation. This ideology permeates throughout this nation's economic, judicial, and legislative components of this democratic system. It is not just isolated people's concerns.

It is understandable that people with money want to protect it. But the greatest grievers of sharing in the economy are the wealthy. I listen to the reports of many wealthy Americans who are choosing to support the notion of overthrowing our fragile democratic process, I started paying attention to the reasoning some of them gave. One was that they are seasoned Republicans. I thought, Democracy governs Republicans, Libertarians, Members of the Green Party, Independents, Progressives, Democrats, members of no party and Conscientious Objectors.

Every American citizen has the right to vote. The fundamental principle of Democracy, that every American citizen has the ability to use is our voice, i.e., the vote. This means that we still have the opportunity to express our desires to this nation. Do you believe that our community is in the state of mind that keeps us optimistic about our strength during this election cycle? Nayib Bukele said that "We are not defined by our political ideologies, but by the results we achieve for people." If only we could act on this idea.

Chapter Thirteen - Vote

As I spent time pondering this matter, I remembered how elated Moma told us her mother just believing the day would come when we, "Colored women," in her time, would be able to vote. The conditions in the south in the early 1900s were very dangerous for Black men to vote even though they could defend this country with their lives.

I would sit in earshot of Moma and her friends during their visits on Sunday afternoons, after church. The stories they told about their lives and the way they were mistreated and disrespected sounded foreign to me. But they were intriguing to hear. Now, I smile, because I have lived long enough to tell stories of my childhood in the segregated South and realize that when I talk with young people who were born in the mainstream of our country, I probably sound just as foreign to them as Moma, and her friends sounded to me.

The statement, "Times have changed" is true in every generation. That is why we must keep telling our story. We may be the only ethnic group of people who may not be able to trace our families back more than 100 years. I also believe that we may be the only ethnic group who can look back on the progress we have made in this country and see the level of our development and merges into the mainstream of America over the past 50 years. Our progress in education and employment are very tangle examples.

During our conversation you may have heard of people whose contributions to our nation and community that you may not have known. It is important that we keep generations before us in perspective. The ever evolving Whether we move forward or backward is left up to us. I say "us" because our history proves that when we put our minds to succeeding, nothing stops us. Here I go again with another of Moma's favorite poems. This one is by Walter D. Wintle titled…

It's All In The State of Mind

If you think you beaten, you are

If you think you dare not, you don't

If you like to, but you think you can't

It is almost certain you won't.

If you think you'll lose, you're lost

For out in the world we find, Success begins with a fellow's will

It' all in the state of mind.

If you think you are outclassed, you are

You've got to think high to rise,

You've got to be sure of yourself before You can ever win a prize.

Life's battles don't always go to the stronger or faster [wo]man,

But soon or late the man [wo]who wins Is the man WHO THINKS [S]HE CAN!

Why vote? The vote is more than your name signed to a voting ballot. It is your voice. Your vote exponentially resonates for your children's children. Even as much as some legislative and judicial branches may lag, the examples of 2024 are apropos as ones to never emulate. That must not, however, stifle your voice. The people we put into these seats hear us, they choose not to honor our collective wish over the lobbyist dollars for their votes or their personal beliefs override the voice of the people. The good news is we can pay close attention to what our elected officials do and vote them out or to remain. On this leg of our Relay, it is time to elect more Black and Brown people to every local, state, and national. But first we must vote.

The United States' Democratic Process

We are constantly told to vote, but have we given our people enough history of its relevance to their daily lives? Do they really know that the vote decides who makes the rules and regulations that govern our society? Do we correlate the value of the vote to the value of industry for our jobs or for the issues of inflation that change the value of our finances? Do we know that the vote determines the way that our schools are run based upon finances and its relationship to staffing, curriculum, and co-curricular in each school district? Do we understand the impact of the vote on what and how our children are taught? Do we understand that being educated requires formal and vicarious learning experiences?

Since the beginning of our democratic process, many of the ideals espoused in the Naturalization Act of 1790 are revealed in present-day White sectarian votes. This is also true relative to local, state, and national governances. Inherent in the statement which reads, "White people are to be citizens of America" is the implication that only White people would vote. Since this is the case, based upon this implication, there must be more emphasis placed upon our history, and we must pledge not to assume that our people understand nor that they are being negligent. To know is power. To assume that one knows, is poison.

Three Types of Elections

There are three types of elections: general elections, primary elections, and special elections.

1. General Elections. In general elections, we vote for federal, state, and local officials.

    - Elected federal officials and U.S. Senators and U.S. Representatives to Congress.

    - Elected state officials are the Governor, Lieutenant Governor, General Assembly, Attorney General, Auditor, General, and State Treasurer.

    - Elected local officials are county and city officials, judges, and magisterial district judges.

2. Primary Elections. In primary elections, a party selects a candidate for a General Election, and you vote for a candidate who will be nominated to be on a ballot. Article1, section 4 of the U.S. Constitution give individual states the right to decide when and how elections are conducted. As a result, every state had different dates for their elections and follows different rules.

The U.S. Presidential Election Voting Process

The following instruction is provided in Article II Section 1 of the U.S. Constitution. It says…

"The President together with the Vice President, chosen for the same term, be elected, as follows: Each State shall appoint, in such Manner as the Legislature thereof may direct, a Number of Electors, equal to the whole Number of Senators and Representatives to which the State may be entitled in the Congress. No Senator or Representative, or Person holding an Office of Trust or Profit under the United States, can be appointed as an Elector."

Chapter Thirteen - Vote

There may still be people who think that our individual votes do not count in the U.S. Presidential election every four years. Let's dispel that notion in this conversation. The way we vote is designed by the Constitution to inform the U.S. Electoral College of our desire for the U.S. President and Vice President for the next four years. Unlike local and state elections where one vote determines who wins an election, voting to elect a U.S. President requires a two-step process. The first step happens when individual citizens go to the poles in their local areas and cast what is known as the Popular Vote for the candidate of their choice. This Popular Vote (your vote) is counted and sent to the second step and becomes the basis for the State election process.

In step two, the Popular Vote goes through what is called the State Election process. Members in this process are called Electoral College Voters (ECVs). The ECVs represent their individual States in what is called the United States Electoral College. Their responsibility is to be informed of the collective popular vote (my vote is included) then they vote to ratify their State's Presidential selection and convey that decision to the U.S. Electoral College in the U.S. Congress where the Vice President presides as its President.

The total number of Electoral College Voters and members of the U.S. Congress (Senate and House of Representatives) is 583, respectively. The number from each State is determined by the number of members of their State in the U.S. Senate and the U.S. House of Representatives. These Electors receive the popular votes from their respective States, and generally vote along with the district they represent. The presidential and vice-presidential candidates who receive 270 of the 583 votes wins the presidential election for the next four years. With the exception of Maine and Nebraska, the Electors vote along the line of the majority of votes received during their state's majority popular vote. Remember that our popular vote is important because it informs our state Electors of our preference. We must never forget that each vote is the voice of an eligible citizen of the United States. In each State, this is the most important election. It is important that we keep up with the date this occurs in our State and vote.

Historically, Who Holds the Most Elected Positions?

Historically, most elected positions in all governmental levels, are held by White men, most of whose sentiments are rooted in the rulings stemming from the Nationalism Act. The fanaticism about local and state redistricting and gerrymandering has a strong relationship to the words transcribed in the Naturalization Act. The White sectarians know the issues of inequality and inequity are subject to change if Black and Brown men and women hold enough seats to enact governmental rules of equality for all citizens in our society.

Family, I remember so well how excited my late daughter was at 18 years old. She was away in college when it was time to vote. On a call one night she told me who she would vote for as U.S. President on the next day. I wish I had words explicit enough to express her eagerness. She was talking fast while telling me about her experiences with other Black students. Some of whom had no understanding of our history because their lives had not been fraught with the kinds of prejudices, their parents, especially from the South, had endured. They knew violence more as a way of life, yet, they had never equated it with Systemic Racism.

Many of her peers did not know the antics White supremacists used as a means for keeping us out of the ballot box. They had not correlated the relationship of violence and death to the Black community's voting rights. Margi told them stories she learned from her elders about how we were beaten, dragged, fired from our jobs, set out of our homes, bombed, tortured, and murdered because of our struggle to vote—in order to obtain our

Civil Rights. Please, never forget that on July 2, 1964, U.S. President Lyndon Johnson signed the Civil Rights Law which prohibited discrimination in public places. It provided for integration of schools and other public facilities and made employment discrimination illegal. The President

Relay to Liberty and Justice

had at one time told Dr. Martin Luther King that he (Martin) would have to push him to sign this legislation. Dr. King pushed; President Johnson signed.

The leaders of our government have always known that the vote is the main tool to change inequality and Systemic Racism in America. It is the voice of the people! This is what the late Congressman John Lewis was talking about when he said, "I gave a lot of blood on that Bridge in Selma, Alabama for the right to vote." It was also the sentiments of Reverend DeLaine who said, "I am not leaving my home because of justice, but, because of injustice."

Each of the following is a segment of America's Democratic process. It is our responsibility to tutor our people and to uphold:

- Direct Democracy is where constituents elect the local and state representatives for their specific townships, cities, and states.

- Representative Democracy is at the state and federal levels where the constituents vote for representatives to speak on their behalf. [NOTE: in Representative Democracy, our legislators are not lawfully bound to vote the will of their constituents.]

- Constitutional Democracy is the governmental structure where the process that is voted upon cover citizens' rights and creates laws.

The United States Republic

What is a Republic? According to the Black's Law Dictionary, "a Republic, is a form of government in which laws are made by representatives chosen by the people. These laws must follow a constitution that specifically protects the rights of the minority from the will of the majority."

This applies today in America, but it does not stand for a democratic process. Millionaires of the minority population vote for U.S. legislators to protect their rights. The rich are getting richer, the middle class is shrinking, and the poor remain a sad reality in this nation of wealth. This does not seem to be the intent of a Republic aligned with Democracy.

At three years old, I pledged allegiance to the U.S. Republic that placed me in an inferior education system, with tattered books, and an under-par curriculum. Do you remember me telling you this in Chapter Two? This may sound far-fetched, but I am concerned that if our history is just information to you, something similar may be your history for your generations. Let me repeat… If I wanted water while in public, I had to drink from the "Colored Only" dirty, dingy fountain. While I was no longer "property," I was still not welcomed to vote at eighteen.

Can you imagine my disappointment when I found out that I was pledging allegiance to a "Republic" that did not include me? Can you imagine what happens if your generations find you in a cyclical situation? You do know that gerrymandering and redistricting are attempts to make our votes illegal in 2024! You do know that this history may report bloodshed again for the governance of our country. I see a group of highly intelligent activists, who may not have realized that the "sleeping giant" awaited your protests while they took away your right to vote. This, too, has the opportunity of becoming the New Republic. God forbid.

A Plausible Origin of Black Voter Suppression

"There are no mistakes in life. There are only lessons to be learned. The lessons keep coming until we learn them."

An African Proverb

Chapter Thirteen - Vote

After the Emancipation Proclamation was signed on January 1, 1863, members of the Northern Union Military were permitted to stay in the south and Black men were allowed to vote. After the Civil War Louisiana remained an occupied territory under the command of General Philip Sheridan. In 1864, General Ulysses Grant sent a Union lieutenant colonel whose name was Henry Clay Warmouth to New Orleans as the U.S. Congress was attempting to heal the nation. At a State election, Lieutenant Colonel Warmouth was elected by the Union Republican Party in Louisiana to represent this occupied territory as a nonvoting member of the United States Congress. He posited himself as a non-politician who represented the common man and claimed that powerful politicians would attack him. As for his honesty, Warmouth was said to have told a Chicago Tribune reporter, "I don't pretend to be honest… I only pretend to be as honest as anybody in politics. And more so than those fellows who are opposing me now."

Warmouth ran for election in Louisiana with promises to be partisan and was able to get a bloc of votes from Black men. When Warmouth defeated his Confederate opposition in Louisiana, Confederate southern men decided to do whatever it would take to stop Black men from voting. In December 1865, the Ku Klux Klan was begun as a secret fraternity in Pulaski, Tennessee. Let's decide, for the conversation that this little story gives us insight as to the birth of voter suppression in these United States.

The origin of stopping the rights of Black eligible citizens of America to vote may have begun in 1885. The lessons to be learned have not happened in 2024 and continue the threat of bloodshed. It is time for this lesson to be learned. We will refuse to have our right to vote be taken from us! It remains the responsibility of our community to tell our story, to continue to break down the White Supremacy Ideology, and to expand our knowledge regarding the inclusive American history of citizens. It is our obligation to maintain the Relay to Liberty and Justice until we grow our Democracy into "a more perfect union." Our ancestors voices ask us to really learn our truest value as members of this society. We can learn this civic lesson as this generation of Black American experience the attributes of the ancestral indelible spirit that has led us from slavery into this century. The Relay to Liberty and Justice for all people has to continue until the White Supremacists' machinations to prevent the vote of Black people are broken.

We Must become Persistent Citizens

I ask that you listen to the remote possibility of my concern and investigate it, even if your proclivity is to dismiss it. I ask that you make a conscious effort to change the constituency of politicians in the first two areas of Democracy. While it is imperative to include more Black and Brown politicians, it is important to form a vigil watch so that their campaigning policies and pledges that you voted for are met. Once chosen, like their White contemporaries, if they choose not to keep their word, then, they should be ousted. This is a reason for us to become faithful lobbyists. Regardless of ethnicity or political party designation, our politicians must uphold the will of the people who elected them to serve, if Democracy is to prevail and grow.

Through The Eyes of This Black Woman

Left to Right: Andrew Goodman, James Chaney, and Michael Schwerner gave their lives in Mississippi for social justice, 1964.

Have you ever wondered about the courage and tenacity it must have taken for the young Black children who were the first to desegregate the South public education system? Has it ever occurred to you to consider the social alienation and sacrifices which they must have felt as they endured the racial slights from both White students and adults in the White establishments that did not want them there?

At 22 years old, W.E.B. DuBois began college on a scholarship to Harvard University. That was as early as 1890. Five years later, he graduated with a Ph.D. Degree. Can you imagine the level of injustices this man of such great intellect must have experienced? At age 33, what do you think gave Autherine Lucy the courage to integrate into the all-White University of Alabama?

Autherine Lucy, 1962;   *Dr. W. E. B. DuBois*

Have you ever wondered how our ancestors came right out of slavery into national political leadership? There was no public education that included the masses of us. So, what do you imagine prepared these.

Chapter Thirteen - Vote

The First Colored Men in the U.S. Senate and the House of Representatives.

Release of Hope

In 2021, the State of Georgia elected the first Black man and first Jewish man as their Senators to the U.S. Congress. Our community came together and proved that the Relay to Freedom and Liberty is still our community's signature.

U.S. Senators from State of Georgia. – Reverend Raphael Warnock and Jon Ossoff, 2021

Let me tell you a story in the words of a man who has dedicated his life to ensuring that our community makes voting a lifestyle. He is an outstanding role model. Attorney Felder's dedication to Civil Rights remains undaunted. After his tenure in the Army, he returned home in South Carolina, became an attorney, then, in 1972 he became the first Black state legislator in his home state and has remained faithful in encouraging others to become politicians and join this legislature.

Innate Ability

Have you ever wondered about the courage and tenacity it must have taken for the young Black children who were the first to desegregate the South public education system? Has it ever occurred to you to consider the social alienation and sacrifices which they must have felt as they endured the racial slights from both White students and adults in the White establishments that did not want them there?

At 22 years old, W.E.B. DuBois began college on a scholarship to Harvard University. That was as early as 1890. Five years later, he graduated with a Ph.D. Degree. Can you imagine the level of injustices this man of such great intellect must have experienced? At age 33, what do you think gave Autherine Lucy the courage to integrate into the all-White University of Alabama?

Attorney James L. Felder

This trailblazer is an orator who never fails to encourage our community members to not just register to vote, but to vote as well. This is a gentleman who has never lost sight of our Relay to Liberty and Justice. He is still a spokesman for social causes in his community, his state, and his nation.

Attorney Felder is the author of the book I Buried JFK. On November 22, 1963, he was stationed at Fort Myer, Virginia. On that day he was on-leave, job hunting, and contemplating his next set of experiences because he was a few days away from being discharged from this tour of duty in the United States Army. This soldier had just left an interview at the Department of Agriculture in DC. When he came out of the building, he saw some ladies standing next to a taxicab crying. He went over to inquire about their distress. The old cab driver said, "They just shot Kennedy, i.e., President John F. Kennedy." Jim responded, "What do you mean they shot Kennedy? He is in Dallas today." The stoic response from the cab driver was, "Yep, that's where they got him."

Jim got into his car and went directly to his apartment. These are his words:

> "As I was walking in the door of my apartment, my telephone was ringing. It was my First Sergeant, who said to me, 'Sergeant Felder, your leave has been cancelled. You need to get out here to Fort Myer and get your team together to go to Dallas to pick up the President's body.'
>
> Let me explain why my leave was cancelled. It was cancelled because it was my turn to serve as the Senior Non-Commissioned Officer (NCO) for funerals at Arlington National Cemetery. By the time I got my team assembled and transported to Andrews Air Base, MD, it was late afternoon.
>
> President Kennedy's Vice President Lyndon B. Johnson had been sworn in as President on Air Force One. He left Dallas immediately, and was in route back to Washington, DC. We didn't make it to Dallas. My team and I were at Andrews waiting for Air Force One to arrive with the President's body. Upon touchdown, we removed the President's casket from the airplane.
>
> Listen, there were two helicopters standing by. One was transporting the President's body to Bethesda Hospital and the other one to transport my team to Bethesda Hospital. Well, we could not get the casket to fit into the helicopter. The President was a former member of the Navy. They, too, were standing by. The backup plan was to put the casket into the Navy's grey ambulance and transport the body over land to the hospital in Bethesda. We did that.

Chapter Thirteen - Vote

My team and I flew ahead in our helicopter to be at Bethesda and were there when the ambulance arrived with the President's body. We took the body out of the ambulance and placed it in the morgue at Bethesda for the purpose of autopsy and embalming.

The responsibility of any team of soldiers from Arlington Cemetery is to guard the body assigned to it and to be readily available to support any efforts needed to accommodate the family until burial. My team managed the security of the body of the President of the United States; therefore, we had to be with the body during the autopsy and the embalming. I saw both of those events. From that moment it was all my job. The autopsy lasted from 8:00 P.M. until 2:00 A.M.

Then, it is now time to embalm the body. Mrs. Kennedy would not allow the body to be removed from the hospital to go to the funeral home for the embalming. The embalmers had to bring their equipment to the hospital to do it.

Meanwhile, Mrs. Kennedy, who was on the 16th floor of the hospital, continued to give directions while making decisions.

The next major decision was selecting a new casket. The casket that the President's body came up in from Dallas was not usable for transporting anymore because one of the handles got broken. At midnight, Jackie Kennedy appointed three of John F. Kennedy's top aides to choose a new one. They were Larry O'Brian, Dave Powers, and Ken O' Donnell.

These men went down the street to Gawlers' Funeral Home and into the display room. The first casket their eyes locked was an African Mahogany one. They chose that one at once. The funeral home staff placed it into their hearse and took it to the Bethesda Hospital where one member of my team, two members from the funeral home, two hospital staff members, and I placed the body into the new casket. We then rolled it to the dock and placed it in the funeral home's hearse.

It is now 4:00 A.M. on November 23rd. There was a long slow procession riding from the hospital down Wisconsin Avenue, Washington, DC to the White House. My six-member team rode in an army sedan following the hearse. We reached the White House and tried to remove the casket. Suddenly, we realized that this casket was heavier than the Dallas casket. That is when we knew we needed more manpower. We struggled to get it into the White House and secured it on a stand. (This stand held President Lincoln's body 100 years earlier.)

Once the casket was secured, I found my First Sargent. While it is customary to have six soldiers on such a detail, I told him that we needed to add two more soldiers to the casket team. For the rest of the funeral, the public would see eight men carrying the casket.

The body was in a state at the White House until Sunday Morning, November 24th. We moved it to the Capital, to the Rotunda. The viewing was supposed to end at 9:00 P.M. Sunday night. At 9:00 P. M. The lines were backed up four abreast for miles. The Capital was not closed. These lines of viewers continued until the President's body was removed to go to St. Matthews Cathedral on Rhode Island Ave., NW., Washington, DC. Following the services there, we placed

My team and I were together for the duration of time from Friday through Monday. My responsibility was to ensure that all orders conducted by my team were according to President funeral protocol. I marched beside the caisson for the

Relay to Liberty and Justice

entire distance. Let me explain. During the march, my position was at the left front of the caisson.

The NCO in charge marches in that position to give commands to the team. Following the last rites at graveside, we folded the flag. I checked it to be sure there was no red showing, then I passed it to the cemetery superintendent, Mr. Metzler, who presented it to Mrs. Kennedy. Our job was over. As an aside: I may have gotten eight hours sleep between Friday and Monday. I tell this story to speak of the prior preparation I had that got me to Arlington Cemetery to begin with. Let me digress a bit. I was drafted into the military. Once it was certain that I had to serve my nation in that manner, I wanted to go into the Air Force but went into the Army instead. My basic training was at Fort Jackson, South Carolina. I spent a lot of time in training from basic through military leadership rigors.

When it was time to be assigned, approximately 1,000 men were awaiting their new assignments. We were told of the requirements to go to Arlington Cemetery. Out of the original number of us, 10 of us qualified. After the training in Arlington, out of the 10 who came from Fort Jackson, one White guy and I made it there.

Why is this story so important? It is because this history is linked to the great mentors I had back home. Growing up in my Southern hometown, I had great role models. From the high school principals, the likes of (your dad) R.E. "Chick" Davis, to J. H. Kilgo, and pastors like Reverends J. Herbert Nelson and Fred James. Two doctors were included in that list. They were S. J. McDonald and William Bultman. Then, there was a professional photographer. E. C. Jones. These men influenced and prepared me for what I would experience when I landed at Fort Jackson, South Carolina then Fort Myer, VA.

I felt that I could do anything in the world. They armed me to be prepared for what was out there--a segregated society. Most importantly, my preparation for life needed to also prepare me to help change that society.

After military, off to Law school I went. I came back to school to find out what I could do in public service to make the difference. My first effort was to increase voter registration among my people. Then I went on to give our "voiceless a voice" in the State of South Carolina's legislative branch of government. I was one of the first three Black legislators in the House of Representatives from 1970- 74; today there are forty-five members.

"Tommye, tell your family while we never know what lies ahead of us, we have a history to prove that many paved our way to come out of segregation into the doors that open for us to enter mainstream America. The doors of greater opportunities are now open for them."

Family, I share this excerpt because this story reveals that a prerequisite to social and political achievements toward what we call our Relay to Liberty and Justice remain demanding. We must include local community activities in our lifestyle as a civic responsibility. Voting is essential. It is the leading. White Supremacists know this and fight to exclude us again from that right; therefore, we fight to not be excluded from our citizenship. Ancestors as late as the 1960s gave their lives for us to have this responsibility. Mini Jean Brown shows us a way to face down adversity when she and eight others integrated into Little Rock Central High School in Little Rock, Arkansas. Like these leaders, we cannot be afraid to continue the Relay to Liberty and Justice.

Chapter Thirteen - Vote

Minni Jean Brown

Relay to Liberty and Justice

CHAPTER FOURTEEN

Leadership

"Let love be without dissimulation. Abhor that which is evil; cleave to that which is good."

Romans 12:9 King James Version

"We are the leaders we are looking for" is the thought-provoking title of Dr. Eddie Glaude's most recent book. He is Chairperson of Black Studies at Princeton University. Dr Glaude contends that the day has passed when we can expect a leader such as Dr. King to speak on our behalf to this nation. With the advancements made by our community over the past 50 years, many more of us have become academically and skillfully prepared as leaders. Our ancestors dared to keep the Relay to Liberty and Justice. This may have been one of the goals they had in mind in the progression of our success in this American life. Hardships, undereducation, and little-to-no education was the history of our people for hundreds of years.

Another Commentary from Me

We have conversed about the areas where Systemic Racism has impacted us for generations. I have shared with you our need to have a greater appearance in the judicial and legislative arenas because we need a presence and votes in all local, state, and national arenas. I have talked about the need to vote as it relates to Systemic Racism. We live in a crucial era in America when our voter and civic participation is imperative if Democracy is to be advanced for all people as our system of government.

Black people, we are the ones who pay the hardest prices when things go wrong with the economy, when jobs close, and when prices increase. There may be a correlation between not educating ourselves about our political fragility and deciding not to vote. When we do not understand, we accept what we hear. Many times, our reasoning is very subjective. Opinions without understanding render us futile.

We speak to people's age or ethnicity as if they are incapable of being intellectually viable and valued. Our interest in our local, state, and national legislators and the issues for us they support are vital. Historically, we have marched, bled, and died for our community and for this country. I suspect the time has come for us to recognize that we, too, must bear some of the responsibility for not grooming more Civil Servants among us. We are capable of helping to make America a more perfect union. We have the ability to help restructure our Democracy.

"Come Let Us Reason Together"

Isaiah 1:18 King James Version

Our history was not on their books, so they may not know our inherent capabilities as builders of the first recorded civilization. The day is past where the voice of the people is the responsibility of predominantly White European men. People who are fighting to keep power are among the wealthiest in this nation and some of the most privileged White citizens. The passage of Scripture in Isaiah 1:18 speaks to our responsibility to make America upkeep of America the ownership of all of its citizens. If we believe we have every right to be here, then we must assume every responsibility to preserve it. Our history was not on their books, so they may not know our inherent capabilities as builders of the first recorded civilization.

Opening Pandora's Box

Engaging in a conversation about the proverbial "Pandora's Box" remains an agonizing and even antagonizing struggle. It raises issues around the sociological, fiscal, and emotional wounds left from the devastating impact of illegal drugs on the lives of our people. These societal factors exist in every segment of the American society. This conversation, however, focuses on the specific segment of the Black people in America, who live from one generation to another, in the sub-culture of our community as described in the chapter on Migration.

The reality that alcoholism and drug addiction are not exempt from any ethnic group is irrefutable. Nevertheless, a part of an article from a Justice Department Report of 2008 on *Decade of Disparity Drug Arrests and Race in America*, still haunts me. The title of that article is: <u>Targeting Blacks: Drug Law Enforcement and</u> <u>Race in the</u> <u>United States.</u> The statement said: "Racial disparities in drug arrests reflect a history of complex politics, criminal justice, socioeconomic dynamics, and emotional trauma our community has endured."

It is true that selling drugs is illegal and that there are legal ramifications for doing so. The proliferation of drugs during the Ronald Reagan Era worsened the issue. The incremental increase of selling drugs became a common way of life in this segment of the Black community. Crack cocaine poured into our community. It was a cheaper and lethal form of cocaine that became the drug of choice.

Mothers, who had been the backbone of the Black families, succumbed to drug habits. Children had to fend for themselves because, it was likely that their fathers were in jail or hooked on drugs, as well. Here are two devastating stories that attest to the fact that the time has come to acknowledge this problem as a systemic issue from inside and outside of our community.

Taking on the Next Relay

As we mount the next hurdle, let it be that by adding more Black and Brown leaders to the US House of Representatives, and Senate, State assemblies and local governing aggregations. I know that we have talked a lot about the seriousness of voting. America today needs us to fight for its survival as a nation of respect for all people. Passivity and expecting someone else to do for us what we can do for ourselves, and others means building our coalitions of judicial and legislative leaders from grassroots through the three federal branches of government. That is the preservation of our country.

"We are the Leaders We are Looking for!"

America belongs to us, too. It is therefore our responsibility to preserve it. The members of our community who fall prey to the lifestyle that either keeps them in a sub-culture or in prison, need our help in taking the next leg of our Relay. Our lives and experiences call us into leadership roles that can build a more diverse Democracy for all humanity. The day has passed when there is one voice to champion our "cause." The conundrum is this.

We expect results for something that we have graduated out of. There is no "they" to save us. There is no one leader to speak for us. But there is a "you" who can take on the responsibility of leadership. You can determine what your leadership role must become as you teach your children how to serve this nation. The collective "You" has become the Pharoah" who gets our sisters and brothers out of bondage.

Voting, Civil Service employment, entrepreneurship, and financial stability can lead to the four- prong education and orientation we must teach our generations. The fight for our country's survival seems to be more internal as it is external. We have come too far to keep relinquishing the internal matters to "them." When we have our responsibilities to preserve that which we helped to build, then, laws to change the trajectory will cause life change.

Drugs - An Archenemy

In the early nineties, the Washington Post was constantly reporting drug raids. One report that made national news was about a young man they referred to as "The Kingpin." He was in his early twenties owning houses, cars, and a helicopter. When the police raided his home, they found cash neatly bundled and in rows, in a room. His drug enterprise was so successful that he became a multi-millionaire. This entrepreneur hired his mother and grandmother and family members to work for him. Now he is in prison for life, without parole, and lives in a private cell alone. His mother and grandmother stood trial as well.

I imagine this young man's IQ is impressive. It is sad that he did not see a way out of the subculture. According to the Post article about his enterprise, this young man established and was CEO of an organization which rivaled some of the largest corporations in America; however, he was reduced to becoming a convicted felon. The fact that he continued to be a pawn in the larger drug culture in America is depressing. Although he probably was not buying nor using the drugs he sold, he, nevertheless, was destroying his community and the lives of the people living there.

It still takes quite a while before the masses of our people can build empires and are financially able to become independent drug buyers from the international drug cartels. This means that, with all the money made, and the pseudo-prestige it may have brought this young man, he still is a "pawn" on the chessboard that brings drugs into the U.S. Now he is in prison for the rest of his life. The question is, "What does it matter that he may be brilliant?" "What does it matter that this young man was a multi-millionaire?"

Opening Pandora's Box

Engaging in a conversation about the proverbial "Pandora's Box" remains an agonizing and even antagonizing struggle. It raises issues around the sociological, fiscal, and emotional wounds left from the devastating impact of illegal drugs on the lives of our people. These societal factors exist in every segment of the American society. This conversation, however, focuses on the specific segment of the Black people in America, who live from one generation to another, in the subculture of our community as described in the chapter on Migration.

The reality that alcoholism and drug addiction are not exempt from any ethnic group is irrefutable. Nevertheless, a part of an article from a Justice Department Report of 2008 on Decade of Disparity Drug Arrests and Race in America, still haunts me. The title of that article is: Targeting Blacks: Drug Law Enforcement and Race in the United States. The statement said: "Racial disparities in drug arrests reflect a history of complex politics, criminal justice, socioeconomic dynamics, and emotional trauma our community has endured."

It is true that selling drugs is illegal and that there are legal ramifications for doing so. The proliferation of drugs during the Ronald Reagan Era worsened the issue. The incremental increase of selling drugs became a common way of life in this segment of the Black community. Crack cocaine poured into our community. It was a cheaper and the more lethal form of cocaine that became the drug of choice.

Mothers, who had been the backbone of the Black families, succumbed to drug habits. Children had to fend for themselves because, it was likely that their fathers were in jail or hooked on drugs, as well. Here are two devastating stories that attest to the fact that the time has come to acknowledge this problem as a systemic issue from inside and outside of our community.

Good Intentions require Better Choices

In the early '90s, while serving as Assistant Superintendent of Public Schools in Washington, DC I received a call from the police captain at the police precinct. He wanted to talk with me about six young men who were truants. The captain asked me what I thought these young men had in common. I said something about them not being in school. His response still hurts my core. He said, "Each of these young men make more money in a week than our salaries might be in a year. You are looking at people who make from $50,000.00 to $100,000.00 or more in a week. In this group of young men is a 14-year-old who pays rent in an apartment building for four two-bedroom family units every month.

According to receipts, this young man pays the rent for these four apartments on time. When I asked him why he was doing this, he said, 'When my mother died, I had to take care of my sisters and brothers. The other three units I got from my people who stayed with us before she died.' Then the Chief said, "This kid told me that he was not going to see his people out on the street, so he deliberately gets suspended from school to protect his territory. The police investigation showed that this fourteen-year-old had formed an organization that mirrors the Army. He was the chief "officer-in-charge."

This young man also told the police officer that his intention was to buy the building when he got to be eighteen so that his collective family would never have to worry about being set out on the streets, again. My heart sank. I knew that in our system was another potential genius who would move from juvenile court into a penitentiary, or worse. There was the possibility that he may have received an adult felony charge, at once. When I drove away from the precinct, I burst into tears.

Social Injustice

People who read stories like the ones just shared are not likely to be the ones who experience such issues in their lives. They may even judge those who do as lazy or irresponsible. The big issue is living in an environment where inequality of human lives prevails. The social injustices Black people face creates trepidation and pain. The devastation increases with the unfair sentences imposed by the judicial and penal systems. The financial returns, and the separation of families do not out-weigh the pain and anguish drugs make to the person, the family, and our community. Our people, who are generationally bound to this sub-culture lifestyle, are perpetually faced with dilemmas like this one.

The negative impact this poison has on the Black family separations through death, incarceration, mental health issues are heart breaking. Could it be that the proliferation of drugs in our community is unfair due to the long arms of Systemic Racism? Is there a correlation between lack of employment, low wage paying jobs and the obligations these young men face as the heads of their household run by their grandmothers.?

Can all members, in every segment of the Black community receive income from jobs in the mainstream that will finance their family obligations? Is it true that "Racial disparities in drug arrests simply reflect a history of the complex political, criminal justice, socioeconomic dynamics, and emotional trauma our community has endured?" Is this not yet another case of Systemic Racism driven by the White Supremacist Ideology?

The argument that we are not the only users of drugs, is not this conversation. In this conversation, the devastations our community incurs through death, personal destruction, and imprisonment because of drugs is astounding. It seems misleading Black people in America. Daily use of legal and illegal drugs is part of the lifestyle of so many members of our community. This conversation is not about cannabis—i.e., marijuana. It is about drugs such as Crack Cocaine, Codeine, Fentanyl, and Heroin.

The drug industry has become a complexity of economic, health, religious, police brutality, education, housing, and climate issues. This drug issue is a lot more than the poor character of our people. There is reason to view this matter as a systemic issue from inside and outside of our community. Drug addiction affects the entire family, not just the user. Selling drugs becomes common place until raided by the police, put in jail, and sentenced some astronomical number of years. Your older child may be in the early teens and left with raising siblings. Orphanages and child services are bulging at the seams.

Has the impact of Systemic Racism become infused into the social construct of our community so deeply that the drug culture has become socially acceptable generationally? Yes! Can the proliferation of the number of parents and children, together in this drug culture, is a way for our community to implode? If so, are we to believe that the perils of Systemic Racism have overtaken this sub-culture of our community? Has a segment of our community succumbed to the indignity of the drug infusion? In this conversation, the answer to that question is, "No!"

Dignity in Action

In Shakespeare's Play Julius Caesar, Marc Antony, the eulogist at Julius Caesar's funeral, makes a statement that ends with "…; The good is often interred with their bones." This line means that noble acts often go unnoticed or that they fade from people's memories.

The people in these photos are here because, in our conversation, it is important for us to remember the work that continues to make America the greatest nation in our times. Our success as a country is due, in part, to people who make outstanding contributions every day on the front-lines of our lives. They are positive community role models who inspire others to become better people. They are members of our communities who ensure that humanity is valued. Their dignity and significance are demonstrated through their direct and indirect services to others.

Their direct services on the local front may be as impactful as the services of state and national figures. These are the people who deliberately make themselves the most accessible. Some are clergy, teachers, coaches, local and state administrators, federal workers, doctors, lawyers, and the list goes on. They mingle among the young and the old on the streets, at community meetings, in church, in local civil and civic affairs. They are the ones who will give a pat on the back to a young person, look them in the eye, and assure them that their lives are worthwhile. In their own right, each of them are mentors. Alongside our national leaders, these people are the ones on the front line of our communities. They make Dr. Dakes' quote a major truth throughout our local and state communities.

There are numbers of people whose names and faces qualify for this next group of photos. The following people represent themselves as they stand in proxy for others. They represent community leaders, members of the medical fields, charitable organizations, clergy, local, and state government workers, entrepreneurs, local county officials, scientists, educators, and the list goes on and on. We must never forget that we are resourceful people. Understanding the value of every contrition to this country is yet another example of our ancestors' legacy.

As you view these faces, there are those who have touched your lives that could be here, as well. They, too, are our most recent contributors to our Relay to Liberty and Justice.

Chapter Fourteen - Leadership

Leroy "Buzzy" Scott

Gwendolyn Clyburn

Coach Coley White

Cassie and Wilfred DeCosta

Benjamin and Dollie Swinton

Hon. James T. McCain Jr.

Rodecia McKnight

Dr. James E. "Buddy" Lee

Rev. Dr. J. Elbert Williams

Dr. Clarence Hill

Lorin Peri Palmer

Dr. Marion Newton

Charlene W. Giles

Dr. Angela C. Hill

Atty. Sherrilyn Ifill

Kimberly McLeod

Herbert McClary

Dr. Joe Albert Bush, Sr.

Remember, Liberty requires collective ambition. Justice is costly. It takes each of us to rub shoulders for support as we seek liberty and then we must maintain our proverbial shoulders

Relay to Liberty and Justice

for others to stand on. You may never know who will add your photo and name among the great members of our community. Yes!! **"We are the Leaders We are Looking for!"**

CHAPTER FIFTEEN

Generative Creativity

"Sing to Him a new song; play skillfully, and shout for joy."

Psalm 33:3 King James Version

What Affects One Affects All?

There is a principle in metaphysics that contends that if a pebble falls into a small body of water anywhere across the globe, every hydrosphere will ripple. So, it is with all humanity. What affects me affects my home; what affects my home affects our community; what affects our community affects our city; what affects our city affects our State; what affects our State affects our nation; and, what affects our nation affects the world.

In each generation we have experiences that expand our responsibilities. Our current requirement is to take a more comprehensive assessment into what our obligations are to ourselves, our homes, our community, our city, our State, this nation, and the world. Even though this has always been true, The Age of Technology instantly connects us with each other in an instant.

A close look at the Civil Rights terrain shows that we are facing another awakening. Leaders for our community come from a myriad of avenues. The unrest about Democracy exists across the globe. In this Era, it is especially important for us to understand the value of the leadership each of us owns, and actively pursue changing laws and economic structures that adversely impact all life.

We must understand that Civil Rights will never exist without Democracy. Democracy is a conscious decision. It exists in a group of individuals who seek freedom and liberty for all people. It does not defend itself. If it ever falls apart in America, we will have failed our ancestors. They always understood that we had to stand for equal treatment for all humanity.

"As I walked out the door toward freedom, I knew that if I did not leave all the anger, hatred, and bitterness behind that I would still be in PRISON."

Nelson Mandela

Chronicling Black American Contributions

In earlier chapters, we discussed our ancestors who made significant contributions to the development in America after The Emancipation Proclamation Period. In the 1900s, our ancestors served in important roles that advanced the growth of America. They involved themselves in the national and global interconnections that affected our nation and the world. The examples our ancestors left for us to follow neither included selfish liberty nor self-centered freedom. Frederick Douglass and Harriet Tubman became Abolitionists after their enslavement.

Today, we can access parts of the world within a twenty-four-hour period. The 21st century communications media connect us anywhere in the world in a matter of seconds. There must be an expanded awareness of this truth, and the indelible spirit, the lies within the Black soul must never allow the intended hurt to break it. That spirit drives away the hurts of unfairness and ignites the determination to make life better for all humanity. This is your genuine self.

Dr. Mary McLeod Bethune

As the Director of African American Affairs and a Special Advisor on Minority Affairs, Dr. Bethune also served as special assistant to the Secretary of War during World War II. This lady continued to give her expertise to U.S. Presidents throughout her life. She gave advice to President Harry S. Truman as she continued to fight for African Americans, particularly for the inclusion of Black women in the armed forces.

Dr. Mary McLeod Bethune was president of Bethune Cookman College, Daytona Beach, FL from 1923-1945. In 1945 she became a Consultant for the United Nations. Her role allowed her to make recommendations to the American delegation on principles and values to guide the Charter.; and she drafted the Charter of the United Nations in San Francisco, CA.

Dr. Howard Thurmond

Dr. Howard Thurmond was an author, philosopher, theologian, educator, and civil rights leader who played a leading role in social justice movements and organizations. In 1936 he led a delegation of African Americans to India to meet Mahatma Gandhi. In 1942, this great leader encouraged James Farmer to form the College of Racial Equality (CORE). In 1957, during his growing stature as a national civil rights leader, Dr. Martin Luther King, Jr., connected as a leader of newly independent countries in Asia and Africa. The White community criticized and alienated him for speaking out about the effects of the Viet Nam War.

In 1965, Dr. King and the other leaders of that Era moved us into mainstream America out of the Jim Crow Era. We moved in greater numbers into the halls of legislative bodies, education, and employment because of the dedicated efforts of earlier fore parents such as Harriet Tubman, Frederick Douglass, Howard Thurmond—leaders who were generationally creative through their presence and persistence for Justice. Their work was followed by modern day leaders such as Shirley Chisholm, and Reverend Dr. Martin Luther King, Jr.

Dr. Thurmond described it best.!! He said,

"There is something in every one of you that waits and listens for the sound of the genuine in yourself. It is the only true guide you will ever have. And if you cannot hear it, you will all your life spend your days on the ends of strings that somebody else pulls."

The Trend Continues

Presently, these members of our 21st century political, judicial, and legislative leadership circles continue to take our representation to a higher level. Here is proof that we are Continuing to Rise as we position ourselves to affect legislative and judicial changes for a better social, financial, and political environment for humanity. Twenty-first leaders are now taking up the mantle of leadership and service in this new millennium.

First Black/South Asian Woman to become Vice President of the United States

First Black Woman Supreme Court Justice Katanji Jackson Brown

Hakeem Jefferies is the First Black U.S House of Representatives Minority Speaker

Through The Eyes of This Black Woman

Benny Thompson, US Congressman from Mississippi, and Chair of the January 4 Committee Racism; Immigration; and Brown people

If people of all ethnicities who believe in Democracy remain passive, this nation will have its first dictator! Racism, a mindset of the chief purveyors of the White Supremacy Ideology, has been ever-present. Remember that their mindset characterizes our community as inferior. Their propaganda and conspiracy theories keep growing. They continue to marginalize us so that they keep their pseudo-status of superiority. This is why we can never give up; their history proves that they never give in. Just as they are persistent over the ages, we must be, as well.

Brown people, please remain alert and diligent. This country has Black mayors in the large cities of New York, New York. Houston, Texas, Los Angeles, California, and Chicago, Illinois, to name a few. As the rage continues about the influx of immigrants in the southern borders of Texas and Florida, their mayors are transporting your ethnic groups in these cities with the probability of the same migration results of the 1930s with our people.

A quote from the Freedom House Report, at face value paints a dismal picture. It says that "Democracy has declined globally because Democratic leaders have done too little to stand for themselves." The onus is as much on us as citizens to remain diligent as it is for the leaders we select to represent us. We, "The People," Fight For Power

Senator Mitch McConnell is a voice of authority in the U.S. Senate. In recent years, he has consistently buried issues concerning Black people as he articulates his mantra that says, "I was not alive during slavery." Neither were we. However, the responsibility to ensure that equal justice prevails for all Americans of all ethnicities, is still the responsibility of all legislators. Let us not forget that as long as the political arena is dominated by White European men, we are likely to continue having the miseducation of our reality spun in a way that fits the opinions of those who still have not dealt with the effects of slavery and its relationship to their lives. Here are great examples of what happens.

As of this writing, the present Minority Leader of the U.S. Senate and the leader of the Republican senators, McConnell opined that "Black Americans vote like all Americans." The distinction of Black Americans from other Americans is a sentiment expressed by those extremists who are proponents of the White Supremacy Ideology. There are far too many of these proponents to name in the House of Representatives led by The Republican Speaker of the House Mike Johnson. These elected officials make decisions which ignore the plight of the Black community.

For them, the issues and costs are more important than gun-control; women's rights to control their own bodies and generational racism. When people who believe in equality and justice engage the legislative and judicial inequities, things change. We must fight for Democracy. In America, "We the people" always retrieve, then maintain the power to change the legislators and the judiciary with candidates who will maintain Democracy in this country. This matter is even bigger that racism. Black people must demand Democracy.

Democracy is Not Perpetual

The day has passed for 77% of the American legislative and judicial systems to be White European male. The Tea Party of the U.S. Congress formed during the Obama Administration made their racist intent clear. Family, we must never forget that the Reformation Era after the Emancipation Proclamation was short lived.

The thorn to perpetuate enslavement continues, thanks to racism. In this story of Black people in this nation, we have never given in to the prospect that Authoritarian or any other tyrannical rulership is to be our lot. Even when our anger, bitterness, and hatred prevail for a while, our goodness overrides it. This is the reality of the indelible spirit, which is the "true guide." Democracy becomes perpetual through us.

Economics' Reality

Each new Era in history builds upon the success of the other and impresses upon us the need to incorporate relevant ideas. Today, a greater number of us understand that our Relay to Liberty and Justice requires the incorporation of economics and the imperative functionality of its fundamental role in the lives of all humanity. Poverty is a deprivation, we have the ability, through economic insurgence, to overcome. This part of leadership removes our indulgence in the drug culture. It has the potential to stop the systemic form of slavery promoted through this nation's penal system. We must insist upon better jobs and wages. We must also learn how to become economically literate within the structure of our government.

Aside from learning economic literacy, we must learn to channel the hurt we have experienced into positive energy. We must also be the role models for generations to build upon. They must not see themselves devoid of their ancestors. We have the obligation to share the succession of events that have led us this far. Our generations must understand that the Black community's sustainability in America requires us to know our history and learn our responsibility as full citizens of America. We have moved into the mainstream that requires each generation that follows to know the relationship of the U.S. Constitution. They must also demonstrate the value of economic empowerment. These are two requirements that we must learn to utilize as we take our rightful place in this American mainstream.

Dr. Heather McGhee

Economic mobility, intergenerational wealth, and more legislative presence have begun to increase in another segment of the Black community in this era. Dr. Heather McGhee is a political commentator and strategist. Her expertise in economic and social policy are examples of the ways we are Generationally Creative on poverty in our community. The knowledge and creativity of our economic experts place them in the ranks of our emerging 21st century Black leaders.

Be the Change We Expect

Members of our community have discovered the requirement for the next leg of our relay. They admonish us to comprehend that we will never really know our power until we become members of this economic society and have more presence in the policy and judicial affairs of our nation.

The power of White supremacy is wielded through the money that supports this governmental structure. We have arrived at this point in our development as American citizens. We helped build this country, and now it is our responsibility to help construct a social order that is made up of ethnicities who own and take care of what has been prepared for us through the blood, seat, and tears of our ancestors. This is the upsurgence of Diversity, Equity, and Inclusion and we must maintain a viable presence in public service so that our voice is coupled with our presence. We cannot justify being disgruntle or just observers on the next leg of our Relay to Freedom and Liberty.

The extent to which we are included at the proverbial "Table" is beckoning us to become more engaged in judicial, political, and legislative areas of government. This is a way to tear down Systemic Racism that continues to keep us living in a fracture nation. I am convinced that the ingenuity of our people is needed in these areas of this American society if DEI is to come into fruition.

Then the possibilities of fair education for all children, affordable housing, equal pay in fail employment, responsible climate change, decrease in police brutality, and an increase in good health have a higher probability of building a stronger nation. When economic development becomes operative for all people, poverty has a chance to diminish, and even if White Supremacy continues to exist its power will no longer have a stronghold in the halls of our government.

Black Entrepreneurship in the 21st Century

We may know about FuBu clothing, but we may not know the story of Daymond John, the entrepreneur who owns that company. This billion-dollar industry, started by a young man of meager means who was raised by a single mom who believed in him and mortgaged her house to help him, became self-employed.

He learned three things. One is that we must not isolate ourselves from other ethnic groups. Secondly, we just moved into the mainstream in 1965, yet, for a nation founded in 1776, as a person, we had a proliferation of pioneering as early as 1492. Thus, as newcomers to this nation, through adverse circumstances, we were determined to rise.

In this story of Black people in this nation, we have never given in to the prospect that Authoritarian or any other tyrannical rulership is to be our lot. The supremacists put up roadblocks, but they did not stop our mobility. Nothing ever will. Even when our anger, bitterness, and hatred prevail for a while, our goodness overrides it. This is the reality the indelible spirit, which is our "true guide."

This third realization is key to our people. Mr. John recognized that much of his success came from learning to operate not just as an entrepreneur but as one who learned how to apply economic literacy.

Chapter Fifteen - Generative Creativity

Daymond John

Jay Morrison, a multi-millionaire Real Estate Entrepreneur and philanthropist verifies the concerns I shared in the last chapter. He is the perfect example of moving from a poor attitude to an awakening. This industrious young man proves that we do not have to continue contributing to the wealth of this economic and capitalistic society through its drug culture.

This gentleman knows both sides of the law. After serving time on a drug accusation, he turned his skills to mainstream entrepreneurship and has become a leading real estate agent who gives back time and resources to his community. While describing the conditions of the jail, Jay Morrison talked about how he had to learn to "beat the trap" inside the system. He talked about learning how to avoid the shank, to move before getting hurt while showering with so many men, and how to overcome the disappointment of a lockdown at the very time when visitors were on the bus ride there.

John Morrison

Mr. Morrison learned a positive way to use the very skills that landed him on the wrong side of the law. He found another way to live in wealth in America and decided that he would use economic intelligence to lead members of our community into positive and productive citizenship. He says that conviction was for selling drugs, he went to jail, served his sentence based upon a multi-generational way to money. This young man makes a distinction between being a drug-dealer and a hustler and shares the way to financial success. Morrison, along with McGhee and John are examples, in this Era, of people who understand how to change the narrative.

Relay to Liberty and Justice

We Rise

We can change the narrative so that we come to view our lives from a more progressive set of lenses. It is time for us to heal ourselves, to celebrate the strides of our enslaved fore parents, and to lay a firm foundation on this plateau for the strides of those who follow us. Our narrative must become one of healing ourselves and forgiving our transgressors. This does not mean becoming passive, but rather, wiser, and more productive.

"HEAL so that you can hear what's being said without the filter of your wounds."

Dr. Thema Bryant

Our collective power has always bred constructive collaboration. Saving democracy requires releasing the anger and the complacency that have kept us shackled. Our time is now. We cannot complain about the current state of government if we do not actively participate in our Democracy by voting and becoming public servants. It is necessary!

Wisdom from the Motherland

There are common practices that are handed down through our African heritage. When faced down, our ancestors learned to become strategic. In adversity, our demeanor can become like this one in this story.

> When Nelson Mandela was studying law at the University, a White professor, whose last name was Peters, disliked him intensely.
>
> One day, Mr. Peters was having lunch when Mandela came along with his tray and sat next to the professor. "Mr. Mandela, you do not understand, a pig and a bird do not sit together to eat."
>
> Mandela looked at him as a parent would look at a rude child and calmly said, "You do not worry professor I'll fly away," and he went and sat at another table.
>
> Mr. Peters, reddened with rage, decided to take revenge. The next day in class he posed the following question. "Mr. Mandela, if you were walking down the street and found a package, and within was a bag of wisdom and another bag with money which bag would you take?"
>
> Without hesitating, Mandela responded, "The one with the money, of course."
>
> Mr. Peters, smiling sarcastically said, "I, in your place, would have taken the wisdom." Nelson Mandela shrugged and responded, "Each one takes what he doesn't have."
>
> "Mister Peters, by this time, was about to throw a fit, seething his anger with fury. So great was the anger that he wrote on Nelson Mandela's exam sheet "IDIOT" and gave it to the future icon of struggle. Mandela took the exam sheet and sat down at his desk trying extremely hard to remain calm while he contemplated his next move. Nelson Mandela got up, walked up to the professor, and told him in a dignified polite tone. "You signed your name on the sheet, but you forgot to give me my grade!

Chapter Fifteen - Generative Creativity

Nelson Mandela

We do not know what happened to Mr. Peters, but we do know that Nelson Mandela proved that he would not allow adversity to stop him from succeeding. This man moved from imprisonment for 27 years to become the President of South Africa.

Relay to Liberty and Justice

CHAPTER SIXTEEN

Poverty: A Human Crisis

"Poverty is the absence of human rights. The frustrations, hostility, and anger generated by abject poverty cannot sustain peace in any society."

Muhammad Yunus

The Systemic Pain of Poverty

Muhammad Yunus' quote begs for pause and contemplation. It requires a definition of humanity that supports the neglect that poor people endure. Poverty transcends ethnicity and lives deep in a place where human beings shun to describe. It works in collaboration with the sense of worthlessness that eats up mental health. It maintains the albatross of poor physical health that overrides grief. It invades the believability of spiritual relief. People who live in generational poverty may view it as a way of life. People who live in situational poverty may view it as a reason for shame. In either respect, poverty is mental, physical, and spiritual pain. No one champions this message clearly and concisely as Dr. William J. Barber, II.

Dr. William J. Barber II, Protestant Minister, and Political Activist: President, Senior Lecturer at Repairers of the Breach, and Co-Chair of the People's Campaign: A National Call for Moral Revival

In a Founder's Day address at Chapman University, Dr. Barber said, "Far too long we have believed the propaganda that tells us the suffering of America's poor is either their fault or the inevitable cost of economic growth. We have refused to see it. The reality of 140 million poor and low-income Americans is breaking through the lies that have hidden in America. Poor and low- wage workers are determined to stand together. Some of our government leaders say poverty is personal failure. Others too often talk about the working class and those trying to make it into the middle class, but they refuse to talk expressly about poverty."

Dr. Barber asks, "Who's to blame for covering up poverty that the nation has refused to face for the past 40 years?" We are to blame. We live in a society where power and privilege are elitist realities. This ethos remains our truth. It has prevailed throughout the history of this nation. Those who have these realities want to maintain their private position. They use their funds to ensure that their positions do not change. They become, or they hire lobbyists to ensure that the regulations that can eradicate poverty are not passed.

The poverty of this country is motivated by greed, selfishness, and the fight for superiority. It is evidenced by laws that our government make that require surplus to become waste instead of provisions for the needy. The subservient ways people in poverty are treated is a testimony to the selfishness of greed. This is a kind of inhumaneness that causes callousness of the heart. It is as evil as the Systemic Racism we have discussed.

Wages and Compensation Packages

The wages that many hardworking Americans receive cannot compete with the cost of living. This is unfortunate. There are members of our community who are diligent workers. They get to work on time, cooperate, and they are competent in their jobs. Yet, their pay is minimal as they do "yeoman's tasks." The work for most people in poverty does not provide compensation packages. There is no health insurance, no 401k or compatible retirement compensation. There is no paid leave.

Most of us know some of these people. They are in our churches, our schools, and they are our neighbors. There is a myriad of inferences to suggest that the poor among us are lazy and welfare cheaters. Our nation could show more consideration if it would provide childcare for working parents and wages commensurate with the cost-of-living index. Rarely do we hear considerations for the impoverished when lawmakers talk of cutting Social Security and Medicare for the elderly and others in need. This contemptuous attitude of legislators regarding the poor is inhumane.

Ethnicity, Discrimination, and Health

According to the Population Division of U.S. Census Bureau Office (Figure #1) and Oregon Center for Public Policy (Figure #2), people in poverty--regardless of ethnicity--are at higher risks for heart diseases, stroke, cancer, asthma, influenza and pneumonia, diabetes, and HIV/AIDS. Moreover, this Office notes that the lack of health insurance is a problem in lower income communities.

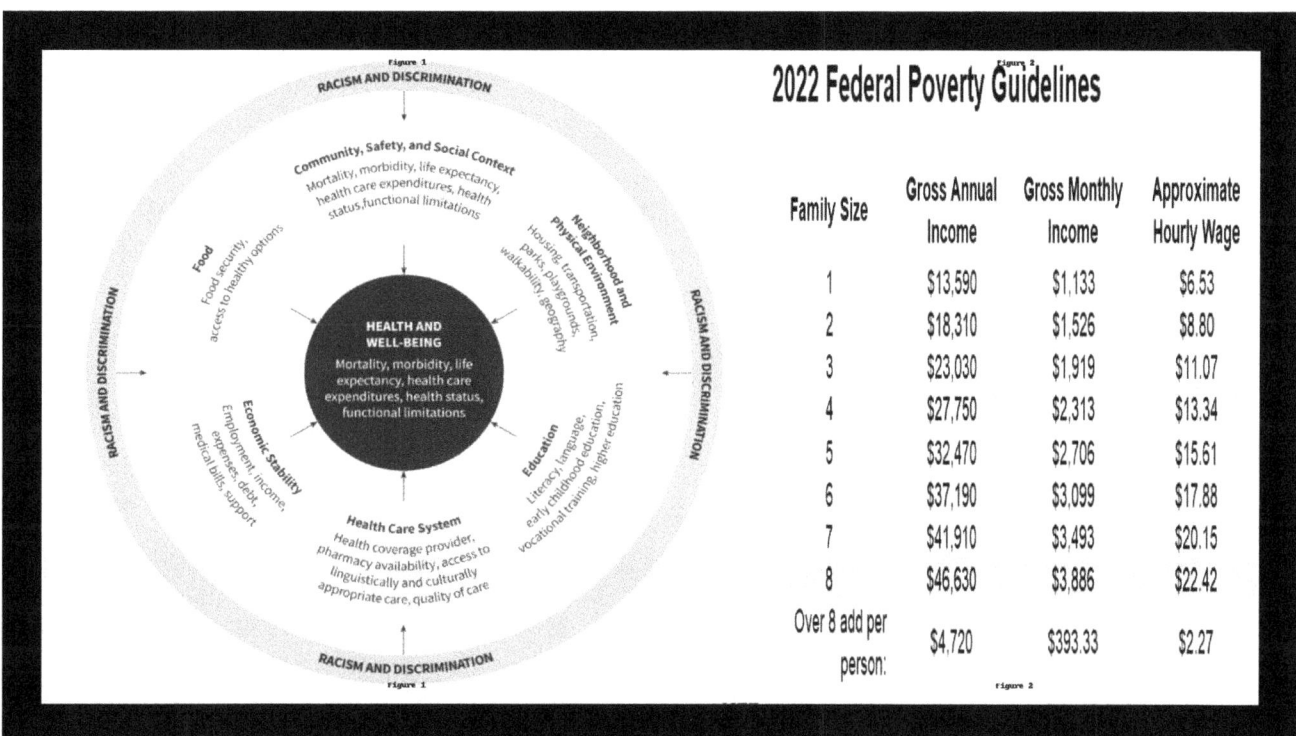

Racism

Since the ending of slavery, Systemic Racism has been the order of the day in America. Our personal experience taught us the voices of Jim Crow. This memory remains with us. It is not the experience of the last two generations of our people. Not knowing this relationship distills Systemic Racism from an Autocratic form of governance. It makes the conversation of our young adults easier to blame a person for the effects of Systemic Racism than it is to focus on a governance that will take away the voice of our citizens. People in poverty are among the major group of voiceless people in America.

Until the 1960s, most of our Black families were not exposed to the economic opportunities of mainstream America. We were not as diversified through classism. Most of us had stories of our survival. We used them as timelines to compare where we were to where we are now. Most of us still knew at least one person who remembered how the obvious tentacles of racism existed in their time.

Our present-day historical message seems to be more into sports and music than about conversations of the new outliers—i.e., people who are detached from the main body of our American system. Politics is more of a curse than a blessing to them. This course of action makes it easier to personalize and blame others for a governing process that does not represent us or our issues.

Greed and Supremacy

Family, the reason for poverty in America is not hidden. Some members of the one percent wealth club require, demand, and stand by using the issues of economics rather than human interest as political issues. Mathematics is not a strong attribute of mine, so I cannot say that numbers lie. They can be manipulated as a means of control. Numbers is a mechanism used to help the rich get richer and the poor remain in a cycle of poverty. Generational enslavement creates a cycle of people who don't know anything but that way of life. The untruth is that they should know how to get out of the cycle.

Beyond the oppressive realities of poverty in the Black community over centuries, keeping fellow American from every segment of our society in poverty is today's form of enslavement. On March 8, 2015, during the speech commemorating the 50th anniversary of Selma, AL Rev. Jesse Jackson theme was focused on eliminating poverty and restoring voting rights. His ten-year old prophecy almost ten years ago was not heeded. Today its sting exponentially impacts this every citizen. His warning is evidenced by the level of polarization and divisiveness America faces.

Rev. Jackson warned that America faces the radical exposure of wealth and poverty and said, "Poverty is the weapon of mass destruction." This Civil Rights leader warned us that the progress some people have made does not mean that there are no problems. He said, "These problems must be resolved from bottom up, not top down." Family, here we are in 2024 facing the repercussions of greed and supremacy. We are facing poverty's ravishing horrors that the destruction of greed and supremacy yield today in this nation. His prophetic words in 2015 are evidenced by this period of devastation our country faces. Greed and supremacy are potentially on the path that can destroy democracy as we have known it. So, what do we do about this? We are known to face challenges with courage and determination to continue the Relation to Freedom and Liberty for all people.

Wages and Compensation Packages

The wages that many hardworking Americans receive cannot compete with the cost of living. This is unfortunate. There are members of our community who are diligent workers. They get to work on time, cooperate, and they are competent in their jobs. Yet, their pay is minimal as they do "yeoman's tasks." The work for most people in poverty does not provide compensation packages. There is no health insurance, no 401k or compatible retirement compensation. There is no paid leave.

Most of us know some of these people. They are in our churches, our schools, and they are our neighbors. There is a myriad of inferences to suggest that the poor among us are lazy and welfare cheaters. Our nation could show more consideration if it would provide childcare for working parents and wages commensurate with the cost-of-living index. Rarely do we hear considerations for the impoverished when lawmakers talk of cutting Social Security and Medicare for the elderly and others in need. This contemptuous attitude of legislators regarding the poor is inhumane.

Eliminating the Poverty Mentality

In the previous chart, poverty remains a systemic and unsettling issue. No one can make this reality clearer than Dr. William Barber. Here is another example of the ethos of White supremacy. If we ever decide to be a nation that affords the opportunity of eliminating poverty, I suggest that it can be done through these two ways. First, keeping and strengthening Democracy should be the priority in elections to poverty becomes less and less impacting on the lives of so many Americans. Second, increasing our presence in the areas of public service where laws are made and carried-out. This is our time. We must never siege opportunities to engage totally in the land that belongs to Black, Brown, and White people. In this Era, we must all have representation in becoming a more "Perfect Union." We may feel like losers sometimes and as winners at others. Our ancestors probably felt these emotions, as well. Like them, our quest remains carrying the baton forward in our Race to Liberty and Justice for all.

Dr. Jamal Bryant

Lifting People Out of Poverty

There is a saying that goes like this, "Give a children fish and they can have a meal. Teach them how to fish and they can feed thousands." At Stonecrest, Georgia, at New Birth Baptist Church, the Pastor is Dr. Jamal Bryant. An impressive component of his strategic plan for the Church is the practical demonstration of "Giving and Receiving" as a way of lifting people out of poverty.

Pastor Bryant has built a strong teaching ministry on how to live a Christian life that is strategically designed to lift people out of poverty. His congregants are learning how to fish on a continuous basis. Just listening to the kinds of practical services that are provided weekly leads to the conclusion that in this Church, the poverty albatross is being lifted off of the shoulders of his parishioners. New Birth is set on around 250 acres of land that includes a medical center, an Arts center, and ground swelling that is allotted to build 250 small houses.

Dr. Bryant uses people who are experts and professions in their fields of endeavor. Perpetual seminars, such as those listed below, are built upon Biblical principles.

- People with credit issues learn how to how to qualify for loans. Often connections have been made with corporations and banks that prepare people to qualify.

- After service, it is not unusual to find farmers giving away fresh fruits and vegetables on the parking lot.

- Scholarships and internships are available to students.

- Dr. Bryant teaches entrepreneurship and shares the example through what he refers to as the Black Wall Street Plaza.

- Lessons on how to understand and utilize Capitalism in daily living are provided.

These and many other examples of ways to eradicate poverty and the poverty mentality are an ongoing practice at New Birth. The principle of giving and receiving are evident. Not only are the members of New Birth expected to tithe, but congregants also exercise the principle of giving and to receiving.

There is so much power in finding examples in the life's work of Drs. Barber and Bryant that is designed to restore human dignity to the masses of people who remain in poverty. Examples such as the one shared by the New Birth Family of Stonecrest, Georgia help to make human dignity a reality of what may be financiaall6 considered "The least of these" in almost every community in America. This a way to eradicate the systemic pain of poverty.

"The quickest way people give us their power is by thinking that they don't have any."

Alice Walker

SEGUE TO SECTION TWO

In Section One Through the Eyes of This Black Woman, my conversation repetitiously depicted the cyclical and parallel paths of the Black Community's Relay for Freedom and Liberty V. Systemic Racism through Climate Change, Education, Health, Police Brutality, Religion, Economics, Housing, and Employment. Of course there are other areas of inequality, but for this conversation, these are the ones I referenced.

We cannot allow ourselves to be lulled into sleep by the common arrhythmic beats inequality. These irregular beats make Democracy fragile in the wealthiest country in the world. Our ancestors are calling from the "deep." They are asking us to make this cycle stop. Can we? My

Family, never forget that since the early 1600s, we have perennially helped to build this country. The economic system, which continues to create America's wealth, happened to the backs of our ancestors in the 1700s. In the 1800s, we gained our citizenship and for the next seven years, some of our men moved into the political structure of this nation.

Jim Crow became the law of the land over those seven years. This heinous system of governance tried to starve us physically and emotionally. We were refused employment, imprisoned for vagrancy, and provided with a poor education. This time created deplorable desegregation statutes. We were indiscriminately killed.

Enter to Sharecropping

For the next 100 years, Jim Crow, through sharecropping, made all attempts to ravage our minds and bodies. We were segregated so that White power and privilege could prevail. Then, after around 100 years of a deplorable reality, our Civil-Rights leaders refused to allow such deeds to triumph. In the mid- 1960s our fore parents' non-violence movement brought us into the American mainstream.

Today, millions of us have taken advantage of the education that was meant for Whites Only in years past. A few of us have tapped into the wealth of the economic system. Many of us have moved into middle classism.

Even after a century of sharecropping and desegregation, the ideals of White supremacy raise their tentacles of Systemic Racism. The physical constituency of national governance has remained predominately White European male. The issues we hold sacred will have a better opportunity for change when we populate these halls, have our voices heard, then makes equality the order of the day. We cannot drop our proverbial baton until our Race to Liberty and Freedom is secured. Our freedom from all cycles of Jim Crow evils must end.

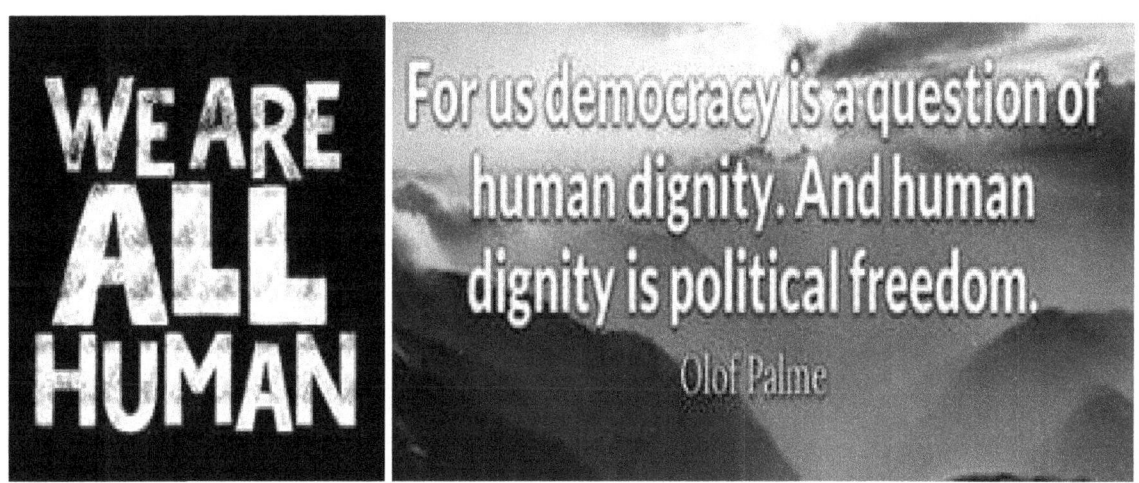

We Are a People of Distinction

"We're all human, aren't we? Every human life is worth the same, and worth saving."

J. K. Rowling

We must never let our history die. Here are the reasons we must tell our stories. We represent a part of the American story about a person who could not be broken or dismissed. We live in varied hues of beauty. These are our first badges of distinction in this society. We are not physical simulators.

Through The Eyes of This Black Woman

This brings us to a real issue that stands to erode our Black community in perpetuity. That saying, "Without knowledge a people perish." This kind of reality opens the door for our country to be governed by Autocracy.

To understand the way Autocracy governs please study the rulership of China, North Korea, Russia, and Hungary. Until our relay is used to increase our ranks in government, the social issues found on the Octopus in Section One of our conversation must not die. The Critical Race Theory we discussed earlier must not erase our story.

A Black People's Story

Mrs. Selentia Q. Moore is an extremely creative and energetic educator. During Black History Month this "daughter" of mine was up by 5:00a.m., she got into character as she puts on her costume and presented a notable Black woman to her students each day for the entire month of February. Her degree in Theatre continues to pay off. She and her husband Anthony are schoolteachers. They are Music and Theatre Directors in the Atlanta, GA area. Look carefully. How many contributors do you identify?

Black People's Story in American History Our Ancestral Story

All enslaved people understood the same drum language regardless of their specific African nation or regional language. When the talking drum was taken the common African communication was not stopped. Our ancestors used songs and hair cornrows to save lives. Songs like "Steal Away to Jesus" signaled escape. Cornrows were, in my opinion, even more ingenious. A hairstyle with curved braids and high buns signaled the desire to escape. Cornrows tight to the head that seemed like designs were showing the routes to leave plantations and the home of slave owners.

Black American families come in all sizes and hues. We have an array of personalities. We work, play, and provide service to humanity. Our roots are in Christianity as a way of life, not as a socio-political venue to teach the exclusion of others. Share portions of your family history as I share some of my family history. Faces connected to history are imperative.

The Peril of American History

Without an American History, which includes the truth about Black contributors to this nation's progress, a little bit of information is as perilous as no information, at all. I repeat, since the inception of this Democracy in 1778, White people have dominated political bodies of power.

I make some conjectures here. Maybe, the writers of the Declaration of Independence and the U.S. Constitution understood that maintaining power and positions, required them to hold most of all political positions. Maybe, this clarifies why our Black fore parents were dismissed from the state legislative branches in the South and the U.S. Congress during the first Jim Crow Era.

These conjectures may also be a way to understand our broken United States through Systemic Racism. (See the octopus in Section I.) Unlike the disconnect of Black history, the White generation of power and privilege is connected through generational systems of legislature and government handed down by their fore parents. Their ideologies of power and privilege may continue to rule this land if they can control our government. Does this help you understand the importance of gerrymandering and redlining congressional districts throughout this country? Here are two more conjectures. Maybe since White history is recorded, it is remembered; since Black history is oral it is forgotten. And finally, just maybe, this objectifies why today's American History remains primarily about the power and privilege of our White ancestors.

The desire for the well-being of one's nation can be - and must be compatible with the welfare of all humanity."

Louis L. Snyder

SECTION TWO

"From the Cottonfield to the White House"

My People - Continuing to Rise!

We are a people of endurance who have moved from enslavement in the cotton fields, to education in one-room schools during Jim Crow. From 1965 until today, we have desegregated Black and White Public Schools, proliferated our enrollment in Black and White Institutions of Higher Education, become viable contributors in Boardrooms across the Corporate and Private Sectors, and into White House of The United States of America as former U.S. President and present U.S. Vice President.

Continuing to Rise

Family Heroes

Some arrived aboard slave ships. They worked from "can, 'til can't,"
rising before day and falling onto
hard pallets for troubled slumber long after the setting of the sun.

Money was in short supply, but
love was always in abundance, for
family and adopted family alike.

If someone dropped in at dinner time,
amiracle meal or watered-downsoup appeared.

Children were nurtured and taught the manners
That would help them make their way, in the hard world that reality and experience would bring,
once the safety of home had been left, and the protection of parents could be no more.

Simple pleasures built one atop the other,
making a solid framework of mind memories,
that would grow like grapevines in the mind,
as everyone sought to make a way, out of no way,
and to survive to smile in the sun.

No one told them the way would be easy,
or that their humanity equally valued,
yet they, whose ancestors came on slave ships,
dared to work, to struggle, to raise families,
to survive in the accomplishments and memories
of those who came behind.
I marvel at their tenacity and the strength of their spirits.

Dr. Barbara Parks-Lee

CHAPTER SEVENTEEN

Endurance

"Blessed is the one who perseveres under trial because, having stood the test, that person will receive the crown of life that the Lord has promised to those who love him."

James 1:12 New International Version

My Story

Section II is about my personal family's story that spans five generations. It begins in a rural community in Richland County, South Carolina in the late-1800s and moves to another rural community in Sumter County, South Carolina toward the mid-1900s. This conversation with you about my personal family is an example of the strength of ancestral indelible spirit in a specific family who is Continuing to Rise.

In the mid-1800s, a White man loved his Black daughter so much that he sent her Black betrothed away to school. Upon his future son-in-law's return to the area, this future father-in-law saw to it that he was made the first Postmaster of the area. That Black daughter became my maternal great grandmother.

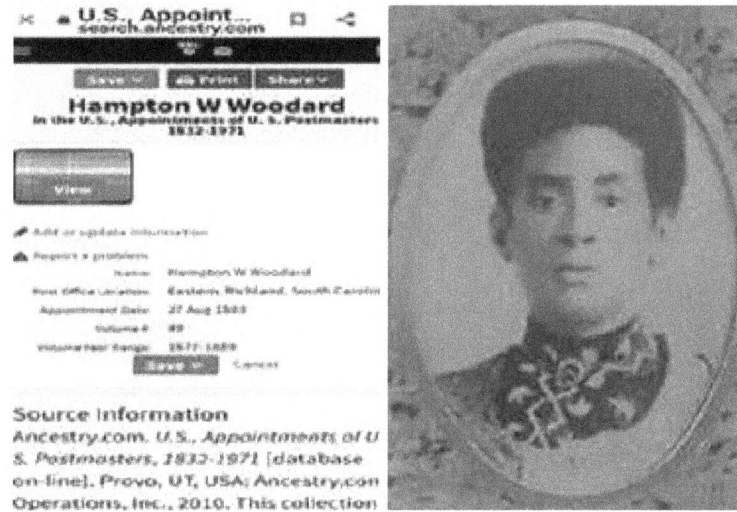

Left: My maternal great-grand father Hampton Woodward: First Black U.S. Postmaster in Eastern [Eastover], South Carolina and right: my maternal great-grandmother Margarette Tucker Woodward

Both of my White great, great grandfathers were generous to their enslaved mistress's children. My paternal great-grandfather Hampton Woodward was a son of the owner of the plantation called the Woodward/Rawlings family in the area now called Eastover. I am not sure if my maternal great great-grandfather Dan Tucker's plantation was also in Eastover or the nearby current areas of Gadsden or Hopkins. Dan's son Jeff Tucker was the father of my great-grandmother, Margarette Tucker Woodward.

When Hampton W. Woodward wanted to marry Jeff's daughter Margarette, he sent Hampton away from South Carolina to get an education. When he finished school and returned home, they got married. Hampton helped Jeff become the first Black U.S. appointed Postmaster in their area. Meanwhile, Margarette was trained to "teach."

Continuing to Rise

Through The Eyes of This Black Woman

This tenacious woman was widowed at a relatively early age and left to raise nine children. Her husband Hampton had been a landowner also. He left her sixty-eight acres of land. After her father's death, she was awarded an additional eighty-three acres of land, a mule, and a donkey. This widow's desire was for her children to "finish college." To ensure that this happened she went to her father's attorney, had her land divided and named eight plots for her children and one for herself.

The proceeds from the crops of the eight children were saved and earmarked to Benedict College in Columbia, South Carolina for each of her girls, Carrie W. Bobo, Louisa

W. Randolph, (Doppie), Ruth W. Rookard, Marion (Ms. Mae), and Margaret Woodward. The proceeds for her three Woodward sons, Hampton (Hamp), William (Bill), and Tucker (Tee) were earmarked for what is now known as South Carolina State University, Orangeburg, South Carolina. Esther, her third daughter, died young.

My Ma (Margarette) included Esther in her portion of the land as a memorial to her. She used those proceeds and her teaching pay to sustain her farm and household expenses. This lady earmarked the funds for her children to continue upon her death so that their education funds would not be touched. When she died, her portion of the land was divided eight ways and given to her children. Some of the land remains in our family.

Ma died when her youngest daughter was three years old. They remained in her home and were taken care of by the older siblings. They followed the plan and went to school. All her daughters graduated from Benedict with what was known as LL Degrees. Hampton and William graduated from the presently known South Carolina State University. Uncle Tee had other plans for his life. Among the accomplishments of her lineage, most of her grand, great-grands and great- great grands are educationally trained beyond high school diplomas. Among us descendants, there are bachelor's, master's, and doctorate degrees. Among our many professions are educators. Here are two of Hampton and Margarette Tucker Woodward's daughters.

Mrs. Ruth Woodward Rookard (Aunt Ruth)   **Mae Marion Woodward Wright McLester (Moma)**

Kinfolk Everywhere

On July 4, 2023, my grandson Aaron Williams is a freelance photographer who was taking pictures during a fourth-of July function at The Frederick Douglass House in Washington, DC. Across from him stood and lady and her young daughter. He went over to her to ask if he could take a picture of them. The young lady looked at him and said, "You look like my family." He was startled. Then she asked if he had relatives in South Carolina, with specific emphasis on the Rafting Creek Area of Sumter, S.C. He said yes. They laughed.

This young lady continued her story. Her home is California. She came to Washington, DC to attend Howard University and stayed on the East Coast. She told Aaron that she visited the Rafting Creek Cemetery to take a picture of her great-uncle who had acquired several hundred acres of land during the early 1900s. He had helped to build the Rafting Creek community and that he died early in the mid-1920s. Then, she said, "My great uncle was TB Wright." My grandson replied, "My great-great granddaddy was TB Wright." It turns out that TB's youngest sibling, Sammie Wright Young was her great grandmother. They laughed. Then, Aaron and the young lady called me.

This is the segue from Richland County to Sumter County. Both counties are in South Carolina's rural areas. TB Wright is my maternal granddaddy.

My Maternal Grandfather: Thomas Boston Wright (TB)

TB Wright, February 1887-May 1925, was born in an area of Sumter County, South Carolina called Claremont near Horatio, SC. Little is known about his early education. The story goes that one day he took a big trunk and placed a pair pants, a shirt, two sets of underwear, and a hat in it. He walked to the train station in Hagood, South Carolina carrying his trunk and owning fifty cents. TB rode the train to Columbia, South Carolina and enrolled in Benedict College where he stayed for one semester. Their daddy lost his sight while TB was in school, so he came back home to take care of his family.

My granddaddy was a genius. I am told that he also had a very gregarious personality. He had a good relationship with all people and provided a home for his dad Jimmy Wright and his mother Agnes Ballad Wright, who was a Black Native American. It is said that there were eighteen children. Many of them died before they were adults. By default, he became the oldest to reach adulthood with nine younger siblings.

So, he began to work hard and to amass land. Next, he built eight houses, a store, a Mason Hall, and a community public meeting hall on his land. After a flood, he gave the land where his church resides today and another plot so that the Black children in his and surround neighborhoods could have a schoolhouse. In time, TB moved his family to the land. He was a more progressive entrepreneur, community leader, and family man. His siblings, who wanted to move on the land, came with their parents. The ones who lived to become adults were his sisters Dinah W. Gregg, Lottie W. Atkinson Boykin, Ella

W. Spann, Millie Wright, Cassie W. Nelson, Bessie Wright, and Sammie W. Young and his brother James Wright (Bubba Son). Most of them moved to the Rafting Creek community and became contributors to the growth and development of that community. As time passed, some of the siblings left this farm and built independent lives. TB's parents, however, remained in the house he provided for them until their deaths.

Mrs. Sammie Wright Young, TB's youngest sister   **Aunt Sammie with some of their sister Ella's grandchildren**

TB and Caroline were independent farmers, homeowners, and Rafting Creek community developers. They were the parents of Mary and Birnie Wright. In the early 1900s, this couple became successful entrepreneurs and sole owners of hundreds of acres-of-lands in the Rafting Creek area of the Rafting Creek Area of Rembert in Sumter County, South Carolina and in Sumter, South Carolina. (See Appendix Three.)

To accommodate his cotton and that of other Black farmers in the Rafting Creek and surrounding communities, TB and Caroline built a cotton gin that housed theirs and his community's bales of cotton. He also built another building to house their cotton seeds until the time came for them to sell these commodities.

The contributions TB and his first wife made to the Rafting Creek Community are well documented. In later years, the Rafting Creek Community Center was housed on land that was originally theirs.

By 1915 this couple had purchased almost one hundred lots in what is presently called the north side of the city of Sumter. From that land, lots closest to Morris College were donated to that school. This is a Historically Black College, mainly funded by the Black Baptist Congregations of South Carolina. When his roommate and forever best friend Dr. John Starks became president of Morris College, TB began making substantial financial contributions there, as well. On the second floor in the Academic building, on that campus, there is a plaque with his name inscribed that honors him.

Caroline died, leaving TB with two teenage children. Before long, he became smitten by my grandmother who was a 19-year-old graduate from Benedict college. He married her.

TB's White House (Moma's children and I were born here.)

Continuing to Rise

Chapter Seventeen - Endurance

Without Money - With Resources

TB built what was referred to as the "big house" up on a hill. It was surrounded by beautiful pecan trees on one side and a fruit orchard on the other. One could see hundreds of acres of land he owned from the three porches of his house.

What is significant about this house built by this Black man in the rural South around 1900 was that it was the only White house owned by a Black family in the area. It had an indoor bathroom, Delco/electric lighting, windowpanes, four bedrooms, and a formal living room. The three of the four bedrooms and formal living room were separated from the kitchen and formal dining room by a large hall.

My family's misfortune is that TB died at such an early age. If he lived, we might have become a generationally Black wealthy family in the South. The fortunate thing that they had was land. Between the Rafting Creek area, Sumter, and Eastover areas, Moma and TB amassed multiple hundreds of acres of land. They were certainly on their way to having at least a thousand or more acres and doing more expansive philanthropic deeds.

Though TB attended Benedict College, Columbia, S.C., he was a founding trustee of Morris College. Upon his death, Moma became one of the first lady trustees of our Alma Mater and later obtained a bachelor's degree there. Some of his sisters and many nieces and nephews, for generations, have matriculated and obtained a bachelor' degree at Morris. Three generations of his direct descendants hold bachelor's degrees from this Historically Black College.

A Saga

Less than a quarter of a mile South of the Wright's farm was a White-owned Cotton gin and cottonseed barn. It remains nestled in an area where a portion of the Confederate War was fought in 1865. By default, if anything happened to the gin and seed barn owned by TB, as he was called, the White owners of the other gin would happily bale his cotton and store it along with the cotton seeds in their facilities.

Remnants of the other gin that was a quarter mile from TB's Gin.
A Confederate monument was posted right next to this gin.

Death from a Massive Heart Attack

During the fall season of each year, TB wrote one check that covered his entire Farm insurance. In 1924 he and Moma were walking in one of the fields when a White insurance agent came to collect the bill. Noting that TB was busy, the "insurance man" said to him, "Do not stop now Tom. I will take care of you. I will come back sometime soon to collect." The insurance policy expired at midnight that night. Before 12:30 a.m., a mysterious fire raged.

Continuing to Rise

The insurance man's saying, "Don't stop now Tom. I'll take care of you. I'll come back sometime soon to collect," came true. TB, and many Black farmers who stored cotton bales of cotton and cotton seeds in his cotton gin were "taken care of." The greater portion of that entire Black community's yearly funds was burned to the ground. Does this sound like a one-man's tragedy? Does this tragedy in Rembert, South Carolina on a smaller scale, replicate the tragedy of Black Wall Street in Tulsa, Oklahoma in 1921?

Aside from his family, many members of this rural community depended on TB. The neighbors stored cotton and cottonseed in his barns; and the houses on the property housed some of his siblings and the other families. The agreement for working the farm was that they would be reimbursed after harvesting. His immediate home life was also greatly impacted. Moma was pregnant with their fourth child, who was my mother, and his first two children had not become full adults, so they, too, were at home.

This man had always paid his bills-in-full. Until this tragedy, he owned everything. For the first time in his life, TB mortgaged his rural farm for $25,000 in November of 1924. In May of 1925, this progressive entrepreneur, humanitarian, and community leader died of a massive heart attack in his sleep.

L-R My cousin/brother William (Junior)   My cousin/brother David (Pab)   Margaret, and I (Moya)

Moma & her daughters   My family   Lil' Randy and Joc

Aunt Ruth's son (Prof)   Aunt Rith's daughter Margaret (Bunny)   Anthony and family (Prof's son)

Continuing to Rise

Chapter Seventeen - Endurance

Junior's son Chris   **Pab's sons Ivan and Omar**

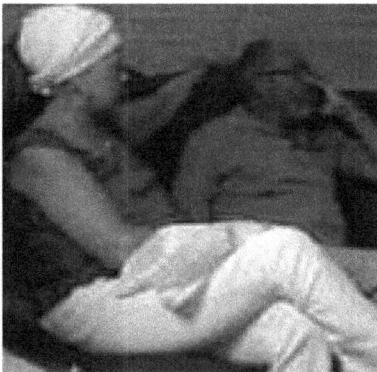

Junior's daughter Davida and children Joshua, Jaylan Pab, and wife, Pat (Kay)

This is my Halifax, VA Family. A beautiful woman, Mrs. Leola Easley Graves instructed me to become her children's matriarch upon her transition.

L to R Dr. Mike and Ce Davis Forest, his Wife Song and Grands Sharon, Ce, & me

Sharon Graves, Le Le Jones Sneed, CeCe Jones, Karen Grave Medley

Continuing to Rise

Don Graves, Greg & wife Angela Graves, Forest and wife Song, Alan, and wife Amber Graves

Family evening at the Kennedy Center, Washington, DC

My Family and my God children at my birthday celebration

A 30-Year-Old Widow's Reality in 1925

Mae Marion Woodward Wright McLester
May 24, 1895 – December 31, 1994

Continuing to Rise

Chapter Seventeen - Endurance

In many ways, my maternal grandmother's story mirrors her mother's life. In 1925, Moma was widowed and became responsible for her children and family members with a mortgaged farm that was previously owned by her husband, it completely mortgaged farm a few months before his death. She was also the principal of the Black school that stood on their land. Along with her LLI degree from Benedict in 1918, she received her bachelor's from Morris College in 1931. Later, this woman received education certificates and began studying for a master's degree at S.C. State. In 1967, Moma was the recipient of an Honorary Doctorate Degree in Morris. Her work as a member of Morris The College's Trustee Board was continued for more than 50 years on the campus with my two aunts Mrs. Magnolia A. Lewis, and Dr. Beatrice G. Sanders. A building on the campus is named after these three women.

Moma's story with TB began in 1918. After graduating from Benedict College, Mae Marion Woodward was introduced to TB by her older brother Hampton. A few months later they were married. She moved from her home in Eastover, South Carolina into the Rafting Creek Community in Sumter County. The only other person she knew in the county was her brother Hamp who was the first "Colored" County Farm Agent in Sumter County, South Carolina. In 1920 she and TB had their first-born that added to his two children. By 1925, TB had three more children with Moma. Additionally, Moma was six months pregnant with their fourth child, who was my mother Margaret, when T.B. died.

This beautiful woman was 30 years old in a community where she was living in the shadow of TB's first wife, pregnant and mothering six children, teaching school, maintaining a farm of several hundred acres, and city lots that had just been mortgaged for $25,000. Furthermore, she was responsible for a major portion of the financial welfare of the ten families who lived on the farm. The proverbial "piranhas" flooded around offering her money for the farm in that community. But she refused to sell.

Moma resolved to stay in this area and to find a way to help the ten families, as well. Mary moved to New York and Birnie moved to Washington, DC by 1935. In the latter part of 1926, Moma remarried to Reverend Leslie McLester, of Camden, SC. To that union in 1928 Celess was born. By 1930 they were divorced. Her five children and the people who remained on the farm worked extremely hard to pay off that mortgage. She paid it off within 15 years, and the property became hers free and clear.

This woman wanted to make sure that her children had the best education possible, so she sold the land in Sumter, sent Big Tommie, Hamp, Jay, and Less to boarding school at Browning Home/Mather Academy in Camden, South Carolina, where I attended years later. My mother was sent to day-school at Lincoln High School in Sumter, South Carolina. She used the rest of the funds to take care of farming and the needs of the people who helped on the farm.

When our Matriarch's area school superintendent discovered that the farm remained in the hands of TB's widow and that she owned a car, he was incensed. He fired the lady who wrote President Franklin D. Roosevelt for a Rosenwald grant for Rafting Creek Colored School. After being fired, she secured and met the requirements by raising matching funds to meet the Rosenwald requirements, released the additional required land so that it would be built, and relocated into her new school assignment outside of the Rafting Creek Rosenwald School District.

Rafting Creek Colored School – A Rosenwald School

My Moma, who was fired as principal of Rafting School, never missed a beat. When she was fired, she immediately found a teaching position at Westbury School, a two-room building near Horatio, SC. She taught the first four grades in one room, while the Principal, Mr. James (Jimmy) Dixon, taught grades 5-8.

When I was three years old, she took me to a two-room school where she taught. The next year I went to school in the Rafting Creek Rosenwald schoolhouse for one year, then moved to the bricked-in school. Moma did not allow her anger to overwhelm her. Her mottos were, "Sticks and stones may break my bones, but words will never hurt me," and "I can do all things through Christ that strengthens me." She lived with them.

Moma led by example. Her life was our lesson of endurance. Moma was a bundle of energy whose life work was being a "Missionary." Her work ethics were remarkable. During the school year, after being demoted from principal, she taught Elementary school, grades 1-4 and at Morris College she served on the Trustee Board for many, many years. At church she was the Sunday School Secretary, Vacation Bible School Director, and President of the Senior Missionary Society.

Each morning, she was up at 4:30a.m. Household chores were accomplished before going off to the two-room schoolhouse. Before breakfast, Moma milked cows and swept the three porches around the house. Around 6:00 a.m. Her favorite wake up tune was "Oh, Where Have You Been Billy Boy, Billy Boy" as she was slamming doors. She would say to anyone who got up after 7:00a.m., "God's sun has been up for hours, and you missed its beauty."

Of course, everybody in the house had assigned chores. They ranged from feeding chickens, hogs, and dogs, to washing dishes after breakfast, working in the cotton fields, to other farm requirements. After school, the routine of farm requirements began again until dusk. Then, when Moma came in the house from the farm, she would grade school papers, work on plans for the next day, read her Bible with me, pray, and then go to bed bellowing a hymn.

On Wednesday nights, she held a Bible study. I know this sounds like a tight schedule. In hindsight, I agree. However, this was our way of life. Momma had a great sense of humor. She asked a lot of questions, too. When asked why she was so inquisitive, her response would be, "Inquiring minds want to know." Then, she would laugh and keep going.

Saturday was always the 'town' day. Moma drove to Sumter to "take care of business." The car could be crowded with as many as eight of us crammed into seats. Sometimes there would even be a flatbed attached to the haul hitch attached to the back of the car. It hauled several 1500 pounds of cotton. On occasion, some of the bales fell off the flatbed. We always had to flag down other cars asking other people to help us put each 1500-pound bale of cotton back on the flatbed. Without an air-conditioned car and packed in like sardines, we were hot.

Upon the return from town, weekend chores included a complete cleaning of the house, washing and hanging the clothes on the line to dry, then ironing things chosen for the next week. Finally, we had to lay out our clothes for church. Chores were divided among the people in the house and supervised by Moma. There was never an excuse for not completing them. My Saturday assignment was to visit a lady in our community who was incapacitated by a stroke. My job was to take care of her personal needs and sing to her.

I forgot to tell you that Moma baked pastries on Saturday evenings and prepared the bulk of the "Sunday dinner" as well. Then after we ate, she would bundle plates of food to take to the elderly and sick throughout the community. This lady knew how to take one chicken and feed an army!!!

We did not do farm chores on Sunday. But we were in church for Sunday School at times when no one else was there. Moma believed our responsibility was to be in "God's house" on Sunday. She would quote: "Remember the Sabbath Day and keep it Holy." If it was cold, we had to bring in wood or coal for the stove then wait for it to warm the church.

Moma was never afraid of a full day's work and taught us that dignity was evidenced in completing tasks that required being done to the best of our ability. This routine was so commonplace that we were accustomed to making it happen. Of course, there were many complaints from us about the pace and demand. Her response was, "Somebody must do it; it might as well be us. If you want something in life, you must prepare to get it done to the best of your ability." She was our model for success in so many ways. For those of us who lived in her house, we never had to wonder how to stick to a task.

Moma maintained her home, took care of her son Jay, and drove until she was over 95 years old. When she died at 99.7 years old, her driver's license was active. Until her late nineties, she also tilled the soil with her garden hoe, planted, and attended vegetables that she grew there.

This remarkable woman taught us the importance of being able to do for ourselves in the world in which we live. She taught, for example, how to manage disappointments by figuring out how to go through them. Moma would say, "Use the brain God gave you. You cannot expect people to be fair to you. You must learn how to be fair to yourself and know that God will show you the way."

In this remarkable woman, I witnessed a tenacious spirit, second-to-none. She was not afraid to stand up for what she felt was right. When people disdained her, she would say, "I must be doing something right. People do not waste time talking about or mistreating people who do nothing." Sometimes, I would get angry with someone who talked about her and reacted with anger. On occasions such as this, Moma would send me to the offender's house to apologize, carry the person some food, and clean this person's house!

Times were financially hard; money was scarce. We lived on a farm, so we had food. When we went to buy groceries, we only needed carnation milk, Maxwell House coffee, sugar, a coconut to bake pies, rice, and seasonings. Everything else we ate was on the farm. The big smokehouse kept meat cured and things like potatoes banked. Beans and peas were dried, and green vegetables and fruits were canned. The cows provided meat, milk, and butter. The chickens, ducks, guineas, turkeys, pigs we raised on the farm, and the deer hunted augmented the meats. Wheat, oats, and barley provided our bread, grits, and oatmeal. Our bedlinen was made from the Purina sacks that the fertilizer for the farm came in and scarps made quilts. Scraps from the table, fed the dogs and pigs; chickens ate ground oats while the larger animals grazed in the pastures. There was never a shortage of resources for us. Why do I tell this story?

When it came to the plight of segregation and the degrading experiences heaped upon our community, Moma would say that our responsibility was to do our best in all situations to show dignity. She was never afraid to do what she thought was the proper way. She got a lot done despite the indecent behaviors she faced from White people.

Ellerbe's Mill is where we brought our oat, barley, and wheat to be ground into cereals.

Moma loved her family and made sure that her children were properly educated and that no one would ever take TB's farm away. Moma taught us by example. This is a typical story of many southern Black people. They taught by example what it means to be warriors. Endurance was one of the ways they kept their lives and families intact. They relied on the indelible spirit and kept their sanity, as well.

Thomas Boston Wright and Marion Woodward Wright McLester's Family.

My maternal aunts and uncles: (Myrtle, wife of Hampton), Hampton September 1921-March 1988; (Hamp), Celess January 1928-March 2012 (Less), Thomasina March 1920-May 2013 (Big Tommie), Moma, Margaret September 1925- 2018 (Moya) and John Paul June 1924-December 2010 (Jay)

Chapter Seventeen - Endurance

Their Grandchildren

L to R Olivia March 1963-April 1986 (Pat), Pamela (Pam), Michael (Mike), Thomasina, (Lil' Tommye), Hampton (Woody), Myra, Derrick (Jack),

L to R Beverly (Ann), Janis, & Larry

Lil' Tommye and Verenander LF Portis, Jr's children are Randy, Ronnie, and the late Tamarinice August 1973- August 2004 (Margi)

The Portis grandchildren are Deysha; Lil Randy, Aaron, Isiah, Caredio, Ayden, Vernard, (Deuce) and Valor (Tre)

Continuing to Rise

L to R: Jason and Ashley Jones; Dr. Eric and Valerie Guthrie Jones and children; Johnathan and Javondra Faith Wright and children Jayah and Jordyn

L to R: Michelle, Kamaya and Johnathan Wright, and Erica Jefferson

L to R Reynard (Ollie) and Jemia Jefferson and daughter; Dacia and Channing Strange and children

Chapter Seventeen - Endurance

Row One: L to R Maurice and Natalie Jones; Janice Wright, daughter Margaret Latoya Williams, husband, and daughter
Row Two: Kamaya and son Kamron; Larry, and Shiela Drakeford and daughters Shiela and Raven

R to L Janis' grandchildren and Jack and Demetress Johnson Wright and their children

Dr. Kimberly Wright   **Christopher Iris Diaz Jones and children**

Family holiday celebration   **Maurice and Natalie Children**

Continuing to Rise

TB and Ms. Mae's Grand and Great Grandchildren: Thomasina *(Tommye)* and her former husband Varenander LF Portis, Jr.'s children are Verenander, III, *(Randy)*, Vernard, *(Ronnie)* and the late Tamarinice *(Margi)* Portis Williams; *Larry* Drakeford and his wife Sheila's daughters are, Sheila and Michelle Drakeford; Beverly *Ann* Hunter has no children, Earl and the late Olivia *(Pat)* Wright Jefferson's children are Erica and Reynard Jefferson; Reverend Stanley and Pamela *(Pam)* Wright Jones' children are, Eric, Maurice, Christopher, Dacia Jones Strange, and Jason Jones; *Janis* Wright's daughter is Margaret *LaToya* Wright Williams; *Hampton (Woody)* and his former wife Sheila Dix Wright's daughter is Kimberly Wright; *Myra* C. Wright has no children; *Michael (Mike)* and his former wife Yvonne Moody Wright's children are Michelle, Jonathan, and Kamaya Wright; and *Derrick (Jack)* and his wife Demetress Johnson Wright's children are Destyne and Derrick Wright.

TB and Ms. Mae's Great and Great, Great Grandchildren: Randy, Ronnie and Margi's children are listed in the first set of family photos; Dr. Eric and Valerie Guthrie Jones' children Sidney, Camille, and Brooke; Maurice and Natalie Quinn Jones's children are Makayla, Trevice, and Madelyn; Christopher and Iris Diaz Jones's children are Carter, Hampton, Cameron; Margaret LaToya Wright and Ya'el Williams's children are Najee; Marquis, Jamir, Aaliyah, and Amari; Dacia Jones and Channing Strange, Sr's children are Channing, Jr., Chanya, Chanlyn; and Reynard and Jamia Keels Jefferson's daughter is Sage; Johnathan Wright and Javondra Faith Wright's daughters are Jayah an Jordyn; and Kamaya Wright's son. Kamron. (Sheila Drakeford, Raven Drakeford, Erica Jefferson, Michelle Wright, Dr. Kimberly Wright, and Jason Jones have no children.)

"I am not what happened to me, I am what I choose to become."

Carl Gustav Jung

The following short stories are set as vignettes about endurance. They speak to the power of these family members who faced unpleasant or difficult situations. They faced them and continued to rise.

V #1 Passing for White

There was another reality. Many Black people passed for White as did one of great grandma Margarette's sisters. I never knew her name, but she married a man from Scotland who was a longshoreman. She moved there, and never returned to the states. Each year she would send her sisters boxes of fine linen tablecloths, with matching napkins, crystal, and silverware. She also sent dainty tea sets.

When great-grandma Margarette's daughters went off to school, they lived on campus from the eighth grade through finishing school. In addition to the rigors of their academics, they were trained in informal social etiquette practices. These women were prepared for homemaking and a professional career. Many young ladies of that era went North to become live-in housekeepers and nannies.

On weekdays, our family ate hot cooked meals together at the kitchen table. Our plates were served from the stove. On Sunday and holidays, we "dressed-up" for dinner. At those times we used the formal linen sets, the finest China, crystal, and silverware on a perfectly set table in the formal dining room. We usually ate together for breakfast, dinner, and supper. During the week and always together on Sundays and holidays.

V #2 Education and Family Next to Christianity

One of the misconceptions held about the Southern Black community is that we were uneducated, uncouth, and impoverished people. In my family, we acknowledge being undereducated, but uneducated, we were not. For five generations our education degrees range from bachelor's to PhD. Our family was a tightly knitted group. We understood that we had each other. That is why I grew up with Bill and an cousins. We lived this quote by Briansolis, which says, "Community is much more than belonging to something: it's about doing something together that makes belonging matter."

V #3 That's a "Fur-in-na" (Foreigner)

My first potentially fatal racist encounter was when I was 13 years old. It was not in South Carolina. It was in Jackson, Mississippi. I rode the bus from Camden, SC to Mississippi, with my roommate from Mather Academy for the Christmas Holiday. We were finally arriving at the bus stop in Jackson, Mississippi, where we were picked up by her parents.

The trip was so long that we completed all of our holiday homework assignments. When I got off the bus, I had to use the bathroom and saw that sign that said, "Women Only." It did not say, "White

Women Only" which was the sign I was accustomed to seeing in SC. With my French homework in my hand, I mad-dashed for the restroom. Two men were running behind me. I did not think they were running after me, so I kept running to the bathroom. When I was about to open the door, they yelled, "Stop, that toilet ain't for you, gal." I needed to relieve myself, so I ran in, shut the door, and dropped my homework on the ground.

The wooden toilet was built with a space between the enclosure and the ground where my homework had fallen. One of the men pulled my homework from the bathroom area, looked at it, and said to his running friend, "Hey, let's go. This ain't no N.... r, she a damn "fur-in-na" (foreigner). I was trembling with fright as I retrieved my books and walked to get to the car that was waiting for me. I must have been traumatized because I did not start crying until hours later. I could not get out of my head that my life was spared because they thought I was foreign.

V #4 A White Reality

One day a driver picked me up from the airport and took me into a mid-west city. I was the keynote speaker for the back-to-school conference in an All-White school district. In fact, I did not see a Black person the entire time I was in the city. The school board members, all central officers, as well as the local faculty and staff were present.

After a most gracious introduction from a newly appointed young teacher, I walked up to the podium reciting "Invictus" by William E. Henley.

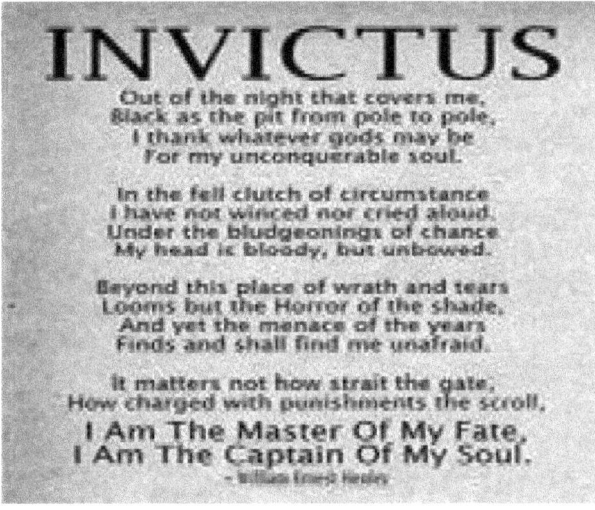

Continuing to Rise

A loud voice from the back attempted to interrupt me. "How did this N— —-r get here?" I continued to recite. He yelled again, "Hey, tell me who sent for you!" I continued to recite. Another yell ensued. "Hey, tell me who sent for you, N— —r?" I continued to move toward the podium. Then he yelled, "Just know I'd rather be poor and White than rich and Black." The man was taken out of the assembly. The situation appeared to be uncomfortable for the people who invited me. I gave the address as if I had been enthusiastically welcomed.

At the end of the session, the chief administrator whispered that he was sorry and thanked me for not stopping my address. My only response was, "Thank you for having me." Such incidents continue to fill my book of life experiences. Paving the way for other others leaves its marks and rewards. I pass this reality forward as I encourage you to find your way the paths of inequity to social justice.

V #5 External and Internal Warring

Jay and his two Montfort Marine friends

During World War II, the federal rule stated that where there were two sons in a family, one could legally remain at home during the war. That did not happen for this independent Black female farm owner. When my Moma petitioned the federal government for one of her sons to remain on the farm to help her maintain it, the request was denied. Her oldest son Hampton Woodward "Hamp" Wright, Sr., was drafted to go into the armed services. Hamp went into the U.S. Army and became an expert shooter. He was sent to the Asiatic Pacific. After his tour of duty, he returned home to resume his farming duties.

Hamp's younger brother John Paul (Jay) Wright was seventeen years old when he too was drafted into the military. He heard that the Marines were recruiting "colored." This brave soul applied and was among the first 1, 200 men recruited in the United States Marine Corp. These men were sent to Montford Point, North Carolina because the White Marines at Camp LeJeune Marine Base refused to train with the "colored." Immediately after his training at Montford Point, the entire crew went directly to the front line. Jay lived much of his time on the firing lines in Iwo Jima.

Jay rarely talked about that time in his life. When he did, he would tell us about how some of the White Marines he fought to save in the trenches and gave them blood, the White Marines then made a mockery of the Black soldiers on the streets. The integrity of these Black soldiers remained the example of our ancestor's indelible spirit. For them, Freedom for one (Marine) meant freedom for all. Ironically, the Marine's motto is, "Always faithful." Jay returned home in 1944 and went back to college. After graduation, he became a high school football coach and social studies teacher at the former Schofield High, Aiken, South Carolina. The pay was so menial he decided to leave the South around 1948 to become a mail carrier in the North. In the fall of 1959, at 39 years old, Jay returned home and was hired at the former Eastern High School in Sumter County, South Carolina where he taught social studies and coached football again.

Jay's coaching skills were equal to his athletic ability. When he was in college, his football coach would say that if the professional football league was hiring Black players, he was sure to be drafted. Meanwhile, both of his high school football teams were division champions. One of his players, the late Reverend McKinley Washington, a former S.C. State Congressman, spoke at Jay's funeral and said that his coach used football to teach his players how to become successful in life.

Eastern High School's football team with Coach John Paul Wright

By 1961, Jay started showing signs of mental fatigue. This time he was inhumanely treated as a veteran. Momma sought help from him. The Veterans Administration (VS.A.) hospitals were filled with White veterans, reaping the benefits of professional care commonly denied to Black veterans. Some of these White veterans never even left the states during the entire war. For the first tumultuous ten years of his failing health, he was denied. All the while, Jay, the proud Marine, would say, "Semper fi!" Jay fought so hard to maintain mental balance.

Finally, Moma wrote to her U.S. Senator. This Senator intervened. Jay was awarded fractional financial assistance from the V.A. However, he was never able to get permanent health assistance from them. Jay died in 2010, in a nursing home on Medicaid, not in a V.A. facility as a soldier of valor. This man owned land. After his death, the nursing home went after his assets. To keep his portion of land in our family that was left to him by his mother, a family member purchased it for $20,000 from the S. C. State Government.

Oh, let me tell you, Jay won! Posthumously, his faithfulness to this nation and loyalty to his team were celebrated. NY3 Robert Lee Dinkins (Navy) and Attorney James L. Felder, (whom you met in Chapter Nineteen), committed themselves to getting Jay recognized as a war hero. Our family is forever indebted and grateful to these two men.

YN3 Robert Dinkins

Family, Jay's story may seem unimaginable. It is inconceivable that the United States veterans, generally, Black veterans specifically, do not get fair treatment from a nation they continue to fight so valiantly to preserve. Despite this reality, this man is an example. He would let nothing stop him from being part of our Relay to Liberty and Justice. Four generations of our family have served this nation through the U.S. Military.

V #6. A Son's and Mother's Experiences - Silence Amid Trepidation

The only way to understand what it means to be silent is to experience it when every fiber of your being is screaming, "Warning! Danger!" Black mothers learn to teach their sons that silence amid danger may save their lives. The expectation is the norm that police will accost them at some point.

One Saturday morning, Ronnie and I drove to surprise Randy and his wife Dee with a visit. We decided to stop at a deli near their home, pick up breakfast, and enjoy being together for a few hours.

I must describe my handsome son Ronnie. He is six'2" and slim built. That day he was wearing tan khaki shorts, a polo shirt, a cap, and sneakers. As we were parking across the street from his brother's house, a siren blew, and a voice on a megaphone demanded me to pull over. The police officer rushed out of the car.

The tone of this White policeman's voice was filled with so much venom that I cringed. I was ready to ask questions. Ronnie was looking straight ahead with his firsthand on the dashboard. Out of the side of his mouth, he said, "Mommie, be quiet and wait to get out of the car after I am out."

The police officer opened the passenger door and asked my son to get out. Ronnie did as was requested and remained quiet. Not once did he or I ask the officer anything. He took my son by his arm, moved him to the trunk of my car, and cuffed him while telling him to stand right there until he returned.

Meanwhile, I wanted to ask why all this vibrato and disrespect. I looked across the street, and my heart sank even more. My other son Randy was standing next to a tree watching his younger brother in cuffs. Instinctively, he must have known not to come across the street, not even in the area where I stood. The police officer got on the phone and stayed for a few minutes.

Time was suspended as my two sons, and I remained "in place." My heartbeat felt intermingled with my lungs, and I breathed as if I had just finished a ten-mile run. Finally, the police officer came back. He informed us that the community store had been robbed by a young man with a darker complexion who was about five'10, wearing long blue jeans. Did you take note of the description of the person that this police officer needed to find?

I asked, "Why was I pulled over?" The police officer said he was driving into the parking area of the store when I pulled out. The call came, so he DECIDED to pull us over. That was his explanation with no apology. He took the handcuffs off Ronnie's wrists, got in his car, and sped off. Not one time did anyone speak disrespectfully to this officer. Not one time did this officer acknowledge the error of his behavior. My son and I walked across the street, hugging. Joining in the hug with my oldest son Randy, the three of us walked into his house.

During this experience, I was consciously aware that my sons must be cautious when stopped by police for the rest of their lives. Another Black man was standing on his porch watching. As we passed him, he said, "Man, that could have gone bad at any second." At this point, my tears began to flow as I began to praise God that my sons were safe.

Randy and Ronnie are continuing to pour into the lives of young people. Their indelible spirit's refuse to allow such disdaining behavior to stop them. My older son and his wife are successful as independent business owners. He has a Bachelors' Degree, is a certified medic, holds other certifications, and is honorably discharged from the United States Army. Ronnie works in his local government. He has a master's degree, and a dynamic wife. Both families have children.

Verenander L. F. "Randy" Portis III, his wife Denise Rivera and their children, Deysha, Caredio, and Lil' Randy

Vernard L. R. "Ronnie" Portis, his wife Cynthia Keith, and their sons Vernard, Jr. (Deuce) and Valor (Tre)

V. #7 Mother and Son

The testing of stamina that Black people acquire is done along our continuum of life. Here are two examples. One of my grandsons was introduced to some in-your-face realities regarding the evils of Systemic Racism when he was fourteen years old. His late mother experienced a harsh reality in her senior year in college.

Son: Ivy-League High School- 2019

My freshman year, my roommate peed in my closet. Our school responded by giving him a "talk," and no further disciplinary action was taken. Even after I requested a new roommate, I was denied. I had to endure the rest of the year with him. I remember walking in on his friends playing the song "My Nigga" and laughing when I was offended.

My sophomore year, some of my classmates make a rap video in the dorm. They kept asking me to show them how to dance and rap. One of them called me a Black roach when I wouldn't help him with his homework. He was the star basketball player, so I didn't have any motivation to tell the administrators. They were protective of this star baseball player.

I was one of seven Black students in my graduating class. If I had a dollar for every time I was called the name of another Black student in these four years, I would be a millionaire by now. How much longer will all Black people look alike and have the same name?

In my senior year when I was applying to colleges, my counselor told me that most of my schools were "a reach" and that I should consider more accessible schools; more HBCU's. I was shocked. My grades were excellent, and I was very involved on campus. First of all, there is nothing wrong with HBCU's. I support them! My counselor's implication was that I needed to lower my standards and that HBCU's aren't as valued as other schools. I was admitted into nearly every school that she said was "a reach." Can you imagine the number of Black students who are told to lower their standards to fit the narratives and stereotypes in some school counselors' heads!

Who, with a heart, would intentionally put a fourteen-year-old through these kinds of devaluing rigors? It did not stop him from moving ahead honorably. This young man was awarded a full scholarship to one of the best universities in this country. He graduated in four years without having to attend a single summer school, maintained his GPA above 3.0, and held leadership roles on campus. Congratulations, world leader!

Mother: College-Level - 1996

My late daughter (his mother) was awarded a full five-year scholarship at an Ivy-League University. In her fourth year she became president of the Black Student Organization (BSO). As President, she was a member of the university's executive leadership team comprised of student presidents of all student organizations, staff, and administration members to include the President. During the first year of her presidency, one other ethnic organization brought the Grand Dragon of the Ku Klux Klan in as a guest speaker.

Later that year, the planning and activities committee of the BSO invited a controversial figure to speak. When the organization advertised under its speaker's name, it caused a great uprising. My daughter was summoned to an emergency executive committee meeting where several people voiced their concerns about the speaker and asked her to change.

Margi shared the concerns with the organization's planning committee because that had engaged the speaker. She reported to the school's executive committee that the BSO's planning committee agreed to move forward with their original plan. They determined it would be appropriate to move ahead since this was not an issue with the other group's speaker. They did. The meeting never occurred because the speaker was unable to come.

I told you that my daughter was on full scholarship. She was completing the fourth of her five-year tenure. Mid-July, before her final year, I received a letter informing me that due to blah, blah, blah, she was shifted from her scholarship funding source for her last four years and placed on a privately funded scholarship criteria to include parent salary. They regretted informing me that my salary exceeded the limit, so my daughter could not receive a scholarship for the upcoming school year.

I was told that neither the school nor I had recourse to this particular private funding source. They wished us well, implying that without the scholarship, Margi would not return. So, they thought! I understood that when grades didn't get many Black students removed before graduation, attrition "by any means necessary," might.

One of the wisest pieces of advice my dad gave me before his death was, "Choose your battles. It does not matter what others may think you ought to do. The question to be answered at all costs is, "What is the best recourse for the situation?" I knew that being a few weeks away from her time to go into her senior year was not the time for me to start a fight. I did not argue the point at all and thanked God for available resources.

The following May, our family watched her walk across the stage. I got the opportunity to speak with, shake hands with, and even take photos with a few of the committee members who sent me that letter at the "ninety-ninth hour." That gave me all the satisfaction I would ever need.

The following May, our family watched her walk across the stage. I got the opportunity to speak with, shake hands with, and even take photos with a few of the committee members who sent me that letter at the ninety-ninth" hour.

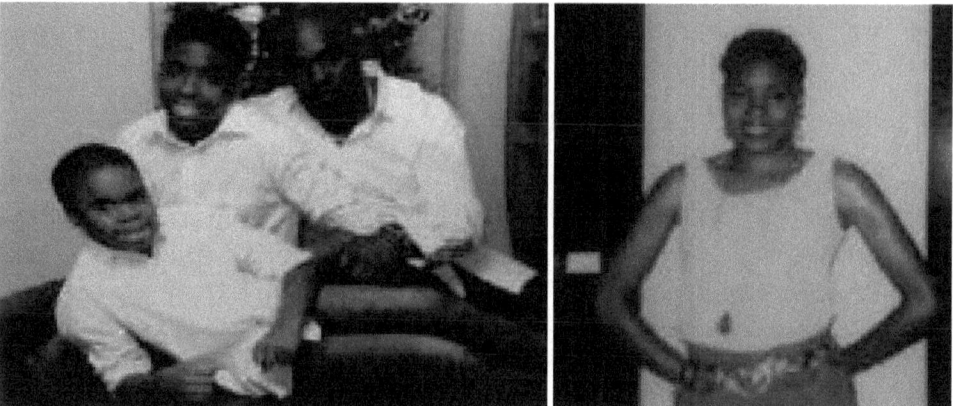

The Late Tamarinice Margaret "Margi" Portis Williams's family: Her husband Anthony and their sons Aaron, and Ayden

V#8 Ignorance Remains a Beast!

One day I got a phone call from a man who came to our home at least once a week. He was hired to tutor my grandsons. I taught voice lessons during the time he tutored. He and I would have conversations about our love for music. Sometimes he reminisced about his high school choir days. Over time, we became platonic friends and exchanged conversations about our lives. He grew up in the Midwest and was never around Black people until college but did not socialize with us then. A few months ago, I got a call from him. During a conversation with his high school music teacher, he told her that he had met a great BLACK musician. He said he described me singing, then told her about his intrigue regarding my vocal teaching strategies.

Then, he said, "I told my teacher I would never have imagined in a million years that I would meet a barefoot Black woman from the deep South, singing and teaching like that." He said, "She is superb. She was an intermediary vocal coach for national actors and singers who performed in prestigious stages. I just had to tell you about her."

This guy was excited. Once he calmed down, I asked, "Barefoot? Do I know this person you are talking about?" "Yes," he said. "YOU!" I took a deep breath and said," I never knew myself without shoes. Who told you I ran around barefooted?" He replied, without hesitation, I might add, "Well, Thomasina, if it wasn't you, it was your grandmother."

I had to respond rather than to react. I stayed quiet until I had permitted myself to feel deep grief for this man's ignorance and the impact it carried. I chose to believe that his quick tongue did not represent his heart. Sadly, ignorance is a beast that will live with anyone regardless of ethnicity or class.

Misinformation and disregard are so inherent in White privilege and supremacy. Our divided lives make this true for the Black community, as well. I long for the day when every human being understands how much this divisive supremacy prolongs dissonance for all people.

Continuing to Rise

V # 9 Clergyman's Social and Ethical Awakenings

The preparations required for a successful national crusade were rigorous. It was fascinating to meet Christian leaders with so many different attitudes and approaches to this form of evangelism. As in every other occupation, some of us worked well together; the others of us walked away from each other. A few of us spent a great deal of time together and formed relationships of comfort. At some point, we would have very in-depth conversations about our lives and what led us into the world of Christian ministry.

I was remarkably familiar with White and Black separations. I was also familiar with not debating with anyone whose theology was quite different from mine. Nevertheless, I had a wonderful experience with a Southern-born White minister.

The suspicion between our two ethnicities had its Southern origin, which we knew all too well. To find myself becoming friends with him and then having open conversations about how we viewed life, despite our Southern codes, amazed me. Even when experiences like this one are short-lived, the impact of our time together remains life changing. In one of our conversations, Jeff (not his real name) started talking about his young years. He said that he was taught that Black people could not carry- on intelligent conversations with White people. Um mm! I never imagined that Jeff and I would have authentic conversations except on issues that might arise during the planning of the Crusade. There was a specific incident where I reacted to an insult and hung up on a White clergy. More than I could have ever imagined about White privilege and self- appointed supremacy had been proven to be true through him!

Later, I shared the fiasco with Jeff. I had the burning desire to show my anger. I needed to make it clear to that man that he was never to approach me in such an authoritative and demeaning way EVER again.

In this all-White man's environment, I remained observant, but never subservient. Life has taught me how to maintain my professional, Christian self. So, I thought. This incident left me wanting to do the very thing that had been done to me. I told Jeff that I needed time to decompress and to pray. I left, did both, and came back to have lunch with him about two hours later. I kept pleading with my indelible spirit to take over. I felt as if an ancestral injury had been awakened.

At lunch, Jeff was pensive. I shared how close I had come to imitating the level of disdain I felt had been heaped on me. Jeff looked at me with tears in his eyes and said, "I apologize for him. I apologize for me, and I apologize for our ancestors."

What he told me next was familiar, but it held my attention. He said, "Let me explain what I mean. We were conditioned to speak to you that way; you Black woman. My dad taught me how to see Black people and how to mistreat women. You represent that double dose of what I was taught, and you must remain my subordinates. Jeff said that the man reacted from a socialized behavior that every Southern White man learns through education and vicarious experiences.

When Jeff turned five years old, his father who was an Evangelical Baptist deacon drove a bus in their Southern hometown. He took his son to collaborate with him to teach him work ethics. As a child, Jeff's job was to hold up a sign that said, "N…. R takes seats in the back." He said that he was proud of his job and did it well. His dad told him that "the N…. R cannot read, so yell at them from your authority."

Continuing to Rise

This young boy did just that. Jeff said he would say, "N…. R, you know you belong in the back, so hurry up and get there!" He said he felt a sense of accomplishment. He also knew that his dad would never tell him anything wrong. Jeff left this Southern town with two lessons from his White American religious dad about people. They were, the way he was to treat Black people, and that same-gender relationships were never to be tolerated.

Years later, Jeff became a pastor. He loved God, his people, and was called to pastoral positions far away from home. For years, this man ministered in a Black community in the West and became respected as a community leader. He learned to love all ethnicities. After twenty years, he was led to move. Based upon his reputation, Jeff was offered a pastoral charge site and sight unseen. He accepted the position which was in another city but in the same State.

The first Sunday in the pulpit, he recognized that the church's membership was made up of people who are gay. He said that he was too shocked to react. He said, "I laughed to myself and thought," God's got jokes!" A couple befriended him immediately. Over time, one of the men stopped coming into the church services. When Jeff inquired about him, his partner said that he was at home dealing with an illness. When told about the disease and its impact on the man, Jeff said his heart became over-whelmed with love and compassion. This pastor visited his parishioner.

This encounter helped Jeff to understand this assignment as, what he called "a God thing." He said that there was no way that this was not divinely orchestrated. This new experience within a gay community meant that he had to learn how to serve with love and without prejudice. He had to accept that all people are human beings made in the image of God. Jeff said that with this understanding, he realized that love was the key that unlocked all prejudices.

This man wrestled with this awakening that might be perceived as a betrayal of his dad's teaching. Jeff told his dad that one of the hardest things to erase was what he had taught him about Black people and how he was instructed to behave towards us. He also shared that he could no longer act offensively toward people's sexuality. His dad never spoke to him again. That was a reckoning experience for me. We lived in an environment that had intentionally isolated us from each other. It had taught Jeff how to exercise his White privilege. I had been taught to suspect a White person's overture of goodness.

The experience helped me to see the inherent truth about love as a choice. It is based upon nothing but giving of oneself. Love is not to be determined by another person's behavior. Often egotistical and selfish conveniences are confused as love.

V # 10 Deep-seated Insecurities

I was given a full scholarship to certify as an Executive Administrator at an Ivy League university. Getting through this process of training and implementation required a lot of time and strategic planning. During our sessions, the director became impressed with my work. She selected me to present a project I had completed to all the school administrators in attendance during that summer program. The participants came from around the world.

Wisdom…. Momma told us, "Always present yourself in the fashion that speaks to your highest quality whether in a bathing suit or a three-piece one. Be sure that you are as prepared for whatever is before you do. Always be physically presentable." I took my grandma's advice.

A flurry of probing questions flowed as I presented. I was confident after a while and felt that the assignment was presented with excellence. I was invited to speak at conferences and conventions throughout the U.S. and internationally.

Little did I know that generational residue of insecurities lurked in my concept of who I was. When I finished the report that day, I rushed off the site. My behavior moved from the demeanor of a Chief Senior Administrator in one of the largest school- districts in the United States into a very childlike one. When I got to the door leading outside of the building, I ran to my room mulling questions. Was this the assignment given to this Black girl who was born in a dot on a Southern County map? Was this Black girl just addressing worldwide education decision-makers? I was sweating, thinking, and running.

When I reached my room, I had become a young girl running down a dirt road, trying to get to my family. I had something to tell them! When I finally got inside, I called my mother. She was not available. I called my grandmother. When she answered, I told her everything I have said here.

This woman was always full of surprises. I said, "Moma, can you imagine me being selected out of all the participants in my program? Can you believe that I stood there without notes and shared the book, answered the questions, and got standing ovations?" There was complete silence on the other end of the phone. Then from what sounded like a reverberating voice of many past generations came a thunderous question. "Madam," Moma said, "Can you tell me whoever told you that you couldn't do what you just did?"

I fell back on the bed and wept. Of all the things I was grateful for in that moment, the greatest of them came in the question full of Moma's wisdom. My answer could have been "yes." I knew of my music and athletic abilities and had always excelled in them. Although I got all as in every degree after the Bachelor's, I did not connect with a comprehensive concept of my own intellectual capability until getting a double Masters in nine months. After that question from Moma, I laid on that bed, anguishing over Moma's question.

My life was not integrated into a daily encounter with White ethnicity. The blatant and residual effects of overt and covert disparities and other messages of despair related to external forces came at me like a tsunami in that room. I remembered painful situations from Black and White experiences. I remembered the eight years and three HBCU matriculations it took me to get out of college. Suffice it to say, that day, the entire experience was exhilarating and agonizing. I still carried years of suppressed "baggage."

After going through the kaleidoscope of emotions that night, I realized that despite my troubling and painful experiences, there had never been a time that I quit. Black people who go through the process of becoming our best selves are not quitters. We are overcomers.

Neither White nor Black people are the exception to intelligence and genius in this human family. I am one who has learned, after two Doctorate degrees, that making a place at the table for others to follow is much more important than giving up. Pressures we face become insurmountable roadblocks when we decide to quit. As Mahatma Ghandi said, "You must be the change you wish to see in the world."

V #11 Moral Dilemma

It is incredible how life experiences come full circle. In the eleventh grade, Joyce Carter Krawczyk, Carole Pickett Williams, and I were chosen for Ms. Van Landingham's journalism class. She was a White missionary from some Midwestern State who had had no experience living among or instructing Black people. I remember her love for what she called "literary appropriations." She said that the two words usually two words meant moral dilemmas. Little did I know that many years later, I would use that lesson.

I was out west in an all-White environment as a guest instructor to a group of people who were a few weeks away from being certified as superintendents of education. Interesting enough, many of the participants expressed that they had never had a Black instructor before. Some of them said that in their professional development process, they had not had a female instructor. A White man, who had never been in the presence of a Black person, was a member of this class. The only thing he knew about Black people was whatever he had heard. He could not reconcile being a student with this Black woman as the lecturer. Yet, there I stood.

This man often prefaced his remarks, telling how the experience challenged him. He would remind the class during discussions about how far he was out of his comfort zone. He admitted his duress about a woman's opinion regarding his ability become a superintendent mattered to him. That she is Black made it even more disturbing. He publicly shared his truth.

During a class discussion on moral dilemmas, this principal decided to raise what he thought was an example. He wanted to know from his classmates how they would oversee a situation if as principal their all-White school enrolled Black children. He explained that an issue would be where to place them. Would these children be seated next to White children who had never been around Black people before? He also wanted to know what to do if a White parent said their children could not sit next to Black children because they are not clean people. All eyes were on me. He was determined to continue probing. He said, "What if you (White) parents would use a specific Black child as an example?" Then he said, "For example," and pointed to me. The hush in the session was thunderous.

Without missing a beat, I had the class role-play his scenario. That cohort was small enough so that each person could role-play, being the student and parent amongst themselves and then bring one example of each back to the full group with a suggested solution to the situation. I reminded myself that this man is typical of so many people. I had signed up for this task. I could not betray it, falling prey to becoming a victim.

When the group reassembled to share their examples, it was evident that some of them had been emotionally involved in their role-playing experiences as both parties. I remained quiet. I was asking God to bridle my tongue and to keep me seated. The "quiet tongue" request was granted. I did, however, walk around the room.

It just SOOO happened that when I stopped, I was standing next to the inquirer's chair and in his personal space. I knew he was uncomfortable. The only way he could have moved away would have been forcing me out of the space I held. Then as an aside, I asked him how he would manage my proximity if he were principal. Before he could answer, I asked what made him more uncomfortable: my ethnicity or my gender?

Moving away from him before he answered any of my questions, I reminded the class that public education in America meant that demographics change all the time. This reality is a situation they would have to consider if they wanted to take the helm on leadership in any school district in our nation. I referred to this man's earlier example and insisted that his honesty was appreciated. As you can imagine, things were quiet. Then I said, "Life has a way of throwing us curves. If not prepared, we may be blindsided or battered by a situation from which we cannot recover." Finally, I asked if today's experience had posed a moral dilemma. The assignment for the next day was to write their opinion and support it.

The class was dismissed. Several people stayed around to find out if I was all right. They wanted to apologize and to assure me that they disapproved of the man's conduct. I smiled. I could not engage their comments. I needed to exhale away from all of them. There we were--Americans from two different experiences. Neither privilege nor White supremacy was in that man's favor. The power was in my pen. Our commonality was that we were professional educators. In the final analysis, I was the visiting professor in that all-White environment with the pen that held the fate of prospective graduates.

V #12 The Gatherings

My dad had three sisters, and every Saturday night, our families got together. The adults played the card game Bridge. When in town, one brother-in-law, the pharmacist of our family, might bring his horn and serenade the crowd. The children were bored and sleepy as we sat in earshot of their conversations. The older I have become, the more I realize that we got together to discuss their weekly experiences in their respective schools. Each of the siblings had one daughter with two of them also having two sons,

Here we are

In these gatherings were schoolteachers. My dad disliked that game of Bridge but loved the conversation about school issues. This school topic invariably touched upon two fundamental issues.

One was the conversation about the disparities between resources for Black and White schools. The other was these three Black principals' finessing approaches to have discussions with their White School District Administrators in "The District

Office." The way these men knew how to work their school districts and to be leaders of their communities were examples of diplomacy. These men were tactful with the all-White officials who governed all Black schools in the county. The officials saw to it that services rendered for the White schools were always on time and bountiful. Then the "negro" schools got what was left unless the principals knew how to "find" solutions.

Conversations were about their adventurous week that sounded like, "Can you top this?" I think that all three of my uncles were Sunday School Superintendents. The absolute rule was that all card games stopped every Saturday no later than 11:50 P.M because we did not play cards on Sunday.

My dad and uncles knew how to get "bees with honey." Their Saturday night conversations always included times to celebrate how they finessed to get the materials and supplies they needed for their schools.

They were leaders who encouraged parents to let their children get an education. They urged teachers to be responsible for teaching subject matters and life issues. They saw to it that the students were participants in cultural excursions and athletic activities. How rewarding it might have been if these generations could have gleaned wisdom from their great "Grindaddy Chick."

If only my dad's great grandsons could have met him and gleaned from his wisdom.

By 1967 the Black high schools and their principals changed. Most Black high schools became middle and elementary schools, and Black principals were sent to some of them. White high schools and their principals remained intact.

The courage of these men was astounding. They were not frontline civil rights leaders; these men were front line educators who kept students in school and out of jail. They helped to finance many high school graduates' college years. I can still remember the names of some graduates from Eastern High School moving into our home to attend college.

Many Black educators gave financial support from their meager wages to Civil Rights leaders who lost their jobs. The tension was incredible. I remember the Black Teachers' Education Association in my hometown finding creative ways to get funds to local Civil Rights Organizations. Had these contributors been reported to their employers, they would have been fired. My parents used pseudonyms to become lifelong members of the National Association for the Advancement of Colored People (NAACP).

V #13 Our Robed Visitors

I never understood why grown White men had to dress up in White robes used for baptism, then, put hoods over their heads. If the intention were to help Black people, then why the outfit? Why hide your face? Why burn crosses; and why carry burning torches? I may have already said that I attended Mather, which was a boarding school. It was run by the United Methodist Church (then, the White sect of the Methodist Episcopal Church) during my high school years.

One summer, a group of our school mates went to a sister school in Tennessee to make repairs. It was a school for White children run by the same denomination as ours. In return, some White students came to our school to do the same type of community service.

In the fall of that year, when all of us returned, we had intruders. They were not visitors. You guessed it. The Ku Klux Klansmen surrounded our campus one night and burned crosses on the grounds around our buildings. Nothing about their intrusion indicated that they wanted to find some unemployed Black people to help.

Nothing about their intrusion indicated that they wanted to find some unemployed Black people to help.

V #14 Moma and Aunt Lottie

Here is a story told about moms and TB's sister, Lottie. They went to Sumter to pay their farm taxes. When they got to the tax office, it was empty except for the White woman who received their payments. The woman looked up from her desk and said, "You girls stand over there until I call you." There were some empty chairs in the office, so Momma and Aunt Lottie sat down.

About an hour later, the lady called them up and scolded them for sitting. She said, with disdain, "Didn't I tell you girls to stand?" Momma looked at her and said, "We saw no girls. The chairs, paid for by our taxes, were empty, so the two of us ladies sat down. We are here to pay our taxes that also help to pay your salary." They paid and walked out smiling with each other. These Black "sistuhs" were courageous entrepreneurs. They owned their farmlands.

V #15 Look for the Light!

You have probably figured out that Moma (my grandmother) was my bonding agent. She was my human anchor. Before I moved into town with my parents, I spent most of my bonding time with her every day. I went to school with her. She and I ate ice cream and her homemade tea cookies every night while we read the Bible together. I went to school with her. Every Saturday morning, she drove to "town" (Sumter) and took me to Mrs. Adelaide McDonald's house for piano lessons. Momma took me to Sunday School and church, to her Senior Missionary meetings and to The Sumter and The Wateree Baptist Associations. I went to the Women's Baptist State Convention of S.C. with her.

Whenever we attended these and other functions, she found a reason for me to play a hymn or two. When she discovered that I could sing, she volunteered me to sing. If I seemed hesitant, she would say, "Mind Tommye; God gave you these gifts. Use them for Him and He'll bless you. Listen to your momma, now."

I went to the Northern and Mid-West States with her. Momma took me to the Sumter County Fair each year. The years when I was 7-10 years old, she made me raise chickens to carry to the Fair to enter them into a contest. However, I never placed in the contest because my chickens were too small. Nevertheless, rarely did she go anywhere without me. I followed her foot-to-foot.

I must interject something here. You might wonder, where was my mother? She was with us. Let me tell you. My very young, loving, and more reserved mother was right here. After her divorce, we lived with Moma. Somehow, she understood that living there would give me a life filled with love tenfold!

Failure was not in my mother's vocabulary, either. She did not allow her marriage at such a young age and the subsequent divorce to keep her from succeeding as a great parent or as a professional woman.

Moya completed her bachelor's degree at Morris College, and earned her master's degree from Temple University, Philadelphia, PA. There is no doubt, she was a responsible single parent who took care of the two of us on her salary as a public-school teacher. She remarried when I was eight years old.

Family, another great attribute in the Black family was taking care of family, which meant extended family as well. I can remember when our house would be bulging over with people. I remember Moma saying, "The more the merrier, and she meant just that. Her nieces and nephews lived with her periodically. Family was a badge of honor in the Black community.

Moma was equally determined to be a civic and community leader and activist. She did it all. And I was following her step by step!!! (In the South we called it "foot to foot.") Our Matriarch worked hard on the farm and as a public-school teacher as she did in all of her myriad leadership endeavors. It remains a mystery to me how she paid off a $25,000.00 mortgage within 15 years during the depression years, 1929-1941, only four years after TB died. I can still hear her telling me, "Baby, the Lord will provide. I know."

The story, among the many Moma shared that impacted my life most, was the one about a dream she had when life was most dismal for her. She remembered being in her early thirties. In the depth of her despair, this devout Christian specifically asked God to show her how she would get the fertilizer and soda needed for the farm, send her children to school, and pay her mortgage bill. She said she asked Him to give her a sign that she would not default on either of these things. She also asked for comfort because she was very distressed.

Though her singing voice was non-descript, this lady would belt out a hymn in a minute! She had no rhythm, so when she sang and clapped, they were never coordinated. Anyway, Moma said she sang the hymn, Count Your Blessings and went on to sleep feeling very calm.

She said that an angel of light guided her while she slept. Her dream that night was that some White men came to her house, dragged her out, dug a deep, very narrow hole in a cemetery, put her in it, and covered her up. She thought that she would die. As she lay there in the blackest of darkness, as she called it, she began to imagine what things would be like for her young children after her death. Then, she said that there was a nudge in her spirit that made her look up. The hole widened. She could move for the first time. She did. Then she looked up. What she saw was a pin light beaming that guided her upward. When she reached the top of the hole, an angel told her not to worry anymore.

The next morning, Moma said that she went to her bank to ask for a two-day extension on her bill. As she stepped inside the door of the bank, a folded piece of money was lying on the floor. She picked it up, gave it to the White lady who always served her, and waited to make her request.

The teller looked up at her, unfolded what was a $100-bill, and handed it back to her. She told momma that the only name on the bill is Benjamin Franklin, and he would not be coming back to claim it.

100 percent authentic

"Whenever life gets you down," Moma said, "Listen to me, Baby, look up and see the light. No matter what, never forget to count your blessings."

Trusting the Light

The light of our ancestral indelible Spirit

"Whenever life gets you down," Moma said, "Listen to me, Baby, look up and see the light. No matter what, never forget to count your blessings."

Segue to Section Three

Dr. Ralph W. Canty

Dr. Ralph W. County is a national and an international clergy icon among other great attributes such as: entrepreneur, pastor, writer, politician, and civic servant. Very early during the Civil Rights Movement of the 60s his leadership and servant's heart were evidenced. He was a teenager who courageously sat down to be served with Mrs. Gloria Montgomery Jenkins and Dr. John Calvin Nelson in the first major chain hotel in our hometown of Sumter, SC. This began what became a notable segment of the National Civil Rights Movement in our town.

His message of love called the <u>Leveling the Playing Field</u> is worthy of sharing. Dr. Canty writes,

> "When reading earlier this morning about the Pope's decision to bar same-sex marriages and his accompanying statement," God cannot bless sin," I was moved. Which led me to ask, how can a church plagued with countless documented cases of gay practices be so intolerant? Especially when so many of those cases have yet to be addressed by the papacy.
>
> Mind you, these are instances of same-gender relationships in the worst context, involving the innocent who were, in many cases, too immature to be "consenting partners."
>
> This conversation may be uncomfortable for some of us, and we do not have to engage in any serious discussion about it. But it is important that we begin to look at our inconsistencies. I agree, God does not bless sin, but the term is included, it implies all. The sin we condone and the sin we condemn. Oh yes, we are very partial, biased, and subjective about sin. Sin that is usual and customary to us is acceptable, but sin that is outside the norm of our experience is unacceptable. It is indeed conflicting to be a culprit and to judge. I pray to God that we would all, at least, fine tune our own imperfections and encourage those endeared to us to do likewise before we pass judgment on others and send them to hell.

Hard Work, Intelligence, and Benevolence

There are three qualities our ancestors practiced. First was physical hard work, for their Relay to Liberty and Justice. Second, the continuation of education and civic responsibility while Continuing to Rise. The third quality that was required for the utmost success of the other two is called benevolence. My greatest desire is for people who understand that benevolence is not for the faint- at-heart. It is a virtue that requires a tough resolve to complete challenges even when giving up is reasonable. It tasks us to always respect humanity. I want to dispel the misnomer that benevolence is a "soft" emotion. On the contrary benevolence is a discipline of quiet rather than rage. It might have been the skill our ancestors employed as an emotional and sometimes physical transfer to a place of pause before responding.

The Power of Benevolence

Benevolence is the indestructible composite of dedication, integrity, love, respect, responsibility, determination, commitment, and excellence. Black people have always known that benevolence is manifested through a character trait for the charitable actions it produces. Unlike kindness, it does not expect a return in- kind. Our ancestors believed that benevolence was one of the strongest and most enduring character traits in all humanity. They believed that it is incubated in the heart as a part of who we are. It was also believed to be an inner strength that forges courage and defies giving in to evil.

The functions of benevolence are persistence, strength, bravery, and caring simultaneously. We will examine the portrayal of the power of benevolence as the indestructible place where dedication, integrity, love, respect, responsibility, determination, commitment, and excellence function.

We are amazing people! White supremacists remain perplexed and angered because it is impossible to degrade one who refuses to be degraded. Black people continue to rise despite attempts to keep us in bondage! The infusion of the indelible spirit is inherent. We are taught that winning is defined by "not giving up." Even when hurt or depressed, most Black people are neither bound by a mental script regarding mistreatment nor unclear of its existence.

The weapons of information and honoring ourselves and all humanity have netted greater strides to our community. In the essay The Race, attributed to Dr. D.H. "Dee" Groberg, he shares an important lesson that I hope will become etched into the memory of each of you. Then, promise yourselves that you will share it with other members of our Black family. It is called The Race....

The Race

Whenever I start to hang my head in front of failure's face, my downward fall is broken by the memory of a race.

A children's race, young boys, young men; how I remember well, excitement sure, but also fear, it was not hard to tell.

They all lined up so full of hope, each thought to win that race or tie for first, or if not that, at least take second place.

Their parents watched from off the side, each cheering for their son, and each boy hoped to show his folks that he would be the one.

The whistle blew and off they flew, like chariots of fire, to win, to be the hero there, was each young boy's desire.

One boy in particular, whose dad was in the crowd, was running in the lead and thought "My dad will be so proud."

But as he sped down the field and crossed a shallow dip, the little boy who thought he'd win, lost his step, and slipped.

Trying hard to catch himself, his arms flew everyplace, and during the laughter of the crowd he fell flat on his face.

As he fell, his hope fell too; he couldn't win it now. Humiliated, he just wished to disappear somehow.

But as he fell his dad stood up and showed his anxious face, which to the boy so clearly said, "Get up and win that race!"

He quickly rose, no damage done, behind a bit that is all, and ran with all his mind and might to make up for his fall.

So anxious to restore himself, to catch up and to win, his mind went faster than his legs. He slipped and fell again.

He wished that he had quit before with one disgrace. "I'm hopeless as a runner now, I shouldn't try to race. "But through the laughing crowd he searched and found his father's face with a steady look that said again," Get up and win that race!"

So, he jumped up to try again, ten yards behind the last." If I'm going to gain those yards, he thought, "I've got to run really fast!"

Exceeding everything he had, he regained eight, then ten… but trying hard to catch the lead, he slipped and fell again.

Defeat! He lay there silently. A tear dropped from his eye. "There is no sense running anymore! Three strikes I am out! Why try?

I have lost, so what's the use?" He thought. "I'll live in disgrace." But then he thought about his dad, who soon he would have to face.

"Get up," an echo sounded low, "You have not lost at all, for all you must do to win is rise each time you fall.

Chapter Seventeen - Endurance

Get up!" THE ECHO URGED HIM ON, "Get up and take your place! You were not meant for failure here. Get up and win that race!"

So, up he rose to run once more, refusing to forfeit, and he resolved that win or lose, at least HE WOULDN'T QUIT.

So far behind the others now, the most he had ever been, still he gave it all he had and ran like he could win.

Three times he'd fallen stumbling; three times he rose again. Too far behind to hope to win, he still ran to the end.

They cheered another boy who crossed the line and won first place, head high and proud and happy – no falling, no disgrace.

But, when the fallen youngster crossed the line, in last place, the crowd gave him a greater cheer for finishing the race.

And even though he came in last with head bowed, low, and unproud, you would have thought he'd won the race, to listen to the crowd.

And to his dad he sadly said, "I didn't do so well." To me, you won, his father said, "You rose each time you fell,"

And now when things seem dark, bleak, and difficult to face, the memory of the little boy helps me in my own race.

For all of life is like that race, with ups and downs and all. And all you must do to win is rise each time you fall.

And when depression and despair shout in my face, another voice within me says, "Get up and win that race!"

Continuing to Rise

"Life is not a holiday but an education. One eternal lesson for all of us: to each of us how better we should love."

Barbara Jordan

"The kind of beauty I want most is the hard-to-get kind that comes from within-strength, courage, dignity."

Ruby Dee

SECTION THREE

OPERATING IN THE RIGHT VENUE: Healing our Nation

Ancestors

Along thecenturies, my ancestorshave worked, learned, and taught.
Somehad it easy; most did not.
Many cried, and others died while trying to make life better for their children and their children's, children's children.

Today, I wonder if what I've done and what I've taught will make any difference to those of my family that has grown to include the world.
How many will cry because someone died a senseless death, a sacrifice to the new slavery that binds us to addictions and to material things?
I wonder just what the missing links in the chain of humanity that has preceded me to think about what we think and where wego and with whom we talk and how we obsess aboutthat which, in the long run, will lie in tatters before we're debt-free.
What mustthesepredecessorsthink whenthey see the lack of love, we show for ourselves and for others when we practice, "Me first" and violence on a grand Scale?
Do they wonder if all they endured went for naught? or do they see a brighter day coming about which we know not?
1

Barbara D. Parks Lee

CHAPTER EIGHTEEN

General "Can't" Is Dead

"To withhold judgment, condemnation, and unforgiveness is to act generously, and, in God's economy, it is rewarded with the same kind of benevolence – pressed down, shaken together, and running over."

Luke 6:37-38 New International Translation

General "Can" killed General "Can't"

The point was clear. The position of defeat I'd taken had to be revised, and I had to complete the task at hand.

We talked about the inherent strength and most used strategy of our ancestors being benevolent. When I think of our nation's current defiant attitude regarding the social disadvantages we face, I think of the years and accomplishments of our ancestors and many ordinary members of our community who are now doing extraordinary things. We must become more diligent with sharing lessons about fathers overcoming.

Family, we have never stopped our Relay to Liberty and Justice. Despite setbacks from the "tacks in our crystal stairs," we are determined to move forward. Like the little train mounting the steep hill with heavy cargo, we move forward, saying, "I think I can; I know I can." Moma always told us that we do what we tell ourselves we can do. She would take that little fist and hit her forehead as she told me to repeat this poem after her.

If You Think You Can by Walter D. Wintle

If you think you are beaten, you are. If you think you dare not, you don't. If you like to win, but you think You can't It is almost a certain you won't.

If you think you'll lose, you're lost.

For out in the world we find, Success begins with the state of mind.

If you think you're outclassed, you are.

You've got to think high to rise,

You've got to be sure of yourself before You can ever win a prize.

Life's battles don't always go to The stronger or faster

man, But sooner or later Life's battles don't always go to the stronger or faster man, But sooner or later the man who wins -

Is the man WHO THINKS HE CAN.

Continuing to Rise

Benevolence in Action Again

Here are three great Black men, you may know. They lay hold to determine and succeed despite the odds they confront. Their lives are beacons of light for our generations to follow. These men demonstrate the strength of character always needed to be humane and dedicated to life greater than self. Here are some of the same ancestral DNA of our fore parents' qualities they carry.

Integrity: "No matter how educated, talented, rich, or fabulous you believe you are, how you treat people ultimately tells all."

Congressman James E. Clyburn: Historian, Civil Rights Leader, Two-term Majority Whip of the United States House of Representatives, and Present 2023 House assistant Democratic Leader

A Hallmark of Benevolence

It is again time to honor and to pay tribute to a man who inspires many people. He is United States Congressman James E. Clyburn, also known as Jim Clyburn. Jim represents what it means to identify oneself through professional preparation, character, and commitment.

Mr. Clyburn honored a commitment that everyone could have understood had he declined. In the summer of 2019, my high school class was having a celebration. As an alumnus of Mather, we asked Jim to be our Saturday morning guest and speaker. The week of our celebration Jim's wife Emily died. In the midst of preparing to memorialize her the next day, Jim honored his word.

He came and spoke to our gathering, our class, and other schoolmates. He demonstrated integrity as the hallmark of benevolence.

History will label Jim Clyburn as one of this nation's greatest historians and politicians. His voice of reason serves his people as well as his country with dignity and integrity. He spoke to our classmates and other schoolmates from his heart about our Democracy. He reminded us of our responsibility. This Congressman urged us not to forget who we are. Then he spoke of the imperative need for us to use the power of the ballot and the power of our collective voice.

History will probably record the opinion of this political and civil rights leader as one whose influence propelled positive change in his home State of South Carolina and this nation. His single endorsement changed the trajectory of the U.S. Presidential race of 2021 when he announced his support for Joseph R. Biden.

Chapter Eighteen - General "Can't" Is Dead

The Congressman's address to our class and other Matherites that day was the highlight of our celebration. My only regret is that multitudes of people missed the experience of his strength of character under such personal duress. The fidelity of commitment to his word continues to demonstrate his integrity and leadership.

No forms of violence will waylay this political giant's integrity and commitment to freedom and liberty. In his book "Blessed Experience," he tells what it means to be a Southern young Black man in the Jim Crow Era. It is no surprise that Jim received the highest civilian honor from President Joe Biden May 2024. This is an historical badge of honor befitting for America' great statesman Congressman James E. (Jim) Clyburn.

LeBron James's championship social and civic change looms as impressive as his record as the all-time point scoring champion for the National Basketball League (NBA).

Dedication: the quality of being committed to a task or a purpose People's passion and unwavering determination can conquer anything.

My children tease me because I always say that I love LeBron James. I mean it as a deep respect for his leadership, courage, and care for humanity. One day, while watching the HGTV Network, a lady was renovating a house when "in" walked LeBron. He helped her with the renovations. His commitment to help others included, in this instance, buying homes and placing Black families in them.

This man, one of the greatest athletes of all time, played basketball for his home team for years. The franchise and city made far more billions of dollars from his talent than he received in his multimillion-dollar salary and bonuses. When LeBron left his hometown, they criticized him as a traitor and treated him as if he had turned his back on those who gave him his start. Never forget the financial rewards they received from his talent. This young man went forward, played on a team that won a National Championship, and returned as a professional basketball player on the same team in the same hometown that scorned him.

LeBron grew up in meager circumstances, worked hard, and became one of his sport's highest regarded men. Over the years, this entrepreneur has started a school, upgraded communities and p272their services, and has become a social activist who speaks up about the politics of our time. Not only has he become vocal, but he is dedicated to effecting change, starting with his community.

This innovative young man is an excellent example of forgiveness conquering adversity. LeBron is a celebrity mouthpiece that encourages people to vote and to rise above the unfair hands dealt them in this nation. He is using his influence to help young people understand the value of how we are interwoven into the fabric of citizenship. His dedication to humanity is inspiring and another example of benevolence.

Determination: firmness of purpose; resoluteness the wake-up call to humanity makes positive changes in our lives.

Judge Ronald A. Wilson

Judge Ronald A. Wilson is a distinguished Tribal Court Judge, Elder, and Mediator serving two indigenous nations, bringing extensive expertise in restorative justice to his roles. Formerly, he held pivotal positions as the Vice President of Equity & Inclusion at The University of Arizona, Chief Diversity Officer at Edinboro University, Executive Dean of Porreco College, and Crime Prevention Specialist for the Pima County Prosecutor's Office. Notably, Judge Wilson's community leadership journey began in 2002 when he was appointed Chief Presiding Judge at the age of 33 for the City of South Tucson in southern Arizona, marking a historic milestone as the first Chief Magistrate of African American descent in Arizona's history.

Judge Wilson is originally from Springfield, Massachusetts, and was reared in a foster home, where he lived for 16 years. His foster parents were incredibly kind and loving people who, during his time in their care, fostered over 400 children. The home always had at least 20 children, coming from a variety of racial and ethnic backgrounds. It was in this environment that Judge Wilson learned the importance of integrity and empathy, values that have guided him throughout his distinguished career.

While in foster care, Judge Wilson was reared as an Orthodox, Roman Catholic and often considered pursuing a calling as a priest or a monk. However, his path took a different turn after reading The Autobiography of Malcolm X while in high school. This powerful book inspired him to pursue a career in law and social justice, setting him on the path that would define his life's work.

Throughout his career, Judge Wilson has garnered numerous accolades and honors, including a Fellowship at the Urban Law and Public Policy Institute and Senior Fellowship at the Center for American Culture and Ideas. He is a graduate of the FBI's Citizen Academy, recipient of the Martin Luther King Jr. Drum Major Award, the Rosa Parks Living History Makers Award, and the Asa Philip Randolph Social Justice Award among many others. He is a former National Chair of the American Bar Association's Judicial Division Mental Health Court Committee, Faculty for the Arizona Supreme Court Judicial College, Editor of the Judges Journal, founder of the National Justice Foundation, President of the Southern Arizona Mentoring Coalition, and member of the National Organization of Black Law Enforcement Executives.

In addition to his judicial duties, Judge Wilson is deeply involved in charitable endeavors, serving as a current or former advisor, mentor, and board member for various local and international organizations, including the United Way, Big Brothers Big Sisters, Casey Family Programs, Devereux, the NAACP, the Center for the Philosophy of Freedom, and United Nations.

Judge Wilson hosted and planned in coordination with the National Center for State Courts, the first statewide conference on Restorative Justice in Arizona. He was also responsible for establishing some of the first Homeless Courts, Veterans Courts, Community Courts, Drug Courts, and Mental Health Courts in Arizona.

With a commitment to education, Judge Wilson has taught college courses on constitutional law, American slavery, criminal procedure, Jim Crow, the First Amendment, the civil rights movement, Title IX, gangs as an American enterprise, urban problems, effective mentoring, and American history. He is a Department of Homeland Security certified incident commander, transformative mediator, and arbitrator.

Judge Wilson holds a Bachelor of Arts degree in Black Studies from Syracuse University and a Doctor of Jurisprudence from Northeastern University School of Law. He is a member of Omega Psi Phi Fraternity, Sigma Pi Phi Fraternity, and the Sovereign Military Order of the Temple of Jerusalem.

Perseverance: persist in doing something despite difficulty or delay in achieving success.

Katherine Johnson
Mathematician

Dorothy Vaughn
Computer Specialist & Engineer

Mary Jackson
Engineer

Features of Grit

Everyone who has Smart Televisions and Telephones, for instant communications ought to be sure to view the movie <u>Hidden Figures</u>. Just as our ancestors were the first to give us commodities for our economic system, these three ladies proved that courage and desire are necessary qualities for success. That was launched in 1957. Though their work was imperative, they were not acknowledged by name. Because they preceded the machine called "Computer," they were huddled into a room together. Each worker was referred to as, "Computer" at the NASA Space Center in Cape Canaveral, Florida.

It is accurate to say that America's first space launch might not have happened were it not for their grit and perseverance. One of the noteworthy characteristics of these women is that they were all ambitious, smart, and competent. They exhibited magnificent work ethics when snubbed and initially overlooked for promotions. Their egos paled in comparison to their determination to succeed.

Black women have always provided steadfast and responsible value to the United States. From nannies to the present Vice-President of these United States, we have broken glass ceilings directly or because of our insistence. Our influence on White America is astounding.

Katherine Johnson, Mathematician; Dorothy Vaughn, Computer Engineer; and Mary Jackson, Engineer all proved that the substance of their determination was to do their best work at their jobs at Langley Air Force Base, VA even when they were discriminated against and met with a host of other adversities. Each of these ladies rose to acclaim during this mission because of their direct contributions to the specific project. These ladies had grit, a firmness of character, and a spirit of perseverance which allowed them to achieve despite difficulties and delayed recognition. It is possible that the first flight in space would not have been accomplished at that time were it not for their genius and generosity.

There are hopes and light at the end of our tunnel. These ladies remained undaunted even when called "computer" until their contributions to the mission distinguished them by their names. Immediately after being called "computer" they were called by their first names.

When the first United States launch into space occurred, these geniuses had Gained respect from the White employees. They were given the title "Ms." This was in deference to them. In this White European male environment, they changed the reference to these three ladies from "Computer." They learned that without their genius, the first U.S. Flight into space with humans would never have happened in 1962 without them. The ladies were benevolent; they never wanted anything except the right to do the quality of work they were capable of doing.

There are many stories just like these which prove that our Benevolent character forbids Systemic Racism to be a deterrent to our success. Is it time for you to begin journaling or drafting your story?

CHAPTER NINETEEN

Our Best Selves

"The best self is wise, caring, and fearless... there is a big difference in every aspect of our lives when we settle the notion to persevere toward excellence with integrity to the end."

Thomasina M. Portis

What They call Us - What We call Ourselves

Many people thought that the description we were given by the people who enslaved us, was our truth. The truth is, we came into a country with another native tongue, and another culture and were given the unfavorable nomenclature "n   r." Even today this term implies dehumanization and the denigration of intelligence, so according to the Whiter supremacists, we remain an inferior person. In her send edition of <u>Post Traumatic Syndrome Disorder</u> (PTSD) Dr. Joy DeGruy tells us the difference in enslavement in Africa and America.

Our ancestors came from an advanced civilization, and about 54 countries, that they ruled for thousands of years, and were brought into a new developing country on the North American Continent. These multiple cultures were also distinctly different from the emerging culture in this new nation. Our fore parents were not ignorant. It remains unknown just how much intelligence and genius came over on the ships from Africa to America. Among them were multi-generational leaders such as national and local politicians, war and policing strategists, legislative and judicial officers, scientists, mathematicians, literary and fine artists, astrologists, architects, orators, college professors, engineers, etc.

Many of the enslaved people were not illiterate. According to the United Nations, there are 54 countries in Africa today. Each of these countries has a different language and culture. On any given ship to America, there may have been people from several African countries linked together in chains and thrown into the bottom of the ships. Pregnant women delivered babies linked in chains. People contracted deadly viruses linked in chained. Men, women, and children eliminated bodily wastes linked in chains.

Two Pejoratives – N----r and Minority

The North American Continent was a developing continent when these experts arrived. The same year that the influx of Black people was brought in chains and sickness, the slave owner declared all of them inferior and treated the masses as if they were animals. They wrote laws that entitled White people to declare our differences inferior and to consider us ignorant.

The attempt to demoralize us came White supremacists demand that we be classified as and called "N-- r. This term" replaced the African names of our ancestors. The White supremacists considered the enslaved to be "minority" beings rather than human beings. This gave them the authority to treat our fore parents as chattel and animals. "Nr" and "minority" remain the inferred belief through the legal policies that are legislating many rulings today. White supremacists still find rulings that mean N -- r, three-fifths of a person, pickaninny, etc., to Black and now Brown people. (The refusal to pass the Congressman John R. Lewis Voting Rights Act is an example.)

The terms I have shared have psychological power. When they are internalized, they mold our beliefs about ourselves. In the Movie Roots, the character named Kunte Kinte ran away from his slave owners because he did not want the American name "Toby." An old Black man named Fiddler watched Kunte Kinte run away, get caught, and then receive a more severe punishment each time he ran. One day after being brutally beaten This young man sat under the tree with Fiddler bleeding after a brutal whipping. He complained about his new name. Fiddler told Kunta Kinta, "It doesn't matter what they call you, what matters, is what you call yourself." This is a profound statement. Throughout this conversation, imagine yourself moving through the Relay to Freedom and Equality. Think of the times that you have faced discrediting nomenclatures or innuendos.

"Our Rights - Our Responsibility"

I am a Black woman who was a participant, not a student-leader, in the Civil Rights Movement of the 1960s. My name appears on the jail records as documentation of my arrests. It is gratifying to know that somewhere along the line, my fore parents and members of my Black community taught me that there are times when responding to others is a significant factor in decision making and personal behavior. I was taught and strive to live by these principles:

There are causes great enough for sacrifice, even with death. Each of us is endowed with the potential to hate the sin while loving the sinner. There are times when principle will override position. Neither a profession nor its title must ever override self-worth. Hope and love are attributes that the faint-at-heart cannot model.

First Photo: Students behind a fence heading into The White Castle, a jail that had not been opened since 1925. This was when I knew that I could die for the cause of freedom.
Second photo: Women of different decades were also jailed.

I, Too, Sing America: White Supremacy Has Never Stopped Black People From Continuing to Rise

In the 1800s Wiley Jones, from Pine Bluff, Arkansas, was one of the wealthiest Black men in his State. He was a Civil Rights activist who helped more than eight hundred enslaved people escaped to Canada through the Underground Railroad.

Chapter Nineteen - Our Best Selves

In 1838, Bass Reeves was the first Black Cowboy. The Lone Ranger series was patterned after his life. He was a wealthy man who learned to speak the language of several Native American Tribes. This deputized Ranger killed 3,000 outlaws.

In 1848, enslaved Bridget "Biddy" Mason walked over 1,700 miles from Utah (then Mexico) to Los Angeles behind a 300- wagon caravan of Mormons where she settled and became a wealthy realtor. Upon her death, she was worth three million dollars. In 2023 her wealth equals ten billion 374 million dollars

Between 1869 and 1870, Joseph Rainy, S.C. Republican, was the first Black U.S. Congressman in the 41st and 42nd Congress where he presided over the House of Representatives.

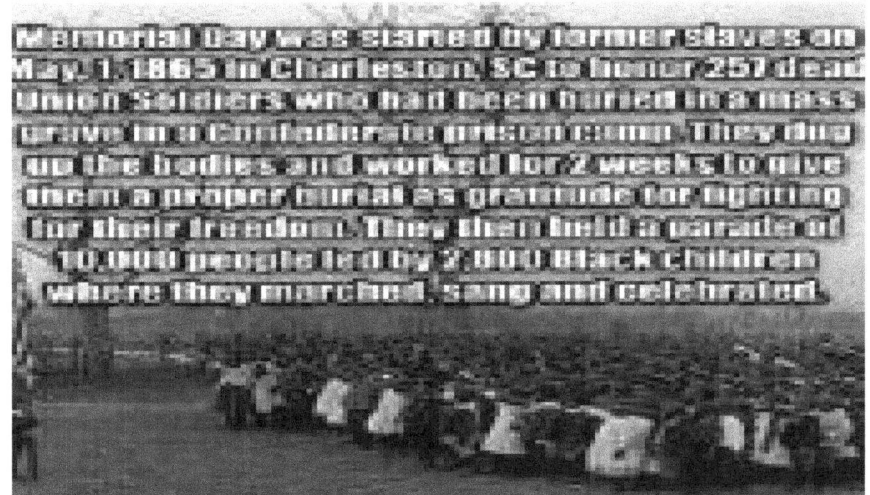

In 1865 Black people in Charleston, South Carolina started Memorial Day.

Continuing to Rise

From late 1800s thru early 1900s, 107 Historically Black Colleges and Universities came into existence because of the American Black Churches' financial sacrifices.

In 1915, Frederick Patterson of C.R. Patterson & Sons entered the ranks of automobile manufacturers, launching the first Patterson automobile.

In 1940, Bayard Rustin formed the first National Civil Rights March in Washington DC for jobs and social justice.

In 1950, Dr. Charles R. Drew, the first Director of the American Red Cross after developing blood transfusions, died from a car accident after being denied a blood transfusion in Burlington, North Carolina.

In 1963, the March on Washington, D.C. that focused on civil and voting rights, as well as labor, was organized by A. Philip Randolph and Bayard Rustin. It featured Dr. Martin Luther King, Jr.

Continuing to Rise

Chapter Nineteen - Our Best Selves

In 1992, this woman, Dr. Mae Jemison became the first Black astronaut to go into space.

In 2013 Black Lives Matter, a global movement, was begun by these three women.

In 2018, Stacey Abrams was the first Black woman to run for the governor of the State of Georgia

The Founding Documents provoke Consternation

The truth of who we are has become a consternation to the White supremacists because of the Preambles to The Declaration of Independence and The U.S. Constitution. Provocation comes with the term "We." These founding documents were written by White men who never dreamed that segregation would ever be abolished, and these documents would provide a Rule of Law for their White American Democracy only. The Framers, from the South or North, could not have imagined that Black people would have the audacity to run a Relay to Freedom and Equality for all humanity.

Diversity, Equity, and Inclusion (DEI)

The rise of Diversity, Equity, and Inclusion (DEI) has caused White women and the Gay community to be included with us our Relay. The American mainstream requires the White supremacists to include using the compromises inherit in the U.S. Constitution to keep us stalemated. These legislators and jurors are frantically making every attempt to destroy the

Continuing to Rise

present Democratic process that was originally written for them to possess power and privilege. DEI forces them to destroy our present Democracy.

In Chapter Two, I shared my truth about segregation and admonish you to learn the difference between an issue and a system. A system can be considered the structural foundation of our government. Issues can be considered as the floors we dislike and demand to be changed. Democracy is the American system. LBGTQ+ community presents issues they want the system to change. If there is no system, then issues become moot. We must be as diligent about knowing the machinations of our American Democratic system as we are adamant about changing issues. Both are urgent and important in that order. Our system belongs to us, and the sitting President can be held responsible for its demise. We, the people, are responsible.

No One defines Us But Us

Family, here is our truth. No one can define who I am but me. No one can define us as an ethnic community, but us. I encourage us to never take our focus away from this leg of our Relay to Freedom and Equality. As we journey through our conversation, you will witness that this fight with White supremacy is not new nor is it over.

This leg of our relay is to disavow ensure that all people are treated equally in all areas of the democratic process. Now, we must increase our presence as politicians on the local, state, and national levels. This leg of our relay invites us to turn away from voting for other ethnic representation in our government. The time has come in 2024 our Relay to Freedom and Equality must be to increase our presence in the legislative and judicial branches of government. This must begin to happen on the local, state, and national levels.

Our second and third generations into the American mainstream are afforded greater educational and economic opportunities to successfully live in this American mainstream. It may be that Systemic Racism exists because since the ratification of the U.S. Constitution, White men of European decent have dominated our political and judicial components of this American Democratic system. As we consider national and global opportunities for employment, here are considering opportunities in these components of this present-day American political arena.

Family, when we become more actively involved as citizens of America, includes becoming more pro-active in politics. Our ideas of who represents our community in these components of the American democratic system will turn around from "them" to "us." Black and Brown people, "Too, sing, America." Politics is our responsibility as American citizens. It is also the only way to the ethos of our legal and judicial systems from the White American Ideology to one that represents all American citizens. We can do this.

Our Country

The fanaticism and fear of losing the rightful place of White supremacy are everywhere. We are a people who have faced horror. Despite this intense reality we triumph by moving onward. My conversation with you journeys us through many struggles and celebrations. I have this conversation with you because we say that we want to change America's legal and judicial systems to provide equality and equity for all ethnicities.

The ethos of the legal and judicial components of this current American system of Democracy must remove the ethos of White supremacy and replace it with one that represents our local, state, national, and international duties to our country and our international allies. We must join with the Brown community's representatives to change the composition of these systems. Since the U.S. Constitution was ratified, the judicial and legal components of this democratic system remain dominated by White men of European descent.

I challenge you not to be too afraid or too angry to channel your anger into productivity and believe that no one will stop us from continuing our Relay to Liberty and Freedom for all humanity. We recognize the deliberate intention of the White supremacist ideology to prove that we are subordinate.

We are not an Intellectually "Slow" People

There is a distinct difference between intelligence and lack of information. Our people have not done well on the Standardized Test mainly because we have not been in schools (public or HBCUs), or community environments subsumed with this this conversation. The declaration of Black students being "slow" and "lack the IQ of White students" is a perpetuation through the absence of Economics studies, Logic, Critical Thinking, Debates, etc. These are the things that provide the language and vicarious experiences that prepare all students for a successful life in America's mainstream. Many American-born White students, on the other hand, live in generational communities whose training began almost after the cradle and continued throughout their educational experiences and their community. This was both formal and vicarious learning in their community.

Where are We Headed?

This question is posited to those of us who have become members of the mainstream culture. Today, members of the Black community are being educated in what were once all-White institutions. Now, let's learn something about how the attempt to divide our community was built upon a principle of divide and conquer.

Erbie Suggs writer for AJC.com said, in "The Talented Tenth" Dr. W. E.B. DuBois argued that the best way to uplift the race was to bolster the efforts and education of the brightest and most talented who would then bring along the others." Dr. DuBois' notion might have worked except the Talented Tenth in 2024, the Black educated members of our community have proven that we are not limited to the talented tenth concept. Even among our educational leaders, the brights and most talented, far exceed one tenth of our people. Our deficiency is the lack of opportunity in generations past to be given the same curricula of our White counterparts from public schools through HBCUs.

Ethnic Separationists Who uphold Authoritarianism.

This ideology of ethnic separation is for the White people who despise Democracy. Taking the oath to uphold the Constitution while trying to dismantle it is a simplified version of a complex matter. It is fair to say that many people in the upper class, especially the owners of major corporations, hold conservative views that help to advance their wealth and power. I will not say that they all are White supremacists and disposers of Democracy. However, history will name some wealthy donors who allegedly bribed Supreme Court Justices and the members of The House of Representatives, in particular, who spent more time seeking evidence of unlawful behaviors, rather than attending to matters for which they are responsible and which they swore to uphold.

The American society has never had an equal playing field based on the academics and all other experiential commonalities. Only then would the meritocracy system become a fair one. The determination of Black intelligence by White research per Herrnstein's definition of IQ is a lie and racist! Even today, the strive for human equality does not bode well with White Supremacists and a meager number of people from other ethnicities.

Generational Inequities

Our generational inequity exists through the perpetuation of the White supremacy lie that refers to Black people as a sub-human and intellectually inferior ethnicity. This misinformation is inferred by the Framers of the U.S. Constitution. The writings of Thomas Jefferson, Abraham Lincoln, and other national leaders throughout the history of this nation reiterated the need for the suppression of Black people.

Poor People's March   Depressed Housing   Living where possible

Framers of the Constitution

Leaders' Messages

Leaders' messages sanction beliefs and solidify behaviors, whether good or evil. It is logical to conclude that the perpetuation of the White Supremacy Ideology might have lost its vitality and strength if there had been leaders to denounce it as un-American. Because the nature of people is to follow the message from their leaders means that our community needs to become very observant and careful listeners to the messages the come from the people we place in legislative positions. This reality might be an impetus for more Black people to take public offices in civic and legislative issues. This idea will be revisited later during our conversation. Many White U.S. Statesmen have perpetuated the ideas that Black people are inferior human beings. Their common theme reiterates separation of Black and White people and their belief in White superiority.

Thomas Jefferson-U.S. President 1801-1809

Thomas Jefferson was highly revered for working towards the principles of freedom. Simultaneously, he owned several hundreds of enslaved people. His Black mistress Sally Hemings bore six of his children. Yet, Jefferson said the following: "Nothing is in the book of fate stating that <u>these people</u> are to be free."

Although Jefferson acknowledges freedom for all, there is a duality of thinking, which is clear in the following statement: "… Nor is it less certain that the two races, equally free, cannot live in the same government. To clarify, Jefferson wanted Black people deported and separated from Whites so that they would be, as he said, "beyond the reach of mixture."

James Madison-U.S. President 1809-1817

James Madison said he wanted the U.S. government to buy up every slave and deport them. After serving his term as President, he ran the American Colonization Society, which sent Black people back to Africa, originally known as The Society for the Colonization of Free People of Color of America. This would be equivalent to our current U.S. Immigration and Customs Enforcement organization.

Henry Clay-U.S. Secretary of State 1825-1829

Clay said at the inaugural meeting of The American Colonization Society that they are "To rid our nation of a useless and pernicious, if not dangerous portion of the population."

Abraham Lincoln-U.S. President 1861-1865

Lincoln said, "I am not nor ever have been in favor of making voters or jurors of negroes, nor of qualifying them to hold office, nor to intermarry with White people…. Lincoln also declared,"… there is a physical difference between the White and Black races which I believe will forever forbid the two races living together on terms of social and political equality."

James Garfield-U.S. President 1881

Garfield wanted the immediate removal and cleansing of the Black population. Garfield announced, "[I have] a strong feeling of repugnance when I think of the negro being made our political equal and I would be glad if they could be colonized, sent to heaven, or gotten rid of in any decent way."

Theodore Roosevelt-U.S. President 1901-1909

Roosevelt thought Black people were a "problem." He said that he had "Not being able to think out any solution to the terrible problem offered by the presence of the Negro on this continent."

William Howard Taft-U.S. President 1909-1913

William Taft declared, "Your [Black] race is adapted to be a race of farmers, first, last, and for all times."

Warren Harding-U.S. President 1921-1923

Harding stated, "This is not a question of social equality, but a question of recognizing a fundamental, eternal, inescapable difference."

Harry Truman-President 1945-1953

Truman noted, "I am strongly of the opinion Negroes ought to be in Africa, yellow men in Asia, and White men in Europe and America." He referred to the Black servants in the White House as, "An army of coons."

The Age of Technology is Now!

Technology is revolutionizing every facet of our lives. The Industrial Age is fading into history, as did the Agrarian Age before it. Public education is lagging in the studies and visibility of technology, while many colleges and technical schools are advancing it. Job preparation and daily living in technology is not a wave of the future; it is now. Every education facility that is not equipped beyond computer classes is obsolete. The curricula and instruction must be updated in its formal and vicarious viability in every facet of our lives—from high schools to elementary school.

The most common denominator for many of the people cited in this document is education. All of them were not privy to private, parochial, and even charter schools. Public education, as of today, remains the mainstay for educating many people from many walks of life.

We live in a time period that demands changes in the way things are done in almost every aspect of our lives. This means that our public education system is being required to restructure and to train staff and faculty who may not be technologically prepared to meet the learning needs of students. It means that facilities require technological transformation as well. The most well- intended educators who have been on school staffs for more than 10 years but are not retirement age are greeting students who no longer view textbooks, pens, pencils, and paper as basic requirements. Library assignments may be foreign and seem a bit archaic to the astute "techies" who navigate their world based upon technological principles.

Bill Gates' statement is very factual. He says, "The advance of technology is based on making it fit in so that you don't really even notice it, so it's part of everyday life." This is a truth that America must begin to view as an everyday life necessity.

Teach Curriculum and Instruction through Technology - Make Education Relevant

Some things become the wave of the future. That is, at first, they were very foreign to us; but later, they made sense. When I was a little girl, Moma told the story about the first time she and her sister Ruth saw a car. It tickled me. She said it was either 1910 or 1911, and they were walking home from school one day when they heard a strange sound coming toward them. These sisters ducked behind some hedges for safety. Moma said that the loud rushing sound came closer and passed right by them.

"It was the first time we'd ever heard a sound like that." Frightened, the sisters ran home and told their brother Hamp. He told them they had just seen a Model T. The Ford Company manufactured it in 1908. I could not believe that they had never seen a CAR! There was always a car in our possession. It was something I took for granted. It was the first time we'd seen a "wagon" that a horse, mule, or Ox was not pulling, she said!

The first car phone I ever saw. It was the first time we'd seen a "wagon" that a horse, mule, or Ox was not pulling!

Continuing to Rise

Fast Forward

One day, I was riding with my cousin Edna Canty Jenkins when my foot bumped into something that looked like a shoebox. I asked, "What on earth is this?" I was amazed when she said that it was a car phone. When I asked my grandsons to identify this picture, they laughed as they tried to figure out what was pictured. They were shocked when they discovered that this was a car phone.

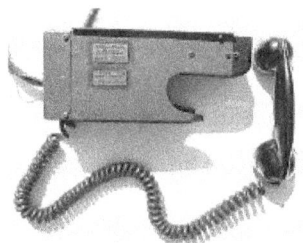

Early car phone

Reynolds E. Davis School

In Sumter County, South Caroling during the 1970s, transitioning from Eastern High School to an Elementary School was painful only because during the desegregation of the schools of that school system, all Black High schools and their principals were demoted to the elementary and middle schools.

The White high schools and their principals received Black high school students. Black Counselors and a few Black teachers were sent along with them. Despite this form of segregation that happened to the Black principals, they opened their doors and received Black and White students.

R.E. Davis School remains the only school in the county named for a Black person in the county. I dream that it will become technologically developed and that the name remains in perpetuity. My dad and the teachers poured educational expertise and financial resources into Eastern High School. The intent was to make it a place of academic and social comfort to ensure that it was educationally progressive for students and teachers. They loved Eastern.

Today, the Alumni extol Eastern High School. My dad's reward was seeing former students become progressive educational and civic leaders in this county, state, and country.

"If future generations are to remember us more with gratitude, than sorrow, we must achieve more than just the miracles of technology. We must also leave them a glimpse of the world as it was created, not as it looked when we got through with it."

Lyndon B. Johnson

I dream that one day soon R.E. Davis School (Officially named Reynolds E. Davis) will become technologically developed to serve and to prepare students for this present and future ages.

Benevolent

"Before you speak, listen. Before you write, think. Before you invest, investigate. Before you criticize, wait. Before you pray, forgive. Before you quit, try. Before you retire, save. Before you die, give."

William A. Ward

CHAPTER TWENTY

Home

"The indelible spirit identifies and preserves the irreversible dignity, goodness, and honor in all people."

Thomasina M. Portis

The idea of home can be an emotional space as well as a physical one. I will share the idea of home from a personal experience of mine and one from Black men and women who serve in the United States military. In both instances, the emphasis of these two stories is on benevolence which preserves the irreversible dignity, goodness, and honor in all people. My story is about someone who was courageous enough to show love to me and to tell me the truth I needed when I needed it most. This truth changed the course of my life change and led me to do a work that helped me to understand the power, whether positive or negative, self-talk can be. In this instance it was genuine love and daring to speak the truth that led me to make a much-needed change in my life.

Honor and Loyalty to the Military

When I was a member of the National Character Education Partnership Board of Directors, one of our members was a man named Dr. Eric Schapps. One day while talking about the term community, he described it more as a spirit than as a place. While pondering the multifaceted term "home," it may just be that the nature the "spirit" is also embedded in this term.

The Indelible Spirit

"Home" is that place in the heart where social disorders pale in comparison to the importance of nurturing and protecting it. It is the commingling of heart and head that refuses to be entrapped by the notion of fair or unfair practices. The concept of "home" resides in our human spirit and demands its preservation. The hundreds of years of social injustices heaped upon Black people have not been able to stop our protection of "home" because it is not transient or situational.

In the Black community, "Home" is much more than a physical aboard. It includes the qualities of relationship, ingenuity, and protection. These qualities form the bedrock of human respect and refuse to be tarnished by ethnic greed and superiority or fight for power. "Home" is the heart and feelings; "Home" is head and intellect. This concept of head and heart is rooted in more than 5,000 years of civilization that taught nurture and struggle as common experiences. It is failure and regret forged into forgiveness and success. "Home" is the collective ancestral experiences of a rugged road made smooth through the inner determination to make a better life happen for all humanity.

Our ancestors experienced mistreatment through social injustices for centuries. Those maladies did not alter the truth about their humanity. They came to these shores with centuries of history about the value in life that resides in moral character traits. Regardless of the heinous and inhumane enactments that were endured by our ancestors, this specific historical concept of "Home" was brought to these American shores. "Home" resided in their indelible spirit and not exclusively in their social and physical life experiences.

Even though our fore parents came to America under duress, they brought with them their centuries of experiences ranging in scope from leadership and royalty to tribal enslavement. They knew war and peace. They were the intellectuals who provided inventions for every civilization that followed and built upon. They understood and embraced that physical feature brought on by the adaptation to tropical weather required Black skin, broad features, and course thick hair. The rich African soil made them experts in tilling it and developing vegetation to sustain themselves. They learned how to dominate animals around them for survival. Cultivation of land and domination of animals required patience and ingenuity.

Our ancestors were warriors, intellects, and caretakers of "Home." The indelible spirit identifies and preserves the irreversible dignity, goodness, and honor in all people regardless of ethnicity, class, or gender. All these realities were part of the DNA of our African ancestors who were captured and brought to these shores.

America is Our Home

As we have this conversation, it is important to reiterate the generational DNA of the Black indelible spirit. It may help to give perspective of who we are as a people through a prism that incites our hopeful anticipation for freedom and liberty for all people. It may also help to acknowledge and not shy away from the evil reality heaped upon this nation through the negative White Supremacy Ideology.

The ebb and flow of the violent behaviors this negative ideology evokes can be traced upon a long timeline. It gives rise to the existence of the impact of the fragility of the democratic principles in America today. A trace of the historical behavior helps one to understand that the White supremacy belief system is interwoven into the belief system of many White people who continue fighting for its preservation. They believe in their supremacy; therefore, they believe that this nation belongs to them. Conversely, Black people believe in human relationships and continue to rise amid all social and physical impediments. We also know that this nation belongs to all of us.

"My Faithful Friend- True friendship resists time, distance, and silence."

During my college days I experienced a lot of hiccups, failures, and challenges. The mounting of personal events had spun me into a life of depression. Forging through this depressed living was laborious. I owned the self-talk that led me into believing that I had no authority to change situations I had taken on as mine. I had to learn that I could not change another person's decisions even when I was convinced that they were detrimental. I also had to learn that I could not continue to make judgements about the way another person's choices. This did not mean that I needed to be negligent or angry. It meant learning how to allow people to live their own lives without my judgement. My final lesson was learning how to be my proverbial sister's and brother's keeper and understanding that when I failed, I was not a failure. I continue to engage in the kind of interdependent support that makes my quest a reality. These are the lessons I learned as I moved through my healing process. It took me eight years and three colleges before I received a baccalaureate degree. My failures were not in my grades. Failing at what I believed was my responsibility to make life different for someone else was my downfall.

Depression assumed residence in my life for eight consecutive years. When I believed that I could not go on, I closed myself up in my single room in a dormitory for seventeen days. It was dark in the room; my soul was as dark. My forever sister/friend Leola Louise (Le- Lu) Kersey Benjamin must have gotten the key from the dorm matron. On the seventeenth day of my hiatus, she stormed into the room, let light into that dark place, and screamed, "Tommye, I forbid you to try to kill yourself by staying in this room doing nothing!" She continued. "You're too stupid to know that you are one of the most intelligent, talented people on this campus. It is time for you to learn it for yourself. Now get up, get cleaned up. Let's go get something to eat. You will not make a liar out of me. You are going to learn who you are, and you will not die on my watch!"

Le-Lu's words (expletives explicit) reverberated so deeply into my dark soul that they drew out a penlight that showed me a flicker of hope. (Could that have been Moma's light?) Le-Lu's behavior was so unlike the demeanor I knew, it shocked me. Somewhere in the recesses of my being, her words took root. I had to self-assess my pain, my self-disappointment, and my years of hurt that had become my truth.

That was the second college I had attended. My behavior had been much like this in my first college matriculation. I moved through those two institutions walking in the misunderstanding that to get therapy did not mean that I was crazy. Therapy is not something to be embarrassed to experience. The brain is a physical organ that houses our emotions, and it needs check-ups just as physical therapy on other parts of the body. My depression was not clinical, so I did not have to be medicated. I did, however, must want "different" to get it. It was exclusively my choice. Seeing myself as negatively "different" was also my high hill to climb. It took hard and consistent work and time for me to overcome. Had it not been for Le-Lu's tenacity and audacity, I am not sure that I would have gone to therapy at all.

Her tenacious emotions struck me as coming from someone who understood what I was experiencing. I heard her caring, not condemning me. She sure did express concern about my welfare. I came through as authentic, non-judging and uncondemning love. Her opinion of me finally became one that I learned to own without self-condemnation. I also learned how to operate my life in congruence with it. I went through a lot of prayer, therapy, hard work in my inner sanctuary, and perseverance. Those were my down years.

I got back up! It is true that once I put my mind to something, I do it. I got myself educationally equipped. So, I am now this beautiful Black woman whose intellectual competence and professional acumen have taken her across six of the seven continents public speaking, consulting, providing community services, preaching, and singing. I am grateful to my sister/friend who dared to tell me the truth about myself, and I love her forever. Her heart was big enough to provide me with a "home.

Le-Lu and her family

America Our Home: The Sworn Oath

My son Randy and I were in a restaurant in Washington, DC the night that President George H. W. Bush announced Desert Storm. Randy was in the Army and visiting with me. I became so overwrought with tears that we had to leave the restaurant. Walking down the street with his hand on my shoulder did not provide me with much solace. So, he stopped, turned me towards himself, and with so much tenderness in his voice he said, "Mommie, if I am called, I must go. I swore an oath." The assurance of his commitment was so resounding that amid my tears, I was overwhelmed with respect for his position. He swore an oath.

The more I ponder Randy's statement, the more respect I gain for all Black men and women who take the oath to protect this nation on the domestic and international fronts. Their social and political experiences from childhood until today are rifted with stories of injustice and heinous inequalities. Despite this inhumaneness, every day they willingly lay down their lives based upon an oath taken to protect "home."

The integrity to uphold your oath must have become your Steadfast Resolve. You epitomize the Scripture that says, "… But I say unto you, Love your enemies, bless them that curse you, do good to them that hate you, and pray for them which despitefully use, and persecute you; (Matthew 5:44 KJV) This is not to be misconstrued as fear, trauma, or weakness, but rather understood as a demonstration of pure strength that comes with loving all humanity.

Buffalo Soldiers

After the Civil War of 1866, six all-Black regiments were established to help rebuild this country. These men fought on Western frontier against American Indians who were tired of life on reservations and the broken promises of the federal government between 1860 and 1870. Like their ancestors who could face adversity and live, these men were outnumbered and outgunned, and yet, they won. They were among the most loyal, decorated soldiers of their time. The 10th Calvary was kick named Buffalo Soldier when they fought to protect settlers, mail, wagon trains and stagecoaches as they battled outlaws, wagon. Rumor has it that the American Indians gave this regiment the name Buffalo Soldiers because of their hair and the amount of time they spent near buffalos.

Mounted Buffalo Soldiers at an unidentified ceremony at the U.S. Military Academy at West Point.

These men were the first Black professional soldiers in a peacetime army. Their backgrounds varied to include formerly enslaved men and veterans from the service in the Civil War. This is another example of the benevolent spirit of Black people. The ancestral understanding of humanity transcends the social injustices and inequities they faced. They became the extended example of loyalty the finds its place in integrity and commitment. They are examples of the many Black men and women who service in the U.S. Military and take the oath to defend our country.

Continuing to Rise

Chapter Twenty - Home

The Montford Point Marines

Now, I understand my uncle Jay, whom I mentioned in Section Two, would recall times when he was placed in harm's way. He was taken directly from Montford Point, where he was trained, directly to the foxholes during World War II's battle at Iwo Jima, Japan, and Okinawa. A glimpse at the VA's treatment these new Black Marines received upon return to their homes, remains incomprehensibly inhumane.

In an NPR report on July 18, 2022, called "All Things Considered," one of the original first Black Marine recruits shared this account of their abuse. He said, "It was a swamp right near Camp LeJeune. In the evening, just at dusk dark, the drill instructor would take the recruits to that swamp and make them stand at attention. And he would say, "You N…. S, did you eat? "Yes, sir" would be our response. "Well, let the [expletives] mosquitoes eat," would be his command as we continued to stand at attention. The bites were reported to be so bad that they were smallpox."

The verbal and physical abuse directed at these men was endless. Recruits who smoked were forced to smoke with a bucket on their heads and blankets over the buckets. It was rumored that someone was forced to drink his own urine.

Directly out of basic training with the Colored Unit in Montford Point, NC, the recruits who could not be trained with White enlisted Marines at Camp LeJeune, NC.—Like Jay—were sent to the front lines and directly into foxholes. Once there, these young men—some like Jay as young as 17—fought and saved people's lives regardless of their ethnicity. Finally, when White soldiers needed blood and the supply had run out, the Black Marines donated their blood. After experiencing all this evil treatment, Jay would be asked, "Why did you save the lives of the very ones who did these things to you and who refused to sit down to eat with you in the Mess Hall?" The essence of his mantra was, "They are people who needed someone to protect them, too. That's what it means to me to be a Marine. The Marines build men!"

Although there were thousands of Black Marines in Iwo Jima and Okinawa, there was neither any evidence of them is shown in the photos nor movie reels made about the U.S. Marines' presence in the South Pacific here is no doubt about the inequalities and inequities we face. There is no question about the violence that is stoked by fanaticism of White supremacy. But we have an example. Of our Steadfast Resolve regarding "home." America is the home of many of us Black people. Our citizenship is of consequence and the preservation of a human and just society remains the intent of our Relay to Liberty and Justice for all ethnicities. Our Black men and women in uniform really seem to actualize loyalty above inequality and injustice they faced in civilian and military life.

My uncle Jay is the face in row six (6) column fourteen (14)

Salute to the Women and Men in Uniform

I salute the men and women in uniform. You choose to take the oath to protect "our" Home. Your benevolence and determination to uphold your oath speaks to a level of integrity and dignity that I recognize and honor as the height of moral character traits. You are examples of what the guiding indelible spirit provides. There is no way around struggle, but there are ways to successfully go through it while Continuing to Rise. Even those who may not have known anything about the Bible understood, on some level, the reality of evil V. Goodness and its perpetual existence throughout the history of humankind.

Men and women of the military, you are to be honored and celebrated. You knowingly took an oath to go into harm's way for the cause of a better humanity while struggling with the social, judicial, and political injustices heaped upon us just because of the color of our skin. I suspect that even as you faced the prejudicial and other unwanted practices that resided in whatever branch of service you entered, you must have become even more resolute in upholding your oath. There is no call to arms, even in the face of violence and death, which has caused you to waver from the determination to preserve and to protect "Home." I apologize that it has taken America so long to appreciate your level of courage and to recognize your benevolence; kindness without expecting a return.

Chapter Twenty - Home

Four Generations In order: Hampton A. Woodward, Generation one; Hampton W. Wright, Sr., and John P. Wright, Generation two; Hampton W. Wright, Jr., Janis M. Wright, and J. Michael Wright, Generation three; Verenander LF Portis, III, Christophe S. Jones, Generation four and Ayden M. Williams Generation five

These four generations of our family's Woodward-Tucker ancestral family-line, along with these other military warriors in this chapter stand in proxy for their courageous and distinguished colleagues from Crispus Attucks, 1770, who fought alongside the men from the American Colonies against British soldiers to the people on active duty today.

Your Reason for Being

I speak to my generational sisters and brothers in uniform. The integrity to uphold the oath, I believe, is one of the best examples of what might have happened to Black men and women. Your decision to serve a nation where mental and emotional trauma remains inherent in our

Continuing to Rise

social construct is phenomenal. Despite the social, judicial, and political injustices you have faced, your reason for being remains focused on protecting all human beings.

Lieutenant General Nadja Y. West (U.S. Army)

Ret. Major General Marcia Anderson (U.S. Army)

Ret. Brigadier General Hazel Brown Johnson, (U.S. Army)

Retired Major Dr. Michele Balmani (U.S. Air Force)

Ret. Chaplain (Major) Andrea M Foster (U.S. Army)

Retired Sergeant Leroy Bowman (Tuskegee Airman), and son Ret. General George Bowman

Retired Sergeant William C. Wright, son, Brigadier General Wayne A. Wright (Both U.S. Aire Force)

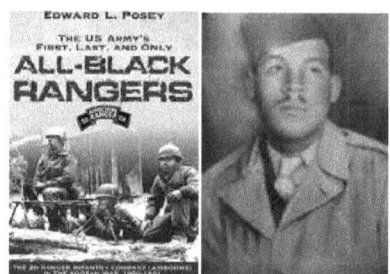
Major James C. Queen All-Black Ranger (U.S. Army) and

The integrity to uphold your oath must have become your Steadfast Resolve. You epitomize the Scripture that says, "... But I say unto you, Love your enemies, bless them that curse you, do good to them that hate you, and pray for them which despitefully use, and persecute you; (Matthew 5:44 KJV) This is not to be misconstrued as fear, trauma, or weakness, but rather understood as a demonstration of pure strength that comes with loving all humanity.

Post-Traumatic Stress Disorder

I am not sure that Post Traumatic Stress Disorder (PTSD) was a general diagnosis when Jay, at 40 years old, began to show signs of emotional trauma. Jay had begun evidencing erratic behaviors when he was a high school social studies teacher and a leading football coach with championship teams in his division. Eventually, his behavior became very erratic; and because he was such a big man in statue and strength, many times during his traumatic episodes he would have to be heavily sedated. However, even during those times, he could be brought back into some semblance of reality if someone talked about the Marines.

Unfortunately, Jay endured mental torture for 40 more years. The wear and tear of the strong medications eventually rendered him unable to walk. This great athlete, teacher, and coach had to rely on others to feed him and care for his personal needs. He lived with Moma from 1959 until her death in 1999. Then, his son took care of him until he died at 80 years old. Sadly, his children; and most of his nieces and nephews never knew this vibrant intellectual who played the piano and enjoyed his life until he was 40 years old. After then, he started showing signs when Jay of being emotionally and mentally removed from us. But, if someone talked about the Marines, on occasions he was known to struggle to raise his body to get up. Then, using his worn fists, he would salute and say, "God Bless America, my" Home, sweet "Home"!"

When Jay took the oath to enter the Marines, he upheld it to the fullest. John Paul (Jay) Wright goes down in the history of America as a Montford Point Marine who received a United States Congressional Award from President Barack Obama. The inscription on the back of the medal reads, "For outstanding perseverance and courage that inspired social change in the U.S. Marine Corps." John Paul (Jay) Wright's legacy lives in perpetuity.

JOHN PAUL WRIGHT "JAY"

IN THE EARLY 1940'S THIS WARRIOR WAS IN THE FIRST GROUP OF U.S. MARINES TO BE TRAINED AT MONTFORT POINT, N.C.

Despite all the inhumane treatment Jay endured, he is among our family warrior and will stand tall in United States History forever. John Paul Wright is the recipient of the United States Congressional Gold Medal of Honor bestowed by President Barack Obama as one of the brave Montford Marines.

Men and women of the Armed Services, your uncompromising loyalty to the oath to defend and protect our "home" makes it even more compelling for me to say:

Thank you for your service.

Continuing to Rise

EPILOGUE

"Great occasions do not make heroes or cowards; they simply unveil them to our eyes. Silently and imperceptibly, as we wake or sleep, we grow strong or weak; and at last, some <u>crisis</u> shows what we have become. "Never let a good crisis go to waste."

Winston Churchill

History Informs

Well Family, you have seen photos that are of people from generations who are awaiting replications through your uniqueness. Mainly photos of Black people who have made and who are making historical contributions to include politics. They move through all phases of our country as entrepreneurs, leaders, and other reputable contributors to our rich heritage. They bear witness to our intellect, genius, courage, and benevolence. I salute them and you. My aim is to prove that our people continue to matriculate in every facet of this American life with purpose and perseverance. I hope that when you write your history that you will include others of us who dare to succeed despite the odds. Moma's voice from her eternal rest still inquires. She is asking, "Who told you that you couldn't succeed?" History informs.

This is why I have made it a point to speak to the history of our ancestors and the legacy of strength, endurance, and benevolence they gave to us. I hope that you have been able to imagine some of the personalities of our lineage. I hope that you also see how they paved the way for us to continue being leaders. On each leg of our Relay to Liberty and Justice, we march toward equality for all people. This, too, represent show we are Continuingto Rise.

"Evil People Plot; Good People Plan"

There was a saying during the Civil Rights Movement that said, "While evil plots, good plans." Family, I know that we are diligent about our family, work, and religious obligations. I ask that we consider making our civil obligations, beyond voting, apart of lifestyle responsibility, as well.

In the Prologue, we shared the concept of needing to have a foundation before building a floor. The concept applies here. Our ancestors' contributions (foundation) are available to inform our future decisions (floor). It is incumbent upon us to connect to our generational story. It provides a continuum that helps us to understand and to respect our lineage. It helps us to see ourselves as viable members of this American society. It also helps us to become involved in civic responsibilities that affect the changes we say that we deserve. We cannot be a person who will dissociate ourselves from the moral obligation of becoming involved in our government.

During our Relay to Liberty and Justice, we have been able to identify the tenets of inequalities that keep *Systemic Racism* viable. We discussed how we have made great strides in education, employment, entrepreneurialship, and economics. Have we ever stopped to think about the efforts White supremacists place on voting, gerrymandering, and strategic placement of people into the judicial and legislative systems? We do know that a vote equals numbers and issues are resolved through the vote. What I ask you to seriously consider during this leg of our Relay to Liberty and Justice, is building a viable representation among these two branches of government.

We cannot expect anyone to do for us what we can do for ourselves. Our moral obligation is to build a plan that will help strengthen the Democracy. It started as a segregated White American Democracy, by the late 1960s we entered the mainstream. It is now a Democracy that challenges the validity of the White American Democracy. We know why there is a movement afoot to tear down this fragile democratic process.

Family, instead of tearing this democratic process down, please consider it an urgency for us to make our presence felt while changing this Democracy. If we vote and take on more political roles, then, we have the opportunity to turn on the beacon of light that shines on "We the People." For the first time, we can help make the statement true. The election of 2024 is only as bleak as our reticence allows it to be.

In Reverend Al Sharpton's Book, *Rise*, he shares a compelling story that the former Congressman Tim Ryan of Ohio told him about Muhammad Ali. It describes who we are! Seeing Ali on the street, a man called out, "Hey, champion, saw you get knocked out at the Garden. You were flat on your back." He laughed and jeered his friend. Ali said, "Wasn't me." The man continued, "What are you talking about? Of course, it was you. I saw it. I had a ringside seat." Ali said, "No, you either saw me standing or getting up. I've never stayed down." We march on until victory is won. I ask that you vote to save a fragile system of governance and make it your business to work toward an American Democracy that celebrates all humanity.

Seeing Ali on the street, a man called out, "Hey, champion, saw you get knocked out at the Garden. You were flat on your back." He laughed and jeered his friends. Ali said, "Wasn't me." The man continued, "What are you talking about? Of course, it was you. I saw it. I had ringside seats." Ali said, "No, you either saw me standing or getting up. I've never stayed down."

Muhammad Ali, *"The Greatest," was a professional boxer, activist, entertainer, poet, and philanthropist.*

We Get Up!

I have hope. I see hope. How can I see hope during these complex times? Since we were brought to these shores as enslaved people, nothing has stopped our Relay to Freedom and Liberty. We have never let a good crisis go to waste. Amid the daily evidence of inhumane behavior and the evidence of militia forming in our country, we must continue to believe and act upon our indelible spirit's direction.

Pictured above are wealthy Freedmen in Edingsville, South Carolina, in the early 1800s. Some of our ancestors always lived well and were successful entrepreneurs.

Singing On One Accord

In 1900 our ancestor James Weldon Johnson was principal of the segregated Stanton School in Jacksonville, Florida. One day he was working on ideas for a student assembly to celebrate Abraham Lincoln's birthday. He came up with the idea of authoring a poem and titled it "Lift Every Voice and Sing." The idea for the poem morphed into a song when James Weldon invited his brother J Rosamond Johnson, a music composer, to set his poem to music.

An in-depth study shows that "Lift Every Voice and Sing" is an ageless component of the human, not just Negro experience. It was written to celebrate a White man, who suffered and Black people, who were suffering. Inherent in these lyrics is the plight of all people; their truth contains hardships and setbacks. The song, relegated as The Negro National Anthem more comprehensively resonates humanity's truth. This moving masterpiece could be considered as **The American Hymn**.

"Lift Every Voice and Sing," E Pluribus Unum, and the Statue of Liberty

The lyrics of this song express the ideals of E Pluribus Unum, i.e., "out-of-many- one." This song's chordal progressions describe all ethnic struggles as well as, hope for everyone from the wealthiest and empowered to the most recently naturalized immigrant. Human situations are different; human behavior is the same.

The Statue of Liberty remains the gateway to America! The invitation penned in her inscription is for every immigrant and for all American citizens.

Read The Statue of Liberty's inscription carefully:

*"Give me your tired, your poor Your huddled masses yearning to be free.
The wretched refuse of your teeming shore. Send these, the homeless, tempest tossed to me, I lift my lamp beside the golden door!"*

The inscription in The Statue of Liberty speaks to the struggles of Native Americans and to all others who at some point migrated to a land that had been inhabited for hundreds of centuries by them. Immigrants include the first Europeans seeking a better life than that of indentured servitude, Black were people brought here as enslaved people. We were never considered as migrants. We are "Home" with earned rights to sing, and Brown people of every culture who come for safety and a better life.

Lift Every Voice and Sing;" and America's Democracy

Regardless of ethnicity or class, this song invites everyone to sing and to ignite hope. Inclusion and hope are two attributes of Democracy.

While there are multiple beautiful renderings of this message, I invite you to listen to these words and music through this rendition of "Lift Every Voice and Sing" as composed and directed by Dr. Roland Carter, on YouTube. He remains a voice for civil rights in Memphis, TN. Dr Carter's composition is a masterpiece expressing the agelessness of hope.

Lift Every Voice and Sing

Stanza #1

Lift every voice and sing, Till earth and heaven ring, Ring with the harmonies of Liberty Let our rejoicing rise High and the listening skies, Let it resound loud as the rolling sea!
Sing a song full of the faith that the dark past has taught us,
Sing a song full of the hope that the present has brought us.
Facing the rising sun of our new day begun Let us march on till victory is won.

Stanza #2

Stony the road we trod Bitter the chastening rod, Felt in the days when hope unborn had died.
Yet with a steady beat Have not our weary feet, Come to the place for which our fathers sighed.
We have come over a way that with tears has been watered We have come, treading our path, through the blood of the slaughtered.
Out from the gloomy past Till now we stand at last. Where the White gleam of our bright star is cast.

Stanza #3

God of our weary years, God of our silent tears Thou Who has brought us thus far on the way Thou Who has by Thy Might Led us into the light Keep us forever in the path, we pray.
Lest our feet stray from the places, our God, where we met Thee
Lest our hearts drunk with the wine of the world, we forget
Thee.
Shadowed beneath Thy hand, may we forever stand True to our God, True, our native land.

James Weldon Johnson (Poet)
J. Rosamond Johnson (Composer

Continuing to Rise

Epilogue

"Tell our story to those who follow us."

Continuing to Rise

APPENDICES

Appendix One.

NBC news. com reports that on May 20, 1967, the NBC correspondent Sander Vanocur sat with Dr. Martin Luther King, Jr. in Ebenezer Baptist Church, Atlanta, GA for this interview called *CIVIL RIGHTS: BLACK POWER*.

Vanocur: "Dr. King, this church is as good a place as any to go back over your commitment to the Civil Rights Movement. When you went out from here in the university and then you went to Montgomery, Alabama and started the bus boycotts there, what was the philosophy of the Civil Rights Movement as you saw it then, more than ten years ago?"

Dr. King: "Well, I would say, then, the philosophy was that we must go all out to use legal and nonviolent methods to gain full citizenship rights for the Negro people of our nation. Now of course that struggle and that philosophy centered on breaking down all the barriers of legal segregation. So, I would say that in that period, the basic thrust for the gaining of citizenship rights for Negroes was to end the humiliation surrounding the whole system of legal segregation."

Vanocur: "Dr. King, was there something peculiar to the place where you started and the kind of people you attracted? I mean by that, there was a strong attachment on the part of your parishioners in Montgomery to the church. They were older people, weren't they?"

Dr. King: "Yes, I would say, by-in-large, they were older people who participated in the boycott because they were the ones using the bus more than anybody else. And Montgomery was "community Church-centered" so that it was very easy to get to most Negroes because they were, in some way, connected with a church in the community."

Vanocur: "Sir, in addition to your commitment to the idea of non-violence, wasn't it also the only thing you could do, the White community having the monopoly on violence… that if you had tried violence, they would have met it with violence? It was the only device open to you, wasn't it?"

Dr. King: "Well, I'll put it another way, that morally, I was led to non-violence because it was the best moral way to deal with the problem. We were seeking to establish a *just society*. And, it was my feeling then, and it is my feeling now, that violence is certainly much more socially destructive, and it creates many more social problems than it solves. So, I was led to non-violence for deep moral reasons. Now there is no doubt about the fact that in our struggle in Montgomery, and all over the United States for that matter, non- violence is also sound. It would just be impractical for the Negro to turn to violence. He has neither the instruments nor the techniques of violence.

We are about ten or eleven percent of the total population of the nation, and I would say, we own about one-tenth of one percent of the firepower. So, it would just be impractical and unwise and unrealistic for the Negro to think of violence. Well, I saw this in the beginning in Montgomery. But this wasn't the basic reason that I turned to non-violence and that I believed in it as a philosophy. I turned to it because it was the morally excellent way to deal with the problem of racial injustice in our nation."

Vanocur: Is there something about non-violence that made it, and I used that in the past tense, that made it more useful amongst other Negroes than the ghetto Negroes of the North?"

Dr. King: "I wouldn't say there's anything that makes it more useful to Southern Negroes.

It is true that we've had more non-violent movements in the South because the problem for many years was more crystallized and, in a sense, more visible in the South. We didn't have many civil rights activities on a massive scale in the North until three or four years ago. So, I would say that we just haven't had a chance to experiment on a broad scale with non-violence in the Northern ghetto.

I have the feeling that non-violence is as applicable and workable in the Northern ghetto as it is in the South. Now, there's a larger job there. The frustrations, at points, are much deeper. The bitterness is deeper, and I think that's because in the South we can see pockets of progress here and there.

We've really made some strides that are very visible, and every Southern Negro knows that he can do things today that he couldn't do four or five years ago where, in the North the Negro sees only retrogress and he doesn't find it as easy to get his vision centered on his target -the target of opposition as he does in the South. Consequently, this has made for despair and, at many points, cynicism, a feeling that you can't win, and it simply means that we've got to develop in the North a massive job of organization and mobilizing forces and resources to deal with the problem. And there have been ghettos of the North just as we've done it in the South."

Vanocur: "In the South, particularly in Alabama, you had visible villains Jim Clark, Bull Connor, cattle prods, police dogs, but in the North, you don't have those visible villains. Isn't it hard to get your people aroused and directed at something that isn't visible?"

Dr. King: "Well, that's exactly right. And this is what I was saying when I said it's harder to see your target. In the South, in the non-violent movement, we were aided always overall, by the brutality of our opponent. It isn't the same way in the North. The other thing is that you don't have legal segregation in the North as you do in the South. So, it is much more difficult to get people to see exactly what you're doing. But it isn't an impossible job.

It's a hard... it's a tedious job at times to get people to be aroused from their apathetic slumbers. But I still feel that Negroes in the North can be motivated just as they were motivated in the South. And I think as time goes on, with the growing economic deprivation in the Negro community, it will even be easier because people will come to see that not only is something wrong in general, but something is wrong, in their own economic and housing situations."

Vanocur: "Well, what is it, I mean, how do you find it? It's very subtle in the North, is it not?"

Dr. King: "It's subtle but it's becoming much more visible. Anybody can see that the schools are more segregated in the North today than they were in 1954 when the Supreme Court rendered its decision declaring segregation unconstitutional. Anybody can look around the ghetto and see that ghetto schools are predominantly segregated and devoid of quality. Anyone who moves through a major ghetto of our nation will see the housing conditions.

People don't have to be reminded that they are forced to live in slums. In many instances they are often rat-infested vermin filled slums. And they didn't have to look hard to see the exploitation that the Negro is confronting in the ghetto where he is forced to pay more for less and constantly trying to make ends meet. But because of either having no job, because of unemployment, or a job that is so economically unprofitable that the person can't make ends meet. I think they see all these things. And more and more they are coming to see them because before the people of the North were looking to the South and they supported the struggles of the South. Now they are coming to see their problems are very real and they've got to organize to grapple with them."

Dr. King: "Well, there was no doubt about the hypocrisy of large segments of the nation on the whole question of racial equality. I think the best example is that many of the senators from the North and the West and congressmen generally, who voted for civil rights legislation in '64 and even '65 of the voting rights bill refused last year's vote for civil rights legislation because it dealt with an issue applicable to the North, the whole housing question. And this, it seems to me, was the greatest expression of the hypocrisy of many of our citizens and many of the senators and congressmen of the North."

Vanocur: "But isn't that part of the dilemma now that people who knew that Negroes were being denied what was guaranteed to them by the Constitution, by the fact that they were citizens of this nation? Then when they were given those rights, do you feel the White community said, 'Well, we've given them all that we have now it's up to them?'"

Dr. King: "Well, I think the dilemma is much deeper. And I think, one during this period of transition, must be very honest with America. And honesty impels me to admit that America has a broad racist element still alive. Racism is still existing in American society in many areas of the society, North and South. And the other thing is that there has never been a single solid determined commitment of large segments of White America, on the whole question of racial equality.

I think we must see that vacillation has always existed. Ambivalence has always existed. And this to me is the so-called White backlash. It is merely a new name for an old phenomenon. I see the White backlash as a continuation of the same ambivalence and vacillation of White America on the whole question of racial justice that has existed since the founding of our nation.

I think the other thing that we must see, at this time, is that many of the people who supported us in Selma and Birmingham were really outraged about the extremist behavior toward Negroes, but they were not at that moment, and they are not now, committed to genuine equality for Negroes. It's much easier to integrate a lunch counter than it is to guarantee an annual income, for instance, to get rid of poverty for Negroes and all poor people. It's much easier to integrate a bus than it is to make genuine integration a reality and quality education a reality in our schools.

It's much easier to integrate, even a public park, than it is to get rid of slums. And I think we are in a new era; a new phase of the struggle where we have moved from a struggle for decency, which characterized our struggle for 10 or 12 years, to a struggle for genuine equality. And this is where we are getting the resistance because there was never any intention to go this far. People were reacting to Bull Connor and to Jim Clarke rather than acting in good faith for the realization of genuine equality."

Vanocur: "Do you think White people in this nation, and I'm talking about non- segregationist, people devoid or thinking they're devoid of racism… do you have any idea of what they want the Negro to be in America?"

Dr. King: "Well it depends on the level that we are talking about here. Because I think you must make a distinction between the people who are genuinely and absolutely committed in the White community on the question of racial equality. And I must confess that I think they are a very small minority. I think the vast majority of White Americans will 'go but so far.' It's a kind of installment plan for equality and they are always looking for an excuse to 'go but so far.'"

Vanocur: "Why are they looking for the excuse? What is it about the Negro? In every other group that came as an immigrant somehow, not easily, but somehow got around it. Is it just the fact that Negroes are Black?"

Dr. King: "That's a part of it and growing. That grows out of something else. You can't 'thing-I- fy' anything without depersonalizing that something. If you use something as a means- to-an end, at that moment you make it *a thing* and you depersonalize it. The fact is that the Negro was a slave in this nation for 244 years. That act, that was a willful thing that was done. The Negro was brought here in chains and treated in very in- humane fashion. And this led to the '*thing-i-fication*' of the Negro. So, he was not looked upon as a person. He was not looked upon as a human being with the same status and worth as other human beings.

And the other thing is that human beings cannot continue to do wrong without eventually rationalizing that wrong. So, slavery was justified morally, biologically, theoretically, scientifically… everything else. And it seems to me that White America must see that no other ethnic group has been a slave on American soil. That is one thing that other immigrant groups haven't had to face. The other thing is that the color became a stigma. American society made the Negro's color a stigma, and that can never be overlooked. So, I think these things are necessary.

The other thing is that America freed the slaves from 1619 until the signing of the Emancipation Proclamation by Abraham Lincoln, they had places to stay and food to eat, even though both were of subpar standards. Once freed they owned nothing and were without a place to lay their heads and food to eat. They had owned nothing from the time they landed up until then. In that same year America was giving away millions of acres of land in the West and the Midwest which meant that there was a willingness to give the White peasants from Europe an economic base.

America refused to give its Black peasants from Africa, who came here involuntarily in chains, and had worked free for 244 years, any kind of economic base. And so, for the Negro freedom meant wanderer. It was freedom to the winds and rains of heaven. It was freedom without food to eat and land to cultivate and therefore was freedom and famine at the same time. And when White Americans tell the Negro to lift himself by his own bootstraps, they look over the legacy of slavery and segregation.

I believe we ought to do all we can and seek to lift ourselves by our bootstraps, but it's a cruel jest to say to a bootless man that he ought to lift himself by his own bootstraps. And many negroes by the thousands and millions have been left bootless, because of all these years of oppression and because of a society that deliberately made his color a stigma and something worthless and degrading."

Vanocur: "Apart from wanting to live better, which all of us want to do, to raise one's children in a better way to be better, does the Negro in America know what he wants to be?"

Dr. King: "I'm convinced that almost every Negro in this nation, other than those who have been so scarred by the system that they've become pathological in the process and we all must battle with pathology. Nobody really knows what it means to be a negro unless one can really experience it. And I know we all must battle with this constant drain of a feeling of *nobody-i-ness*. But, despite this, I think most Negroes in this nation know that they want to be people. They want to be men [and women]. They want equality, period. It just boils down to that. And we haven't been able to be people.

We haven't been men [and women] because of all the conditions that we've lived with and the syndrome of deprivation surrounding conditions whether it's in housing, in the economic area, or in schools, in the vicious credit practices that we face in the ghetto, and in all the problems of closed doors and constant defeats. Despite of all this, I think we all know basically that we want to be men [and women}] We want to be persons, judged not based on the color of our skin, but based on the content of our character."

Vanocur: "But you know that many young Negroes don't want anything that smacks of the American White middle class. But do they want something that smacks of whatever is the Black middle class or do they just not want bourgeois values which are, after all, the basis of this Democracy?"

Dr. King: "Well, I think we must see what they are saying. I would be the first to agree that integration does not mean giving up everything that has an Afro- American taint, so to speak, a background. I think there are certain unique things within any culture and certain cultural patterns that when you get to the process of amalgamation, can really lift the whole culture. And it seems to me that integration at its best is the opportunity to participate in the beauty of diversity.

I think the other thing that we've got to see is that these young people are saying that there must be a revolution of values in our nation. As Jimmy Baldwin said on one occasion, *'What advantage is there in being integrated into a burning house?'* And I feel that there is a need for a revolution of values in America because some of the values that presently exist are certainly out of line with the values and the idealistic structure that brought our nation into being.

Unfortunately, we haven't been true to these ideals. And many of the values of so- called White middle-class society are values that need to be reviewed and re- evaluated and in a real sense, they need to be changed. So, I think the young people in the Negro community, who are raising these questions, are raising some very profound questions about our total society. In other words, they are saying that there must be a restructuring of the architecture of our society where values are concerned. And with this I would agree.

So, in the quest for integration, I think we can offer our whole nation something because there are three evils in our nation. It's not only racism, but economic exploitation of poverty would be one, and then militarism. And I think in a sense, and in a very real sense, that these three are tied inextricably together and we aren't going to get rid of one without getting rid of the other."

Vanocur: "When you stood in the Lincoln Memorial that day in August '63 and you said, *'I have a dream,'* did that dream envision that you could see a war in Asia preventing the federal government doing for the Negroes; preventing the society doing for the Negroes that which you think had to be done?"

Dr. King: "No I didn't envision that, then. I must confess that that period was a great period of hope for me. And I'm sure for many others across the nation. Many of the Negroes who had just about lost hope saw a solid decade of progress in the South and in 1954 which was, I mean '64. 1963, nine years after the Supreme Court's decision to be in the March on Washington, meant a great deal. It was a high moment, a great watershed moment. But I must confess that that dream that I had that day has at many points turned into a nightmare.

Now I'm not one to lose hope. I keep on hoping. I still have faith in the future. But I've had to analyze many things over the last few years. And I would say over the last few months I've gone through a lot of soul-searching in agonizing moments, and I've come to see that we have many more difficult days ahead. And some of the old optimism was a little superficial and now it must be tempered with a solid realism. And I think the realistic fact is that we still have a long, long way to go and that we engage in a war on Asian soil which, if not checked and stopped, will bring poison in the very soul of our nation."

Vanocur: "Dr. King even if there had not been a war in Asia would you still not have had this nightmare insofar as the Negro movement for equality then touched on two things that the Relay to Freedom & Liberty White community holds sacred, their children and their property?"

Dr. King: "Oh, I have no doubt that we would have encountered great difficulties, great problems of resistance if the war had not been in existence. So, I'm not going to say that all our problems will be solved at the war in Vietnam. But I do say that war makes it infinitely more difficult to deal with these problems. When a nation becomes obsessed with the guns of war, it loses its social perspective, and programs of social uplift suffer. This is just a fact of history so that we do face many more difficulties because of the war. It's much more difficult to really arouse a conscience during a time of war. I noticed the other day, some weeks ago a Negro was shot down in Chicago. And it was a clear case of police brutality. That was on page 30 of the paper.

But, on page one at the top was, '780 Vietcong killed.' There is something about a war like this that makes people insensitive. It dulls the conscience. It strengthens the forces of reaction, and it brings reaction, bitterness, hatred, and violence. It strengthens the military industrial complex of our nation, and it's made our job much more difficult. Because, I think, we could go along with some programs if we didn't have this war on our hands. That would cause people to adjust to new developments just as they did in the South.

They said they'd never ride the bus with us; blood would flow in the streets. They wouldn't go to school with us and all these things. But, when people came to see that they had to do it, because the law insisted, they finally adjusted. And I think White people all over this nation will adjust once the nation makes it clear that in schools and housing, we've got to learn to live together as brothers [and sisters].

I think the biggest problem now is that we have had our gains over the last 12 years at *bargain rates* so-to-speak. It didn't cost the nation anything. In fact, it helped the economic side of the nation to integrate lunch counters and public accommodations. It didn't cost the nation anything to get the right-to-vote established. And now we are confronting issues that cannot be solved without costing the nation billions of dollars. Now, I think, this is where we are getting our greatest resistance. They may put it on many other things, but we can't get rid of slums and poverty without it costing the nation something."

57 years have passed since this interview and the cycle of White privilege and discrimination continues predominately for the advantages of White men of European descent. As we enter this conversation, as you engage this conversation, please allow yourself to remember that amid the atrocities, our ancestors never lost hope and faith regardless of the social atrocities crises they faced. This is their message to us, they say from their graves, "hate no one, love unconditionally while Continuing to Rise.

Appendix Two

Frederick Douglass' Fourth of July Speech on 1852 at Rochester, New York's Old Corinthian Hall

Mr. Douglass Wrote:

Mr. President, Friends, and Fellow Citizens:

He who could address this audience without a quailing sensation, has stronger nerves than I have. I do not remember ever appearing as a speaker before any assembly more shrinkingly, nor with greater distrust of my ability, than I do this day. A feeling has crept over me, quite unfavorable to the exercise of my limited powers of speech. The task before me is one which requires much previous thought and study for its proper performance. I know that apologies of this sort are considered flat and unmeaning. I trust, however, that mine will not be so considered. Should I seem at ease, my appearance would much misrepresent me. The little experience I have had in addressing public meetings, in national schoolhouses, has given me nothing on the present occasion.

The papers and placards say that I am to deliver a fourth [of] July oration. This certainly sounds large, and out of the common way, for it is true that I have often had the privilege to speak in this beautiful Hall, and to address many who now honor me with their presence. But neither their familiar faces, nor the perfect gage I think I have of Corinthian Hall, seems to free me from embarrassment.

Frederick Douglass' Fourth of July Speech on 1852 at Rochester, New York's Old Corinthian Hall

The fact is, ladies and gentlemen, the distance between this platform and the slave plantation, from which I escaped, is considerable and the difficulties to be overcome in getting from the latter to the former, are by no means slight. That I am here today is, to me, a matter of astonishment as well as of gratitude. You will not, therefore, be surprised, if in what I have to say I evince no elaborate preparation, nor grace my speech with any high-sounding exordium. With little experience and with less learning, I have been able to throw my thoughts hastily and imperfectly together; and trusting your patient and generous indulgence, I will proceed to lay them before you.

This, for the purpose of this celebration, is the 4th of July. It is the birthday of your National Independence, and of your political freedom. This, to you, is what the Passover was to the emancipated people of God. It carries your minds back to the day, and to the act of your great deliverance; and to the signs, and to the wonders, associated with that act, and that day. This celebration also marks the beginning of another year of your national life; and reminds you that the Republic of America is now 76 years old. I am glad, fellow citizens, that your nation is so young. Seventy-six years, though a good old age for a man, is but a mere speck in the life of a nation. Three score years and ten is the allotted time for individual men; but nations number their years by thousands. According to this fact, you are, even now, only in the beginning of your national career, still lingering in the period of childhood. I repeat, I am glad this is so. There is hope in the thought, and hope is much needed, under the dark clouds which lower above the horizon. The eye of the reformer is met with angry flashes, portending disastrous times; but his heart may well beat lighter at the thought that America is young, and that she is still in the impressible stage of her existence. May he not hope that high lessons of wisdom, of justice and of truth, will yet give direction to her destiny? Were the nation older, the patriot's heart might be sadder, and the reformer's brow heavier. Its future might be shrouded in gloom, and the hope of its prophets go out in sorrow. There is consolation in the thought that America is young. Great streams are not easily turned from channels, worn deep during ages. They may sometimes rise in quiet and stately majesty, and inundate the land, refreshing and fertilizing the earth with their mysterious properties. They may also rise in wrath and fury, and bear away, on their angry waves, the accumulated wealth of years of toil and hardship. They, however, gradually flow back to the same old channel, and flow on as severely as ever. But, while the river may not be turned aside, it may dry up, and leave nothing behind but the withered branch, and the unsightly rock, to howl in the abyss-sweeping wind, the sad tale of departed glory. As with rivers, so with nations.

Fellow-citizens, I shall not presume to dwell at length on the associations that cluster about this day. The simple story of it is that 76 years ago, the people of this nation were British subjects. The style and title of your "sovereign people" (in which you know glory) was not then born. You were under the British Crown. Your fathers esteemed the English Government as the home government, and England as the native land. This home government, you know, although a considerable distance from your home, did, in the exercise of its parental prerogatives, imposed upon its colonial children, such restraints, burdens, and limitations, as, in its mature judgment, it

deemed wise, right, and proper.

But, your fathers, who had not adopted the fashionable idea of this day, of the infallibility of government, and the absolute character of its acts, presumed to differ from the home government in respect to the wisdom and the justice of some of those burdens and restraints. They went so far in their excitement as to pronounce the measures of government unjust, unreasonable, and oppressive, and altogether such as ought not to be quietly submitted to. I scarcely need say, fellow citizens, that my opinion of those measures fully accords with that of your fathers. Such a declaration of agreement on my part would not be worth much to anybody. It would, certainly, prove nothing, as to what part I might have taken, had I lived during the great controversy of 1776. To say now that America was right, and England wrong, is exceedingly easy. Everybody can say it; the dastard, not less than the noble brave, can flippantly descant the tyranny of England towards the American Colonies. It is fashionable to do so; but there was a time when to pronounce against England, and in favor of the cause of the colonies, tried men's souls. They who did so were accounted in their day, plotters of mischief, agitators and rebels, dangerous men. To side with the right, against the wrong, with the weak against the strong, and with the oppressed against the oppressor! here lies the merit, and the one which seems unfashionable in our day of all others. The cause of liberty may be stabbed by the men who glory in the deeds of your fathers. But, to proceed.

Feeling themselves harshly and unjustly treated by the home government, your fathers, like men of honesty, and men of spirit, earnestly sought redress. They petitioned and remonstrated; they did so in a decorous, respectful, and loyal manner. Their conduct was unexceptionable. This, however, did not answer the purpose. They saw themselves treated with indifference, coldness, and South Carolina on. Yet they persevered. They were not the kind of men who would look back.

As the sheet anchor takes a firmer hold, when the ship is tossed by the storm, so did the cause of your fathers grow stronger, as it breasted the chilling blasts of regal displeasure. But, with that blindness which seems to be the unvarying characteristic of tyrants, since Pharaoh and his hosts were drowned in the Red Sea, the British Government persisted in the exactions complained of. The greatest and best of British statesmen admitted its justice, and the loftiest eloquence of the British Senate came to its support.

The madness of this course, we believe, is admitted now, even by England; but we fear the lesson is wholly lost to our present ruler.

Oppression makes a wise man mad. Your fathers were wise men, and if they did not go mad, they became restive under this treatment. They felt themselves the victims of grievous wrongs, incurable in their colonial capacity. With brave men there is always a remedy for oppression. Just here, the idea of a total separation of the colonies from the crown was born! It was a startling idea, much more so, than we, at this distance of time, regard it. The timid and the prudent (as has been intimated) of that day, were, of course, shocked and alarmed by it. Such people lived then, had lived before, and will, probably, ever have a place on this planet; and their course, in respect to any profound change, (no matter how great the good to be attained, or the wrong to be redressed by it), maybe calculated with as much precision as can be the course of the stars. They hate all changes, but silver, gold, and copper change! Of this sort of change they are always strongly in favor.

These people were called Tories in the days of your fathers; and the appellation, probably, conveyed the same idea that is meant by a more modern, though a somewhat less euphonious term, which we often find in our papers, applied to some of our old politicians.

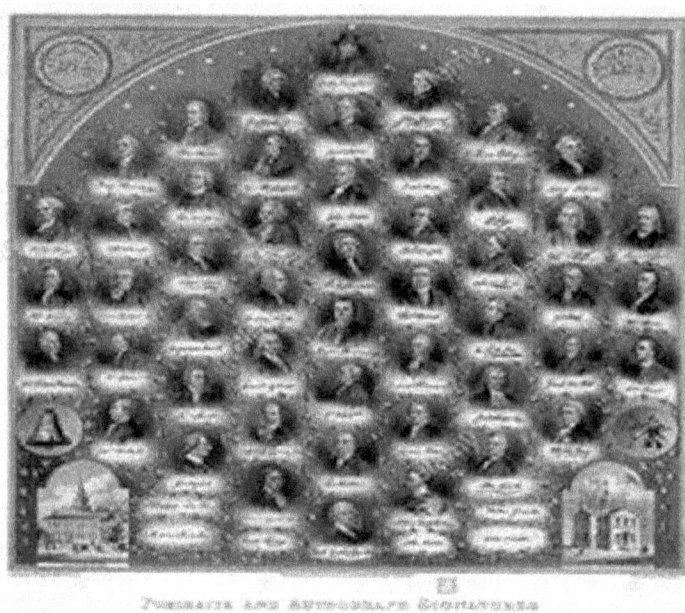

Portraits and autograph signatures of the framers and signers of the American Declaration of Independence in Philadelphia July 4, 1776

Their opposition to the then dangerous thought was earnest and powerful; but, amid all their terror and affrighted vociferations against it, the alarming and revolutionary idea moved on, and the nation with it. On the fourth of July 1776, the old Continental Congress, to the dismay of the lovers of ease, and the worshipers of property, clothed that dreadful idea with all the authority of national sanction. They did so in the form of a resolution; and as we seldom hit upon resolutions, drawn up in our day whose transparency is at all equal to this, it may refresh your minds and help my story if I read it. "Resolved, that these united colonies are, and of right, ought to be free and Independent States; that they are absolved from all allegiance to the British Crown; and that all connection between them and the State of Great Britain is, and ought to be, dissolved. "

Citizens, your fathers made good that resolution. They succeeded; and to-day you reap the fruits of their success. The freedom gained is yours; and you, therefore, may properly celebrate this anniversary. The 4th of July is the first great fact in your nation's history — the very ringbolt in the chain of your yet undeveloped destiny.

Pride and patriotism, not less than gratitude, prompt you to celebrate and to hold it in perpetual remembrance. I have said that the Declaration of Independence is the ringbolt to the chain of your nation's destiny; so, indeed, I regard it. The principles contained in that instrument are saving principles. Stand by those principles, be true to them on all occasions, in all places, against all foes, and at whatever cost.

From the round top of your ship of state, dark and threatening clouds may be seen. Heavy billows, like mountains in the distance, show to the leeward huge forms of flinty rocks! That bolt drawn, that chain broken, and all is lost. Cling to this day — cling to it, and to its principles, with the grasp of a storm-tossed mariner to a spar at midnight.

The coming into being of a nation, in any circumstances, is an interesting event. But, besides general considerations, there were peculiar circumstances which make the advent of this republic an event of special attractiveness. The whole scene as I look back to it was simple, dignified and sublime.

The population of the nation, at the time, stood at the insignificant number of three million. The nation was poor in the munitions of war. The population was weak and scattered, and the nation a wilderness unsubdued. There were then no means of concert and combination, such as exist now. Neither steam nor lightning had then been reduced to order and discipline. From Potomac to Delaware was a journey of many days. Under these, and innumerable other disadvantages, your fathers declared liberty and independence and triumphed.

Fellow Citizens, I am not wanting in respect the fathers of this republic. The signers of the Declaration of Independence were brave men. They were great men too — great enough to give fame to a great age. It does not often happen to a nation to raise, at one time, such several truly great men. The point from which I am compelled to view them is not, certainly, the most favorable; and yet I cannot contemplate their great deeds with less than admiration. They were statesmen, patriots, and heroes, and for the good they did, and the principles they contended for, I will unite with you to honor their memory.

They loved their nation better than their own private interests; and, though this is not the highest form of human excellence, all will concede that it is a rare virtue, and that when it is exhibited, it ought to command respect. He who will, intelligently, lay down his life for his nation, is a man whom it is not in human nature to despise. Your fathers staked their lives, their fortunes, and their sacred honor, on the cause of their nation. In their admiration of liberty, they lost sight of all other interests.

They were peaceable men; but they preferred revolution to peaceful submission to bondage. They were quiet men; but they did not shrink from agitating against oppression. They showed forbearance; but that they knew its limits. They believed in order, but not in the order of tyranny. With them, nothing was "settled" that was not right. With them, justice, liberty, and humanity were "final;" not slavery and oppression. You may well cherish the memory of such men. They were great in their day and generation. Their solid maturity stands out the more as we contrast it with these degenerate times.

How circumspect, exact, and proportionate were all their movements! How unlike the politicians of an hour! Their statesmanship looked beyond the passing moment and stretched away in strength into the distant future. They seized upon eternal principles and set a glorious example in their defense. Mark them!

Fully appreciating the hardship to be encountered, firmly believing in the right of their cause, honorably inviting the scrutiny of an on-looking world, reverently appealing to heaven to attest their sincerity, soundly comprehending the solemn responsibility, they were about to assume, wisely measuring the terrible odds against them, your fathers, the fathers of this republic, did, most deliberately, under the inspiration of a glorious patriotism, and with a sublime faith in the great principles of justice and freedom, lay deep the corner-stone of the national superstructure, which has risen and still rises in grandeur around you.

Of this fundamental work, this day is the anniversary. Our eyes are met with demonstrations of joyous enthusiasm. Banners and pennants wave exultingly in the breeze. The din of business, too, is hushed. Even Mammon seems to have quitted his grasp on this day. The ear-piercing fife and the stirring drum unite their accents with the ascending peal of a thousand church bells. Prayers are made, hymns are sung, and sermons are preached in honor of this day; while the quick martial tramp of a great and multitudinous nation, echoed back by all the hills, valleys, and mountains of a vast continent, bespeak the occasion one of thrilling and universal interest — a nation's jubilee.

Friends and citizens, I need not enter further into the causes which led to this anniversary. Many of you understand them better than I do. You could instruct me regarding them. That is a branch of knowledge in which you feel, perhaps, a much deeper interest than your speaker. The causes which led to the separation of the colonies from the British crown have never lacked for a tongue. They have all been taught in your common South Carolinas, narrated at your firesides, unfolded from your pulpits, and thundered from your legislative halls, and are as familiar to you as household words. They form the staple of your national poetry and eloquence.

I remember, also, that, as a people, Americans are remarkably familiar with all facts which make in their own favor. This is esteemed by some as a national trait — perhaps a national weakness. It is a fact, that whatever makes for the wealth or for the reputation of Americans and can be had cheap! will be found by Americans. I shall not be charged with slandering Americans, if I say I think the American side of any question may be safely left in American hands.

I leave, therefore, the great deeds of your fathers to other gentlemen whose claim to have been regularly descended will be less likely to be disputed than mine! My business, if I have any here today, is with the present. The accepted time with God and his cause is the ever-living now. Trust no future, however pleasant, Let the dead past bury its dead, Act, act in the living present, Heart within, and God overhead.

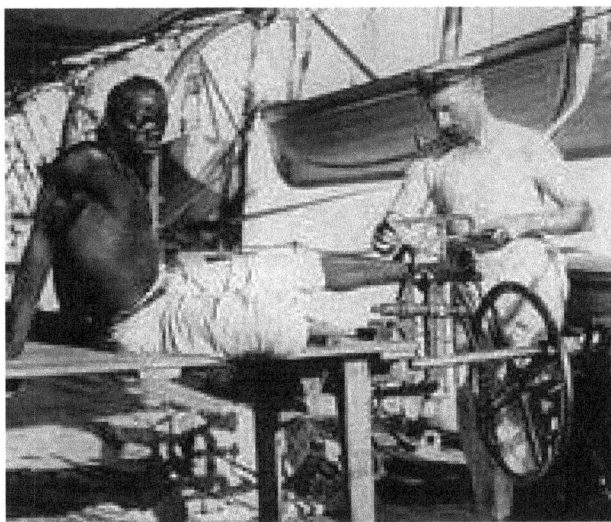

"Trust no future, however pleasant, Let the dead past bury its dead, Act, act in the living present, Heart within, and God overhead."

We have to do with the past only so we can make it useful to the present and to the future. To all inspiring motives, to noble deeds which can be gained from the past, we are welcome. But now is the time, the important time. Your fathers have lived, died, and have done their work, and have done much of it well. You live and must die, and you must do your work. You have no right to enjoy a child's share in the labor of your fathers, unless your children are to be blest by your labors. You have no right to wear out and waste the hard-earned fame of your fathers to cover your indolence. Sydney Smith tells us that men seldom eulogize the wisdom and virtues of their fathers, but to excuse some folly or wickedness of their own. This truth is not a doubtful one. There are illustrations of it near and remote, ancient, and modern. It was fashionable, hundreds of years ago, for the children of Jacob to boast, we have "Abraham to our father," when they had long lost Abraham's faith and spirit. Those people contented themselves under the shadow of Abraham's great name, while they repudiated the deeds which made his name great. Need I remind you that a similar thing is being done all over this nation today? Need I tell you that the Jews are not the only people who built the tombs of the prophets, and garnished the sepulchers of the righteous?

Washington could not die till he had broken the chains of his enslaved people. Yet his monument is built up by the price of human blood, and the traders in the bodies and souls of men shout, "We have Washington to our father." — Alas! that it should be so; yet so it is. The evil that men do, lives after them, the good is oft interred with their bones.

Continuing to Rise

Egyptian Sculpture from the 7th Dynasty 2161-2015 B. C

Fellow-citizens, pardon me, allow me to ask, why am I called upon to speak here today? What have I, or those I represent, to do with your national independence? Are the great principles of political freedom and of natural justice, embodied in that Declaration of Independence, extended to us? and am I, therefore, called upon to bring our humble offering to the national altar, and to confess the benefits and express devout gratitude for the blessings resulting from your independence to us? Would to God, both for your sakes and ours, that an affirmative answer could be truthfully returned to these questions! Then would my task be light, and my burden easy and delightful. For whom is there so cold, that a nation's sympathy could not warm him? Who so obdurate and dead to the claims of gratitude, would not thankfully acknowledge such priceless benefits? Who so stolid and selfish, that would not give his voice to swell the hallelujahs of a nation's jubilee, when the chains of servitude had been torn from his limbs?

I am not that man. In a case like that, the dumb might eloquently speak, and the "lame man leap as a hare."

But such is not the state of the case. I say it with a sad sense of the disparity between us. I am not included within the pale of this glorious anniversary! Your high independence only reveals the immeasurable distance between us. The blessings in which you, on this day, rejoice, are not enjoyed in common. — The rich inheritance of justice, liberty, prosperity, and independence, bequeathed by your fathers, is shared by you, not by me. The sunlight that brought life and healing to you, has brought stripes and death to me. This Fourth [of] July is yours, not mine. You may rejoice, I must mourn. To drag a man in fetters into the grand illuminated temple of liberty and call upon him to join you in joyous anthems, were inhuman mockery and sacrilegious irony. Do you mean, citizens, to mock me, by asking me to speak today? If so, there is a parallel to your conduct. And let me warn you that it is not a sensible idea to copy the ex- ample of a nation whose crimes, lowering up to heaven, were thrown down by the breath of the Almighty, burying that nation in irrecoverable ruin! I can today "By the rivers of Babylon, there we sat down. Yes! We wept when we remembered Zion. We hanged our harps upon the willows in the midst thereof. For there, they that carried us away captive, required of us a song; and they who wasted us required of us mirth, saying, Sing us one of the songs of Zion. How can we sing the Lord's song in a strange land? If I forget thee, O Jerusalem, let my right hand forget her cunning. If I do not remember thee, let my tongue cleave to the roof of my mouth."

Fellow-citizens; above your national, tumultuous joy, I hear the mournful wail of millions! whose chains, heavy and grievous yesterday, are, to-day, rendered more intolerable by the jubilee shouts that reach them. If I do forget, if I do not faithfully remember those bleeding children of sorrow this day, "may my right hand forget her cunning, and may my tongue cleave to the roof of my mouth!" To forget them, to pass lightly over their wrongs, and to chime in with the popular theme, would be treason most Scandalous and shocking, and would make me a reproach before God and the world. My subject, then, fellow citizens, is AMERICAN SLAVERY. I shall see, this day, and its popular characteristics, from the slave's point of view. Standing, there, identified with the American bondman, making his wrongs mine, I do not hesitate to declare, with all my soul, that the character and conduct of this nation never looked Blacker to me than on this 4th of July! Whether we turn to the declarations of the past, or to the professions of the present, the conduct of the nation seems equally hideous and revolting. America is false to the past, false to the present, and solemnly binds herself to be false to the future. Standing with God and the crushed and bleeding slave on this occasion, I will, in the name of humanity, which is outraged, in the name of liberty, which is fettered, in the name of the constitution and the Bible, which are disregarded and trampled upon, dare to call in question and to denounce, with all the emphasis I can command, everything that serves to perpetuate slavery the great sin and shame of America! "I will not equivocate; I will not excuse;" I will use the severest language I can command; and yet not one word shall escape me that any man, whose judgment is not blinded by prejudice, or who is not at heart a slaveholder, shall not confess to be right and just." But I fancy hearing some one of my audiences say, it is just in this circumstance that you and your brother abolitionists fail to make a favorable impression on the public mind. Would you argue more, and denounce less, would you persuade more, and rebuke less, your cause would be much more likely to succeed. But I submit, where all is plain there is nothing to be argued. What point in the anti- slavery creed would you have me argue? On what branch of the subject do the people of this nation need light? Must I undertake to prove that the slave is a man? That point is conceded already. Nobody doubts it. The slaveholders themselves acknowledge it in the enactment of laws for their government. They acknowledge it when they punish disobedience on the part of the slave. There are seventy-two crimes in the State of Virginia, which, if committed by a Black man, (no matter how ignorant he be), subject him to the punishment of death, while only two of the same crimes will subject a White man to the like punishment. What is this but the acknowledgement that the slave is a moral, intellectual, and responsible being? The manhood of the slave is conceded. It is admitted in the fact that Southern statute books are covered with enactments forbidding, under severe fines and penalties, the teaching of the slave to read or to write. When you can point to any such laws, in reference to the beasts of the fields, then I may consent to argue the manhood of the slave. When the dogs in your streets, when the fowls of the air, when the cattle on your hills, when the fish of the sea, and the reptiles that crawl, shall be unable to distinguish the slave from a brute, then will I argue with you that the slave is a man!

For the present, it is enough to affirm the equal manhood of the Negro race. Is it not astonishing that, while we are ploughing, planting and reaping, using all kinds of mechanical tools, erecting houses, constructing bridges, building ships, working in metals of brass, iron, copper, silver and gold; that, while we are reading, writing and cyphering, acting as clerks, merchants and secretaries, having among us lawyers, doctors, ministers, poets, authors, editors, orators and teachers; that, while we are engaged in all manner of enterprises common to other men, digging gold in California, capturing the whale in the Pacific, feeding sheep and cattle on the hill- side, living, moving, acting, thinking, planning, living in families as husbands, wives and children, and, above all, confessing and worshipping the Christian's God, and looking hopefully for life and immortality beyond the grave, we are called upon to prove that we are men!"

"I wake up every morning in this house built by enslaved people."

Michelle Obama

Would you have me argue that man is entitled to liberty? That he is the rightful owner of his own body? You have already declared it. Must I argue the wrongfulness of slavery? Is that a question for Republicans? Is it to be settled by the rules of logic and argumentation, as a matter beset with great difficulty, involving a doubtful application of the principle of justice, hard to be understood? How should I look to-day, in the presence of Americans, dividing, and subdividing a discourse, to show that men have a natural right to freedom? speaking of it relatively, and positively, negatively, and affirmatively. To do so would be to make myself ridiculous, and to offer an insult to your understanding. — There is not a man beneath the canopy of heaven, that does not know that slavery is wrong.

What, am I to argue that it is wrong to make men brutes, to rob them of their liberty, to work them without wages, to keep them ignorant of their relations to their fellow men, to beat them with sticks, to flay their flesh with the lash, to load their limbs with irons, to hunt them with dogs, to sell them at auction, to sunder their families, to knock out their teeth, to burn their flesh, to starve them into obedience and submission to their masters? Must I argue that a system thus marked with blood, and stained with pollution, is wrong? No! I will not. I have better employment for my time and strength than such arguments would imply.

What, then, remains to be argued? Is it that slavery is not divine; that God did not establish it; that our Doctor of Divinity are mistaken? There is blasphemy in the thought. That which is inhuman, cannot be divine! Who can reason with such a proposition? They that can, may; I cannot. The time for such an argument has passed. At a time like this, scorching irony, not convincing argument, is needed. O! had I the ability, and could I reach the nation's ear, I would, today, pour out a fiery stream of biting ridicule, blasting reproach, withering sarcasm, and stern rebuke. For it is not light that is needed, but fire; it is not the gentle shower, but thunder. We need the storm, the whirlwind, and the earthquake. The feeling of the nation must be quickened; the conscience of the nation must be roused; the propriety of the nation must be startled; the hypocrisy of the nation must be exposed; and its crimes against God and man must be proclaimed and denounced.

What, to the American slave, is your 4th of July? I answer: a day that reveals to him, more than all other days in the year, the gross injustice and cruelty to which he is the constant victim. To him, your celebration is a sham; your boasted liberty, an unholy license; your national greatness, swelling vanity; your sounds of rejoicing are empty and heartless; your denunciations of tyrants, brass fronted impudence; your shouts of liberty and equality, hollow mockery; your prayers and hymns, your sermons, and thanksgivings, with all your religious parade, and solemnity, are, to him, mere bombast, fraud, deception, impiety, and hypocrisy — a thin veil to cover up crimes which would disgrace a nation of savages. There is not a nation on the earth guilty of practices, more shocking and bloodier, than are the people of these United States, at this very hour.

Go where you may, search where you will, roam through all the monarchies and despotisms of the old world, travel through South America, search out every abuse, and when you have found the last, lay your facts by the side of the everyday practices of this nation, and you will say with me, that, for revolting barbarity and shameless hypocrisy, America reigns without a rival.

Take the American slave-trade, which, we are told by the papers, is especially prosperous just now. Ex-Senator Benton tells us that the price of men was never higher than now. He mentions the fact to show that slavery is in no danger. This trade is one of the peculiarities of American institutions. It is executed in all the large towns and cities in one-half of this confederacy; and millions are pocketed every year, by dealers in this horrid traffic. In several states, this trade is a chief source of wealth. It is called (in contradistinction to the foreign slave-trade) "the internal slave trade." It is, probably, called so, too, to divert from it the horror with which the foreign slave trade is contemplated. That trade has long since been denounced by this government as piracy. It has been denounced with burning words, from the high places of the nation, as an execrable traffic. To arrest it, to put an end to it, this nation keeps a squadron, at immense cost, on the coast of Africa. Everywhere, in this nation, it is safe to speak of this foreign slave trade, as a most inhuman traffic, opposed alike to the laws of God and of man.

The duty to extirpate and destroy was admitted even by our Doctor of Divinity. To put an end to it, some of these last have consented that their colored brethren (nominally free) should leave this nation and establish themselves on the western coast of Africa! It is, however, a notable fact that, while so much execration is poured out by Americans upon those engaged in the foreign slave- trade, the men engaged in the slave-trade between the states pass without condemnation, and their business is deemed honorable.

Behold the practical operation of this internal slave-trade, the American slave- trade, sustained by American politics and America religion. Here you will see men and women reared like swine for the market. Do you know what a swine- drover? I will show you a man drover. They inhabit all our Southern States. They perambulate the nation, and crowd the highways of the nation, with droves of human stock. You will see one of these human flesh- jobbers, armed with pistol, whip and bowie knife, driving a company of a hundred men, women, and children, from the Potomac to the slave market at New Orleans. These wretched people are to be sold singly, or in lots, to suit purchasers. They are food for the cotton fields, and the deadly sugar-mill. Mark the sad procession, as it moves wearily along, and the inhuman wretch who drives them. Hear his savage yells and his blood-chilling oaths, as he hurries on his affrighted captives! There, see the old man, with locks thinned and gray. Cast one glance, if you please, upon that young mother, whose shoulders are bare to the scorching sun, her briny tears falling on the brow of the babe in her arms. See, too, that girl of thirteen, weeping, yes! weeping, as she thinks of the mother from whom she has been torn! The drive moves tardily. Heat and sorrow have nearly consumed their strength; suddenly you hear a quick snap, like the discharge of a rifle; the fetters clank, and the chain rattles simultaneously; your ears are saluted with a scream, which seems to have torn its way to the "center of your soul! The crack you heard, was the sound of the slave-whip; the scream you heard, was from the woman you saw with the babe. Her speed had faltered under the weight of her child and her chains! that gash on her shoulder tells her to move on. Follow the drove to New Orleans. Attend the auction see men examined like horses; see the forms of women rudely and brutally exposed to the shocking gaze of American slave-buyers. See this drove sold and separated forever; and never forget the deep, sad sobs that arose from that scattered multitude. Tell me citizens, WHERE, under the sun, you can witness a spectacle more fiendish and shocking. Yet this is but a glance at the American slave-trade, as it exists, at this moment, in the ruling part of the United States.

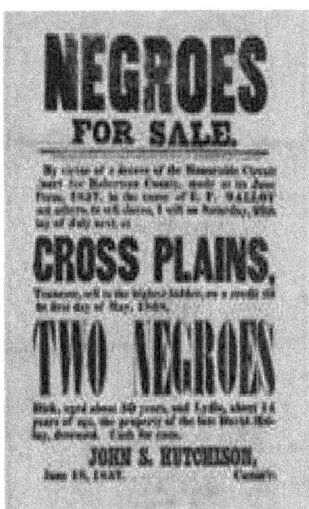

Formal Announcement Public

I was born amid such sights and scenes. To me the American slave-trade is a terrible reality. When a child, my soul was often pierced with a sense of its horrors. I lived on Philpot Street, Fell's Point, Baltimore, and have watched from the wharves, the slave ships in the Basin, anchored from the shore, with their cargoes of human flesh, waiting for favorable winds to waft them down the Chesapeake. There was, at that time, a grand slave mart kept at the head of Pratt Street, by Austin Woolfolk. His agents were sent into every town and county in Maryland, announcing their arrival, through the papers, and on flaming "handbills," headed CASH FOR NEGROES. These men were generally well-dressed men, and very captivating in their manners. Ever ready to drink, to treat, and to gamble. The fate of many a slave has depended upon the turn of a single card; and many a child has been snatched from the arms of its mother by bargains arranged in a state of brutal drunkenness.

The flesh-mongers gather up their victims by dozens, and drive them, chained, to the general depot at Baltimore. When enough has been collected here, a ship is chartered, for the purpose of conveying the forlorn crew to Mobile, AL or to New Orleans, LA. From the slave prison to the ship, they are usually driven in the darkness of night; for since the antislavery agitation, a certain caution is observed. In the deep still darkness of midnight, I have been often aroused by the dead heavy footsteps, and the piteous cries of the chained gangs that passed our door. The anguish of my boyish heart was intense; and I was often consoled, when speaking to my mistress in the morning, to hear her say that the custom was very wicked; that she hated to hear the rattle of the chains, and the heart-rending cries. I was glad to find one who sympathized with me in my horror.

Fellow-citizens, this murderous traffic is, today, in active operation in this boasted republic In the solitude of my spirit, I see clouds of dust raised on the highways of the South; I see the bleeding footsteps; I hear the doleful wail of fettered humanity, on the way to the slave markets, where the victims are to be sold like horses, sheep, and swine, knocked off to the highest bidder. There I see the tenderest ties ruthlessly broken, to gratify the lust, caprice and rapacity of the buyers and sellers of men. My soul sickens at the sight.

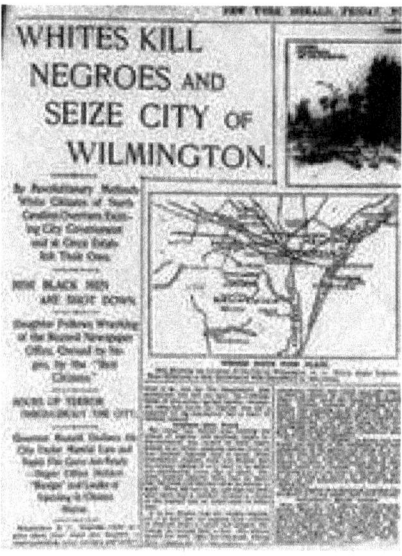

Is this the land your Fathers loved? The freedom which they toiled to win? Is this the earth whereon they moved? Are these the graves they slumber in?

But a still more inhuman, disgraceful, and scandalous state of things remains to be presented. By an act of the American Congress, not yet two years old, slavery has been nationalized in its most horrible and revolting form. By that act, Mason and Dixon's line has been obliterated; New York has become as Virginia; and the power to hold, hunt, and sell men, women, and children as enslaved people remains no longer a mere state institution, but is now an institution of the whole United States. The power is co- extensive with the Star-Spangled Banner and American Christianity. Where these go, may also go the merciless slave- hunter. Where these are, man is not sacred. He is a bird for the sportsman's gun. By that most foul and fiendish of all human decrees, the liberty and person of every man are put in peril. Your broad republican domain is hunting ground for men. Not for thieves and robbers, enemies of society, merely, but for men guilty of no crime. Your lawmakers have commanded all good citizens to engage in this hellish sport. Your President, your Secretary of State, our lords, nobles, and ecclesiastics, enforce, as a duty you owe to your free and glorious nation, and to your God, that you do this accursed thing. Not fewer than forty Americans have, within the past two years, been hunted down and, without a moment's warning, hurried away in chains, and consigned to slavery and excruciating torture. Some of these have had wives and children, dependent on them for bread; but of this, no account was made. The right of the hunter to his prey stands superior to the right of marriage, and to all rights in this republic, the rights of God included! For Black men there are neither law, justice, humanity, not religion.

The Fugitive Slave Law makes mercy to them a crime; and bribes the judge who tries them. An American judge gets ten dollars for every victim he consigns to slavery, and five, when he fails to do so. The oath of any two villains is sufficient, under this hell-Black enactment, to send the most pious and exemplary Black man into the remorseless jaws of slavery! His own testimony is nothing. He can bring no witnesses for himself. The minister of American justice is bound by the law to hear but one side; and that side, is the side of the oppressor. Let this damning fact be perpetually told. Let it be thundered around the world, that, in tyrant- killing, king- hating, people-loving, democratic, Christian America, the seats of justice are filled with judges, who hold their offices under an open and palpable bribe, and are bound, in deciding in the case of a man's liberty, hear only his accusers!

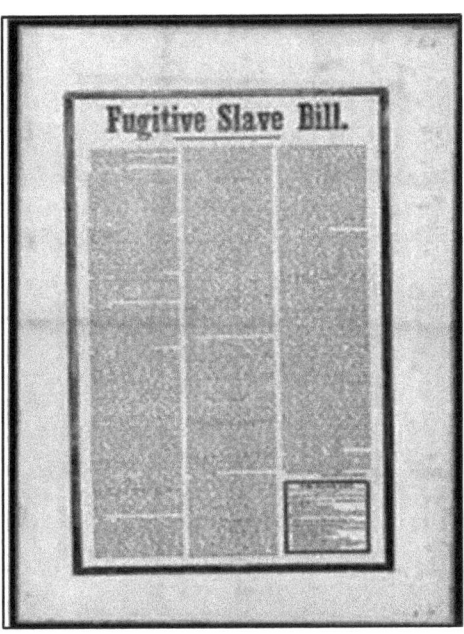

Fugitive Slave Bill was signed by President Millard Fillmore, September 18, 1850

In glaring violation of justice, in shameless disregard of the forms of administering law, in cunning arrangement to entrap the defenseless, and in diabolical intent, this Fugitive Slave Law stands alone in the annals of tyrannical legislation. I doubt if there is another nation on the globe, having the brass and the baseness to put such a law in the statute-book. If any man in this assembly thinks differently from me in this matter, and feels able to disprove my statements, I will gladly confront him at any suitable time and place he may select.

I take this law to be one of the grossest infringements of Christian Liberty, and, if the churches and ministers of our nation were not stupidly blind, or most wickedly indifferent, they, too, would so regard it.

At the very moment that they are thanking God for the enjoyment of civil and religious liberty, and for the right to worship God according to the dictates of their own conscious, they are utterly silent in respect to a law which robs religion of its chief significance and makes it utterly worthless to a world lying in wickedness. Did this law concern the "mint, anise, and cumin" — abridge the right to sing psalms, to partake of the sacrament, or to engage in any of the ceremonies of religion, it would be smitten by the thunder of a thousand pulpits. A general shout would go up from the church, demanding repeal, repeal, instant repeal! — And it would go hard with that politician who presumed to solicit the votes of the people without inscribing this motto on his banner.

Further, if this demand were not complied with, another Scotland would be added to the history of religious liberty, and the stern old Covenanters would be thrown into the shade. A. John Knox would be seen at every church door, and heard from every pulpit, and Fillmore would have no more quarter than was shown by Knox, to the beautiful, but treacherous queen Mary of Scotland. The fact that the church of our nation, (with fractional exceptions), does not esteem "the Fugitive Slave Law" as a declaration of war against religious liberty, implies that that church regards religion simply as a form of worship, an empty ceremony, and not a vital principle, requiring active benevolence, justice, love, and goodwill towards man esteems sacrifice above mercy; psalm singing above right doing; solemn meetings above practical righteousness. Worship that can be conducted by persons who refuse to give shelter to the houseless, to give bread to the hungry, clothing to the naked, and who enjoin obedience to a law forbidding these acts of mercy, is a curse, not a blessing to mankind. The Bible addresses all such persons as "Scribes, Pharisees, hypocrites, who pay tithe of mint, anise, and cumin, and have omitted the weightier matters of the law, judgment, mercy and faith."

But the church of this nation is not only indifferent to the wrongs of the slave, but it also actually takes sides with the oppressors. It has made itself the bulwark of American slavery, and the shield of American slave-hunters. Many of its most eloquent Divines. who stand as the very lights of the church, have shamelessly given the sanction of religion and the Bible to the whole slave system. They have taught that man may, properly, be a slave; that the relation of master and slave is ordained of God; that to send back an escaped bondman to his master is clearly the duty of all the followers of the Lord Jesus Christ; and this horrible blasphemy is palmed off upon the world for Christianity. For my part, I would say, welcome infidelity! Welcome atheism! Welcome anything! In preference to the gospel, as preached by those Divines! They convert the very name of religion into an engine of tyranny, and barbarous cruelty, and serve to confirm more infidels, in this age, than all the infidel writings of Thomas Paine, Voltaire, and Boling broke, put together, have done!

These ministers make religion a cold and flinty-hearted thing, having neither principles of right action, nor bowels of compassion. They strip the love of God of its beauty, and leave the throng of religion a huge, horrible, repulsive form. It is a religion for oppressors, tyrants, man-stealers, and thugs. It is not that "pure and undefiled religion" which is from above, and which is "first pure, then peaceable, easy to be entreated, full of mercy and good fruits, without partiality, and without hypocrisy. " But a religion which favors the rich against the poor; which exalts the proud above the humble; which divides mankind into two classes, tyrants and enslaved people; which says to the man in chains, stay there; and to the oppressor, oppress on; it is a religion which may be professed and enjoyed by all the robbers and enslavers of mankind; it makes God a re- specter of persons, denies his fatherhood of the race, and tramples in the dust the great truth of the brotherhood of man. All this we affirm to be true of the popular church, and the popular worship of our land and nation — a religion, a church, and a worship which, on the authority of inspired wisdom, we pronounce to be an abomination in the sight of God. In the language of Isaiah, the American church might be well-addressed, "Bring no more vain ablations; incense is an abomination unto me: the new moons and Sabbaths, the calling of assemblies, I cannot away with; it is iniquity even the solemn meeting. Your new moons and your appointed feasts my soul hateth. They are a trouble to me; I am weary to bear them; and when ye spread forth your hands I will hide mine eyes from you. Yes! When ye make many prayers, I will not hear. YOUR HANDS ARE FULL OF BLOOD; cease to do evil, learn to do well; seek judgment; relieve the oppressed; judge for the fatherless; plead for the widow." The sin of which it is guilty is one of omission as well as of commission. Albert Barnes uttered what the common sense of every man at all observants of the actual state of the case will receive as truth. He declared that "There is no power out of the church that could sustain slavery an hour if it were not sustained in it. "

Let the religious press, the pulpit, the Sunday school the conference meeting, the great ecclesiastical, missionary, Bible, and tract associations of the land array their immense powers against slavery and slaveholding, and the whole system of crime and blood would be scattered to the winds; and that they do not do this involves them in the most awful responsibility of which the mind can conceive.

In prosecuting the anti-slavery enterprise, we have been asked to spare the church, to spare the ministry; but how, we ask, could such a thing be done? We are met on the threshold of our efforts for the redemption of the slave, by the church and ministry of the nation, in battle arrayed against us; and we are compelled to fight or flee. From what quarter, I beg to know, has proceeded a fire so deadly upon our ranks, during the last two years, as from the Northern pulpit? As the champions of oppressors, the chosen men of American theology have appeared men, honored for their so- called piety, and their real learning. The Lords of Buffalo, the Springs of New York, the Lathrops of Auburn, the Coxes and Spencers of Brooklyn, the Gannets and Sharps of Boston, the Deweys of Washington, and other great religious lights of the land have, in utter denial of the authority of Him by whom they professed to be called to the ministry, deliberately taught us, against the example or the Hebrews and against the remonstrance of the Apostles, they teach that we ought to obey man's law before the law of God.

My spirit wearies of such blasphemy; and how such men can be supported, as the "standing types and representatives of Jesus Christ," is a mystery which I leave others to penetrate. In speaking of the American church, however, let it be distinctly understood that I mean the great mass of the religious organizations of our land. There are exceptions, and I thank God that there are. Noblemen may be found, scattered all over these Northern States, of whom Henry Ward Beecher of Brooklyn, Samuel J. May of Syracuse, and my esteemed friend (Reverend R. R. Raymond) on the platform, are shining examples; and let me say further, that upon these men lies the duty to inspire our ranks with high religious faith and zeal, and to cheer us on in the great mission of the slave's redemption from his chains.

One is struck with the difference between the attitude of the American church towards the anti-slavery movement, and that occupied by the churches in England towards a similar movement in that nation. There, the church, true to its mission of ameliorating, elevating, and improving the condition of mankind, came forward promptly, bound up the wounds of the West Indian slave, and restored him to his liberty. There, the question of emancipation was a highly religious question. It was demanded, in the name of humanity, and according to the law of the living God. The Sharps, the Clarksons, the Wilberforces, the Buxtons, and Burchells and the Knibbs, were similarly famous for their piety and for their philanthropy. The antislavery movement there was not an anti- church movement, because the church took its full share in prosecuting that movement: and the anti-slavery movement in this nation will cease to be an anti- church movement, when the church of this nation shall assume a favorable, instead of a hostile position towards that movement. Americans! your republican politics, not less than your republican religion, are flagrantly inconsistent. You boast of your love of liberty, your superior civilization, and your pure Christianity, while the whole political power of the nation (as embodied in the two great political parties), is solemnly pledged to support and perpetuate the enslavement of three million of your nation men. You hurl your anathemas at the crowned headed tyrants of Russia and Austria, and pride yourselves on your Democratic institutions, while you yourselves consent to be the mere tools and bodyguard of the tyrants of Virginia and Carolina. You invite to your shore's fugitives of oppression from abroad, honor them with banquets, greet them with ovations, cheer them, toast them, salute them, protect them, and pour out your money to them like water; but the fugitives from your own land you advertise, hunt, arrest, shoot and kill. You glory in your refinement and your universal education, yet you maintain a system as barbarous and dreadful as ever stained the character of a nation a system begun in avarice, supported in pride, and perpetuated in cruelty.

You shed tears over fallen Hungary and make the sad story of her wrongs the theme of your poets, statesmen and orators, till your gallant sons are ready to fly to arms to vindicate her cause against her oppressors; but, regarding the ten thousand wrongs of the American slave, you would enforce the strictest silence, and would hail him as an enemy of the nation who dares to make those wrongs the subject of public discourse! You are all on fire at the mention of liberty for France or for Ireland; but are as cold as an iceberg at the thought of liberty for the enslaved of America. You discourse eloquently on the dignity of labor; yet you sustain a system which, in its very essence, casts a stigma upon labor. You can bare your bosom to the storm of British artillery to throw off a three- penny tax on tea; and yet wring the last hard-earned farthing from the grasp of the Black laborers of your nation.

You profess to believe "that, of one blood, God made all nations of men to dwell on the face of all the earth," and hath commanded all men, everywhere to love one another; yet you notoriously hate, (and glory in your hatred), all men whose skins are not colored like your own. You declare, before the world, and are understood by the world to declare, that you "hold these truths to be self-evident, that all men are created equal; and are endowed by their Creator with certain inalienable rights; and that, among these are, life, liberty, and the pursuit of happiness;" and yet, you hold securely, in a bondage which, according to your own Thomas Jefferson, "is worse than ages of that which your fathers rose in rebellion to oppose," a seventh part of the inhabitants of your nation.

Fellow-citizens! I will not enlarge further on your national inconsistencies. The existence of slavery in this nation brands your republicanism as a sham, your humanity as a base pretense, and your Christianity as a lie. It destroys your moral power abroad; it corrupts your politicians at home. It saps the foundation of religion; it makes your name a hissing, and a byword to a mocking earth. It is the antagonistic force in your government, the only thing that seriously disturbs and endangers your Union. It fetters your progress; it is the enemy of improvement, the deadly foe of education; it fosters pride; it breeds insolence; it promotes vice; it shelters crime; it is a curse to the earth that supports it; and yet, you cling to it, as if it were the sheet anchor of all your hopes.

Oh! be warned! be warned! a horrible reptile is coiled up in your nation's bosom; the venomous creature is nursing at the tender breast of your youthful republic; for the love of God, tear away, and fling from you the hideous monster, and let the weight of twenty million crush and destroy it forever!

But it is answered in reply to all this, that precisely what I have now denounced is, in fact, guaranteed and sanctioned by the Constitution of the United States; that the right to hold and to hunt enslaved people is a part of that Constitution framed by the illustrious Fathers of this Republic.

Then, I dare to affirm, notwithstanding all I have said before, your fathers stooped, barely stooped. To palter with us in a double sense: And keep the word of promise to the ear But break it to the heart. And instead of being the honest men I have before declared them to be, they were the very imposters that ever practiced on mankind. This is the inevitable conclusion, and from it there is no escape. But I differ from those who charge this baseness on the framers of the Constitution of the United States. It is a slander upon their memory, at least, so I believe. There is no time now to argue the constitutional question at length— nor have I the ability to discuss it as it ought to be discussed. The subject has been overseen with masterly power by Lysander Spooner, Esq., by William Goodell, by Samuel E. Sewall, Esq., and last, though not least, by Gerrit Smith, Esq. These gentlemen have, as I think, fully and clearly vindicated the Constitution from any design to support slavery for an hour.

Fellow-citizens! There is no matter in respect to which the people of the North have allowed themselves to be so ruinously imposed upon, as that of the pro- slavery character of the Constitution. In that instrument I hold there is neither warrant, license, nor sanction of the hateful thing; but, interpreted as it ought to be interpreted, the Constitution is a GLORIOUS LIBERTY DOCUMENT. Read its preamble, consider its purposes. Is slavery among them? Is it at the gateway? or is it in the temple? It is neither. While I do not intend to argue this question on the present occasion, let me ask, if it be not somewhat singular that, if the Constitution were intended to be, by its framers and adopters, a slaveholding instrument, why neither slavery, slaveholding, nor slave can anywhere be found in it. What would be thought of an instrument, drawn up, legally drawn up, for the purpose of entitling the city of Rochester to a tract of land in which no mention of land was made? Now, there are certain rules of interpretation for the proper understanding of all legal instruments. These rules are well established. They are plain, common- sense rules, such as you and I, and all of us, can understand and apply without having passed years in the study of law. I thought the idea that the question of the constitutionality or unconstitutionality of slavery is not a question for the people. I hold that every American citizen has a right to form an opinion of the constitution, and to propagate that opinion, and to use all honorable means to make his opinion the prevailing one. Without this right, the liberty of an American citizen would be as insecure as that of a Frenchman. Ex Vice President Dallas tells us that the Constitution is an object to which no American mind can be too attentive, and no American heart too devoted. He further says, the Constitution, in its words, "is plain and intelligible, and is meant for the home-bred, unsophisticated understandings of our fellow citizens." Senator Berrien tells us that the Constitution is the fundamental law, that which controls all others. The charter of our liberties, which every citizen has a personal interest in understanding thoroughly. The testimony of Senator Breese, Lewis Cass, and many others that might be named, who are everywhere esteemed as sound lawyers, so regard the constitution. I take it, therefore, that it is not presumption in a private citizen to form an opinion of that instrument.

Now, take the Constitution according to its plain reading, and I defy the presentation of a single pro-slavery clause in it. On the other hand, it will be found to contain principles and purposes entirely hostile to the existence of slavery. I have detained my audience entirely too long already. At some future period, I will gladly avail myself of an opportunity to give this subject a full and fair discussion. Allow me to say, in conclusion, notwithstanding the dark picture I have this day presented of the state of the nation, I do not despair of this nation. There are forces in operation, which must inevitably work towards the downfall of slavery. "The arm of the Lord is not shortened," and the doom of slavery is certain. I, therefore, leave off where I began, with hope. While drawing encouragement from the Declaration of Independence, the great principles it contains, and the genius of American Institutions, my spirit is also cheered by the obvious tendencies of the age. Nations do not now stand in the same relation to each other that they did ages ago. No nation can now shut itself up from the surrounding world, and trot round in the same old path of its fathers without interference. The time was when such could be done. Long established customs of hurtful character could formerly fence themselves in and do their evil work with social impunity. Knowledge was then confined and enjoyed by the privileged few, and the multitude walked on in mental darkness. But a change has now come over the affairs of mankind. Walled cities and empires have become unfashionable. The arm of commerce has borne away the gates of the strong city. Intelligence is penetrating the darkest corners of the globe. It makes its pathway over and under the sea, as well as on the earth. Wind, steam, and lightning are its chartered agents. Oceans no longer divide, but link nations together. From Boston to London is now a holiday excursion. Space is comparatively annihilated. Thoughts expressed on one side of the Atlantic are distinctly heard on the other. The far off and almost fabulous Pacific rolls in grandeur at our feet. The Celestial Empire, the mystery of ages, is being solved. The fiat of the Almighty, "Let there be Light," has not yet spent its force. No abuse, no outrage whether in taste, sport, or avarice, can now hide itself from the all-pervading light. The iron shoe, and crippled foot of China must be seen, in contrast with nature. Africa must rise and put on her yet unwoven garment. "Ethiopia shall stretch out her hand unto God." In the fervent aspirations of William Lloyd Garrison, I say, and let every heart join in saying it:

God speed the year of jubilee The wide world o'er When from their galling chains set free, The oppress'd shall vilely bend the knee, And wear the yoke of tyranny Like brutes no more.

That year will come, and freedom's reign, to man his plundered fights again Restore.

Godspeed the day when human blood Shall cease to flow!

In every clime be understood, The claims of human brotherhood, And each return for evil, good, Not blow for blow; That day will come all feuds to end. And change into a faithful friend Each foe.

God speed the hour, the glorious hour, When none on earth Shall exercise a lordly power, Nor in a tyrant's presence cower; But all to manhood's stature tower, By equal birth!

That hour will come, to each, to all, And from his prison- house, the thrall Go forth. Until that year, day, hour, arrive, With head, and heart, and hand I'll strive, To break the rod, and rend the gyve, The spoiler of his prey deprive — So witness Heaven!

And never from my chosen post, Whate'er the peril or the cost, Be driven.

Appendix THREE

Properties of TB Wright in the City of Sumter, South Carlina

1. Thomas B. Wright
from
Fannie Douglas
Dated: January 9, 1908
Recorded: January 15, 1908, Deed
Book Z.ZZ at Page 154 Located in
Rafting Creek Township

  25 Acres

2. Thomas B. Wright
from
Louise S. Manning
Dated: February 20, 1908
Recorded: April 1, 1908,
Deed Book Z.ZZ at Page 302
Located in Rafting Creek Township

  16 Acres

3. Thomas Wright
from
A. W. Scarborough, et al. Dated:
December 1915
Recorded: December 16, 1915, Deed
Book M-4 at Page 719 Located
Charleston-Camden Road

  86 Acres

4. Thomas B. Wright
from
Mary E. Jackson
Dated: December 28, 1915
Recorded: January 13, 1916,
Deed Book M-4 at Page 772
Sanders Camden-Charleston Rd. Wright

  50 Acres

5. T. B. Wright
from
Louise B. Stubbs, Individually and as
Trustee Dated: March 17, 1920
Recorded: March 22, 1920
Deed Book U-4 at Page 176
Plat Book 0-4, Page 61

  Lot Nos. 19, 20,
21, 22, 23, 26, 29
37, 38, 39, 48, 55,
61, 73, 75, 80, 91,
87, 88, 89, 90, 93,
94, 95, 96, 97, 98,
99, 100, 101, 102,
108, 109, 117, 133,
135, 136 & 154

Continuing to Rise

6. T. B. Wright from Leila N. Nigon Dated: December 11, 1919
Recorded: February 1, 1922,

Deed Book T-4 at Page 380
Several Lots, Streets, etc.

Plat Book 4-A at Page 2

7. T. B. Wright from
J. J. Starks
Dated: January 21, 1922
Recorded: February 1, 1922,
Deed Book W-4 at Page 366
Parts of Blocks Y, M, N, O, P, Q, R, S All of Blocks X, U,T, S, Grantham St, Browler St., Durham St, Carolina
Ave Plat Book 4-A at Page 2

8. Thomas B. Wright
from
Washington S. Williams By Master in Equity Dated: January 29, 1923, Recorded: January 31, 1923
Deed Book Y-4 at Page 74
Claremont, Bowman, Robinson, Sanders McCall
Plat Book F-4 at Page 184

24 Acres

9. Estate of T. B. Wright- Plat
Plat Book G-5 at Page 47
Dated: November 23, 1934
Recorded: May 3, 1934
Plat of 3 Tracts Adjacent to Alston, Sanders, Deacon, Jackson

161 Acres

<u>Partial list of TB Wright's property holdings at time of death</u>

ACKNOWLEDGEMENTS

I recognize that no project can ever be accomplished without a community that shares its gifts, time, guidance, inspiration, conversation, and encouragement to make it happen. I am indebted to my children, Randy, and Ronnie; my grandchildren, Deysha, Caredio, Lil Randy, Aaron, Ayden, Vernard Jr. (Deuce), and Valor (Tre); my friends, Barbara D. Parks Lee, and Joyce Carter; my cousin, Dr. Edna C. Jenkins; and my ancestors who stood with me. Thanks to everyone mentioned throughout this book. Please keep the Relay to Liberty and Justice alive.

About the Author

Dr. Thomasina M. Portis is the CEO of Renaissance Global Ministries. She began her professional career as a public school's teacher in Sumter, South Carolina and retired as an Assistant Superintendent from the District of Columbia Public Schools Following her retirement she was appointed by Judge Judy Clark in Maryland as a Trustee of the former Word of Life Academy in Fort Washington, Maryland, later becoming its Chief Administrative Officer.

As a national and international preacher, lecturer, and author, Dr. Portis has also taught as an adjunct professor at Cabrini College in Radnor, PA, Trinity University, The University of the District of Columbia in Washington, D.C., and Brigham Young University in Provo, Utah. She is an internationally accredited Chaplain and Christian Counselor with a history of civic engagement that began at the age of fifteen. Among her many contributions, she has facilitated the enrollment of over one thousand inner-city promising young Black individuals in HBCUs nationwide, counseled survivors of the Oklahoma City Bombing, and contributed to the development of two National Community Service Projects at the invitation of two U.S. Presidents.

Her philanthropic efforts include raising funds to bring sick individuals from Ghana for surgeries in the U.S. and serving as Chair/President of Sisters-By-Choice, a residential facility for emancipated mothers aged 14-21 in San Diego, CA. Dr. Portis has delivered numerous presentations, including as a Baccalaureate speaker at Brandeis University in Waltham, MA, and as a guest speaker at International Character Education Conferences in South Korea and Germany, and the White House Conference on Children and Youth. She has also been a consultant for The National Education Conference for American Teachers, The National Conference for Guidance and Counseling, and The Music Educators National Conference. Additionally, she has been a keynote speaker for the 100 Black Women and an educational consultant in over 900 U.S. school districts. Dr. Portis has also been a guest plenary speaker at state and national Christian Conferences and was the first African American woman to chair Learning for Life, the educational component of The Boy Scouts of America.

REFERENCES

SECTION ONE

Alberta, Tim, THE KINGDOM, AND THE POWER, AND THE GLORY, Harper Collins Publishers, 2023.

African American History: New York, Black Wall Street www.findBlackwallstreet.com. https: www.nyhistory.org/web/africanfreeSouth Carolina/history/vontext.html

Bonhoeffer, Dietrich, (New Foreword by Metaxas, Eric), The Cost of Discipline the Touchtone Edition, New York, NY, 1995.

Brown, Cole, GREY BOY Finding Blackness in A White World, Arcade Publishing, New York, New York, 2020.

Burke, Tarana, Brown, Brene, YOU ARE YOUR BEST SELF, Random House, New York, 2021.

Butler, Anthea, WHITE EVANGELICAL RACISM The Politics of Morality in America, Marcie Cohen Ferris, and William R. Ferris Imprint, University of North Carolina Press, North Carolina, 2021.

Cheney, Liz, Oath and Honor, Little, Brown, and Company, 2023.

Clyburn, James E., Blessed Experiences, University of South Carolina Publishing Press, 2022.

Cobb, Thomas R.R., ugapress.org/author/Thomas-r-t-cobb. Comparing Governments: Democracy vs. Authoritarianism. Cobb, William Jelani, The Substance of Hope: Barack Obama and the Paradox of Progress, Bloomsbury Publishers, 2nd publication, 2020.

Crenshaw, Kimberle, #SAHERNAME, Haymarket Books, Chicago, Illinois, 2023. DeGruy, Joy, Post Traumatic Slave Syndrome, Upton Press, El Segundo, CA, 2005.

Diangelo, Robin, White Fragility: Why It's So Hard for White People to Talk About Race, Beacon Press, Boston, MA. 2018.

Eig, Johnathan, KING A Life, Farrar, Straus, and Giroux, Broadway, New York, 2023.

Felder, Cain Hope, Troubling Biblical Waters, Orbis Books, Mary Knoll, New York, 1989 Felder, James L., I Buried John F. Kennedy, Lee Books, LLC, Columbia, South Carolina, 1994.

Frankl Viktor E., (Afterword by Winslade, William J.), Man's Search for Meaning, Beacon Press, Boston, MA, 2014.

Frederick Douglass, "What, To The Slave, Is The Fourth Of July" https://www.Blackpast.org/african-american-history/speeches-african- american-

History/1852- Frederick-Douglass-what-slave-fourth-July/

Gladwell, Malcolm. David and Goliath, Back Bay Books/ Little, Brown and Company, Hackett Book Group, Inc., New York, New York. 2013.

Henderson, Rebecca, Reimagining Capitalism in A World on Fire, Public Affairs, New York, 2020. Herrnstein, Richard J., IQ in Meritocracy, Penguin Books/Random House, New York, New York, 1973.

Jefferson, Thomas, quote is published in "White Over Black–1550-1912," by Winthrop Jordan, Omohundro Institute of Early American History and Culture, Williamsburg, VA 1968.

Johnson, Guy, Standing At The Scratch Line, Strivers Row, Villard, New York, 1998. Jones, Nona, Success from the Inside Out, Zondervan, Grand Rapids, Michigan, 2020.

Jones, Clarence, and Stuart Connelly, LAST Of The LIONS An African American Journey in Memoir Redhawk Publications, The Catawba Valley Community College Press, Hickory, North Carolina 2023.

Jones, Robert P., White Too Long, Simon and Schuster, New York, New York, 2020 Lincoln, Abraham, quote is published in Abraham Lincoln Encyclopedia by Mark E. Neely, Jr., Da Capa Press, Inc., New York, New York, 1983.

Maddow, Rachel, PREQUEL, An American Fight Against Fascism, Crown, division of Penguin Randon House LLC, New York, 2023.

McGhee, Heather, THE SUM Of Us What Racism Costs Everyone and How We Can Prosper Together, One World, New York, 2021.

McLester, Marion Whets.edu/oral history program/158/_ 1994. Oluo, Ijeoma, So You Want to Talk About Race, Seal Press, Hachette Book Group, New York, 2019.

Parrott, Les, Love Like That, Nelson Books, Carol Stream, Illinois, 2018. Peonage, www.law. Cornell, edu/code/text/42/1994.

Perryman, Wayne, The 1995 Trial on the CURSE OF HAM, Pneuma Life Publishing, Bakersfield, CA, 1994.

Raboteau, Albert, J., SLAVE RELIGION "The Invisible Institution" in the Antebellum South, Updated Edition, OXFORD University Press, New York, New York, 2004.

Raskin, Jamie, UNTHINKABLE Trauma, Truth, And The Trials Of American Democracy, Harper, New York, New York 2022.

Robinson, Edward W, Jr., No Man Can A-Hinder Me, WWW areativespace.com/ 03669309, 2011.

Sandel, Michaël J., THE TYRANNY OR MERIT What's Becoming of The Common Good? Farrar, Strauss, and Giroux, New York, New York, 2012.

Sandel, Michael, J., WHAT MONEY CAN'T BUY the Moral Limits of Markets, Farrar, Strauss, and Giroux, New York, New York, 2020.

Scott, Dred v Sandford, M.www.history.com/topics/Black- history/dred scott case. Socialism v Democracy, www.thoughtco.com.

The Holy Bible, The New International Version, Biblica, Huntington Beach, CA, 1978. U.S. Supreme Court Racist Decision, https://www.thoughts.com, 2010.

Wilkinson, Isabel, Warmth of Two Other Suns: The Epic Story of America's Great Migration, Barnes and Nobles, New York, New York, 2010.

Wiggins, Phyllis, The CURSE of HAM; Satan's Vicious Cycle, www.xulonpress.com, 2005.

Williams, Patricia J., "THE ALCHEMY Of RACE And RIGHTS: Diary of a Law Professor," Harvard University Press, Cambridge, MA, 1991

References

https://www.Whitehousehistory.org/collections/president-biographies, https://www.Whitehousehistory.org/the-american-colonization-society.

Bash, Dana with Fisher, David, America's Deadly Election: The Cautionary Tale of the Most Violent

Election In American History, Hanover Square Press, Toronto, Ontario M5H 4E3, Canada, 2024.

SECTION TWO

American Psychiatric Association., Diagnostic and Statistical Manual of Mental Disorders, (5th ed.). Arlington, VA, American Psychiatric Publishing, 2015.

Anderson, Carol, White Rage: The Unspoken Truth of Our Racial Divide, Bloomsbury, New York, 2016.

Baptist, Edward E., The Half Has Never Been Told: Slavery and the Making of American Capitalism, Basic Books, New York, New York, 2019.

Berry, Mary Frances, My Face Is Black Is True Callie House and the Struggle for Ex-Slave Reparations, Vintage Book, A Division of Random House, Inc., New York, New York 2005.

Budney, A.J., Sargent, J. D., & Lee, D. C., "Vaping Cannabis (Marijuana); Parallel Concerns to E cigs? Addiction," 110 (11): 2015. p. 1697-704.

Butler, Paul, Choke Hold, The New Press, New York, New York. 2018.

Diangelo, Robin, White Fragility: Why It's So Hard for White People to Talk About Race, Beacon Press, Boston, MA. 2018.

Gergel, Richard, UNEXPLAINED COURAGE the Blinding of Sgt. Isaac Woodard and the Awakening of President Harry S. Truman and Judge J. Waites True Creighton Books, Farrar, Straus and Giroux, New York, New York, 2019.

Haygood, Wil, I Too, Sing America, Columbus Museum of Arts, Rizzoli, NY 1984.

Hall, W. Degenhardt L., Adverse Health Effects on Non-Medical Cannabis Use. Lancet. 374 (9698): p. 1383-91, 2009.

Lopez – Quinton, et al. "Probability and predictors of the transistor from first use independence on nicotine, alcohol, cannabis, and cocaine: results of The National Epidemiologic Survey on

Alcohol and Related Conditions (NESARC), Drug and Alcohol Depend." (115 12): p. 120-30, 2011.

National Institute on Drug Abuse. "Is Marijuana Addictive?" Rockville, MD. National Institute of Health, National Institute on Drug Abuse, Rockville, VA., 2010.

Reid, Joy-Ann, MEDGAR & MYRLIE, Medgar Evans, and the Love Story That Awakened America, Mariner Books, New York, 20224.

Woody, Howard and Thigpen, Allan D., Arcadia Publishing, Charleston, SC, 2005.

SUGGESTED READING

Bell, Derrick B.Ae.Es., At The Bottom of the Well, Hachette Book Group, New York, NY, 1992.

Brazile, D., Caraway, Y., Daughtry, Moore, M., with Chambers, V., For Colored Girls Who Have Considered Politics, St. Martin's Press, New York, 2018.

Brown, Charles L., From Scapegoats to Lambs: How God's Word Speaks to George Floyd's Murder, Author House, Bloomington, IN, 2021.

Butler, Anthea, WHITE EVANGELICAL RACISM, The Politics of Morality in America, The University of North Carolina, Chapel Hill, NC, 2021.

Cheney, Liz, OATH And HONOR – A Memoir and a Warning, Little, Brown and Company, New York, 2023.

Cobb, William Jelani, The Substance of Hope: Barack Obama and the Paradox of Progress, Bloomsbury Publishers, 2nd publication, 2020. Bloomsbury Publishers, 2ndpublication, 2020.

Collier, Walter. V., Dr., Why RACISM Persists – AME Uncomfortable Truth, Dr. Walter V. Collier, PO Box 2024, Oak Bluffs, MA 02557, 2016.

Crenshaw, Kimberle; Gotanda, Neil; Peller, Gary; and Thomas "Critical Race Theory," The New Press, New York 1995.

Crenshaw, Kimberle, and African American Forum Policy, #SAY HER NAME, Haymarket Books, Chicago, Illinois, 2023.

Dates, Charlie, I Can't Breathe, https://www.thegospelcoalition. Org/podcasts/word-of the week/I- can't breathe-a-sermon-by Charlie-dates, June 11, 2020.

DeGruy, Joy, "Post Traumatic Slave Syndrome: America's Legacy of Enduring Injury and Healing," Upton Press, St. Joseph, Michigan, 2005.

Diangelo, Robin, NICE RACISM: How Progressive White People Perpetuate Racial Harm, Bacon Press, Boston, MA, 2021.

DuBois, W.E.B., The Souls of Black Folks, A.C. McClury & Company, Chicago, IL, 1903.

Duckworth, Angela, "GRIT the Power of Passion with Perseverance," Scribner, an imprint of Simon and Schuster, New York, NY.2016.

Eig, Johnathan, KING A Life, Farrar, Strauss, and Giroux, New York, 2023.

Felder, Cain Hope, Troubling Biblical Waters, Orbis Books, Mary Knoll, New York, 1989.

Gates, Louis, "Stoney the Road We Trod: White Reconstruction, White Supremacy, and the Rise of Jim Crow." Gladwell, Malcolm. "David and Goliath," Back Bay Books/ Little, Brown, and Company, Hackett Book Group, Inc., New York. 2013.

Glaude, Jr., Eddie S., "Begin Again," Crown, an imprint of Random House, a division of Penguin, Random House, L.L.C., New York, 2020.

Gillespie, Andra, "Race and the Obama Administration: Substance, Symbols and Hope,"

Manchester University Press, Manchester, UK 2019.Gross, Ariela J., "What Blood Won't Tell: A History of Race on Trial in America, " Harvard University Press, Cambridge, MA 2008.

References

Hacker, Andrew, "Two Nations: Black and White, Separate, Hostile, Unequal," Scribner, New York, 1992.

Hale, Grace Elizabeth, "Making Whiteness: The Culture of Segregation in the South," 1890-1940. Pantheon, New York. 1998.

Henderson, Rebecca, Reimagining Capitalism in a World on fire, Hunt, Raymond G., and Benjamin Bowser, "Impacts of Racism on White Americans," SAGE Publications, Thousand Oaks, CA, 1996.

Isikoff, Michael and Klaidman, Daniel, FIND ME THE VOTES A Hard-Charging Georgia Prosecutor, A Rogue President, and the Plot to Steal an American Election, Hachette Book Group, New York, 2024

Jones, Robert P., "The End of White Christian America," Simon and Schuster Paperbacks, New York, NY. 2016.

King, Martin L., Jr., "Letter from Birmingham Jail," The Christian Century edition Chicago, IL, 1963. Laymon, Kiese, "Heavy: An American Memoir," Scribner, New York, NY, 2018.

Lewis, John R., and Aydin, Andrew, MARCH, Top-Shelf Production, Marietta, GA 2013.

Maxwell, Zerlina, "The End of White Politics: How to Heal Our Liberal Divide," Hackett Book Group, Inc., New York, 2020.

Moore, Wes, with Green Erica L., "FIVE DAYS the Fiery Reckoning of An American City," One World, an imprint of Random House, a Division of Penguin Random House, L.L.C., New York, 2019.

Norris, Michelle, OUR HIDDEN CONSERVATIONS What Americans Really Think About Race and Identity, Simon, & Schuster, New York, 2024.

Obama, Barack, "A Promised Land, " Crown, an imprint Random House, New York, New York, 2020.

Parks, Lewis A., and Birch, Bruce C., Ducking Spears, Dancing Medley: A Biblical Model of Church Leadership, American Press, Nashville, TN, 2014.

Parrott, Les, Dr., LOVE LIKE THAT, Nelson, Books, Nashville, Tennessee, 2018.

Perryman, Wayne, The 1995 Trial on the CURSE OF HAM, Pneuma Life Publishing, Bakersfield, CA, 1994.

Proctor, Samuel D., "The Sound of the Trumpet," Judson Press, Valley Forge, PA., 1994. Raper, Arthur F., "The Tragedy of Lynching," University of North Carolina Press, Chapel Hill, NC, 2016.

Robinson, Edward W, Jr., No Man Can A-Hinder Me, www areativespace.com/3669309, 2011. The University of South Carolina, Columbia, S.C. 2014.

Scarborough, Joe, "Saving Freedom: Truman, the Cold War, and the Fight for the Western Civilization," An Imprint of Harper Collins Publishers, New York, New York. 2020.

Scazzero, Peter with Bird, Warren, The Emotionally Healthy Church, a Strategy for Discipleship that Changes Lives, Zondervan, Grand Rapids, MI, 2003.

Sellers, Bakari, THE MOMENT – Thoughts on the Race Reckoning That Wasn't and Who We All Can Move Forward Now, Harper Publishing, New York, 2024.

Sokol, Jason, "There Goes My Everything: White Southerners in the Age of Civil Rights, 975," Vintage, NY, 2008.Sussman, Robert, W., "The Myth of Race: The Troubling Persistence of an Unscientific," Harvard University, Press, Cambridge, MA., 2014.

The Holy Bible, The New International Version, Biblica, Huntington Beach, CA, 1978. Thurston, Baratunde, How to Be Black, Harper Collins, New York, New York, 2012.

Walker, Vanessa Siddle, "Their Highest Potential: An American School Community in the Segregated South," The University of North Carolina Press, Chapel Hill, NC, 1996.

Ware, Carl, Portrait of an American BUSINESSMAN: One Generation from Cotton Fields to Boardroom, Mercer University Press, Macon, GA, 2019.

Wheatley, Margaret J., "How New Science: Learning about Organization from the Orderly Universe," Berrett-Koehler Publishers, Inc., San Francisco, CA., 1991.

Wiggins, Phyllis, The CURSE of HAM; Satan's Vicious Cycle, www.xulonpress.com, 2005. Wilkerson, Isabel, "CASTE the Origins of Our Discontents, Random House, a Division of Penguin Random House, L.L.C., New York. 2020.

Williams, Cecil, Out-of-the-Box in Dixie: Cecil Williams' Photography of the South Carolina Events that Changed America, Orangeburg, SC, 2010.

Williams, Kidada, "They Left Great Marks of Me: African American Testimonies of Racial Violence from Emancipation to World War I," University Press, New York NY, 2012.

Williams, Patricia J., "The Alchemy of Race and Rights: Diary of a Law Professor," Harvard University Press, Cambridge, MA, 1991.

Wilson, Willie Dr., What Shall I Do Next When I Don't Know What to Do? The Extraordinary Story of a Man, His faith, and the Building of Financial Empire, Willie Wilson Publishing Company, Mattison, IL, 2008.

Woodson, Carter, G., "The Miseducation of The Negro," No reference.

Woodward, C. Vann, "The Strange Career of Jim Crow," Oxford University Press, NY 2002.